CD-ROMS:
Breakthrough in Information Storage

FREDERICK HOLTZ

TAB TAB BOOKS Inc.
Blue Ridge Summit, PA

FIRST EDITION
FIRST PRINTING

Copyright © 1988 by TAB BOOKS Inc.
Printed in the United States of America

Library of Congress Cataloging in Publication Data

Holtz, Frederick.

CD-ROMs : breakthrough in information storage / by Frederick
Holtz.
p.   cm.
Includes index.
ISBN 0-8306-1426-5   ISBN 0-8306-9326-2 (pbk.)
1. CD-ROM.   I. Title.
TK7882.C56H65   1988
.621.397'3—dc19   88-9424
CIP

Questions regarding the content of this book
should be addressed to:

Reader Inquiry Branch
TAB BOOKS Inc.
Blue Ridge Summit, PA 17294-0214

Contents

Introduction

CD-ROM. Does that expression conjure up imaginative thoughts of a highly compact, infinitely dense storage media? Or does it painfully bring to mind another technological obstacle that one must study for months or even years to be brought up to date with the newest "trend"?

Hopefully, your answer to this question is the former. Compact disc read-only memories (CD-ROMs) are still an infant technology. However, they are now at the point that the standard magnetic hard disc had attained less than one decade ago. If you can recall those days in the late seventies, then you are probably aware of how exotic the idea of a hard disc drive was, especially for microcomputer users who were still using cassette tape storage or the far more sophisticated (and still a bit exotic) floppy disc medium.

CD-ROM storage is not a thing of the future. Rather, it is a highly efficient and useful storage device of the present, one with far more storage capabilities than previous technologies have offered. CD-ROM devices are only now beginning to make inroads into the everyday world of computer users worldwide. Fortunately, CD-ROM storage parallels many of the basic precepts of technologies that have preceded it. To learn about this new, super-high density storage medium, all that is necessary is to grasp the principles of optical storage as opposed to magnetic storage.

This text walks you through this new technology with the very able assistance of many persons who are at the forefront of this industry and have contributed articles and even entire chapters that explain the exciting world of the

CD-ROM. Additionally, they include listings and overviews of some of the most modern CD-ROM titles currently available. These are pre-loaded databases that contain thousands upon thousands of data items.

Yes, CD-ROM is here to stay. And, its' beginning to make its presence heavily felt throughout the industry. Chances are that in the very near future, all of modern society will be interfacing with CD-ROM databases. Perhaps you already have and don't even know it.

1
Overview of
CD-ROM Technology
and Hardware

CD-ROM, which stands for compact-disc read-only memory, is an extension of CD audio, the high-quality optical disc technology that has literally revolutionized the music industry. Its promise lies in the fact that a single CD-ROM, measuring a mere 4¾ inches, is capable of storing the equivalent of up to 250,000 pages of text, 1500 floppy discs, 74 minutes of audio, or thousands of images, any of which can be retrieved in seconds by means of software. This tremendous storage capacity has caused the prediction of a similar revolution in the information industry that will change forever the manner in which we manipulate information.

Information on a CD-ROM disc is encoded in the form of pits and spacings on a spiral track that amounts to three miles long. The disc spins on a laser-equipped drive. As the disc moves, the pits and spacings modulate the reflected laser beam, forming binary ones and zeros—the language of computers. A highly sophisticated form of error correction is built in during all phases of manufacturing, reducing the probability of error far below that on tape or floppy disc.

CD-ROM is the brainchild of Philips and Sony, the same companies that brought CD audio to the forefront of the music industry. The technology has already been proven to be reliable, secure, and of high quality. Standards, already available for CD audio, have now been developed for CD-ROM to ensure compatibility among hardware and data storage formats within the industry, and CD-ROM products are now available in a wide variety of fields.

CD-ROM MARKETS

CD-ROM technology is targeted toward markets where large amounts of static (or semi-static) information must be accessed on a regular basis. These include:

- **Libraries**—CD-ROM has probably generated more excitement and interest in this field than any other, with many library professionals embracing the technology as *the* solution to many of their information-handling problems, both in managing and disseminating the vast amounts of information they are responsible for. Bibliographic databases, among the first CD-ROM products to come to market, are fast finding acceptance with libraries, with the Library of Congress at the forefront of this movement in developing a single CD-ROM that contains a complete bibliography of everything in their card catalogs.

- **Education**—A companion to the library market, the education market also fully realizes the potential of CD-ROM. However, because schools at all levels must adhere to budgets, this market should realize the fruits of this technology as soon as possible, but they will probably be slow to implement it. Regardless, the educational impact is tremendous and holds great promise.

- **Publishing**—Publishers are already making use of CD-ROM to some extent, with McGraw-Hill, Prentice-Hall, Groliers and other publishing giants beginning to release encyclopedias and other types of static information on CD-ROM.

- **Online Database Services**—Virtually all online database providers have accepted CD-ROM as the wave of the future, with numerous online databases already converted to CD-ROM. When CD-ROM was first introduced, a shock wave was felt throughout the online industry because it was feared that CD-ROM would replace the need for online databases. It is now generally accepted that the two will complement each other. CD-ROM is certainly appropriate for online database conversion, but because the information these databases contain can and does change and requires regular updating, online providers are approaching CD-ROM as an addendum rather than a replacement for their current online services. A subscriber to a company's CD-ROM product is offered updated discs on a regular basis (quarterly, semi-annually, or whatever is appropriate), plus access to the company's online service for access to updates not yet available on compact disc. Online providers are also taking advantage of CD-ROM's versatility and modifying the manner in which a user interacts with the system.

- **Government**—Government at all levels has taken an extremely active position with regard to CD-ROM. Numerous prototype projects are underway, and developers are already in heated competition in their attempts to get a piece of this lucrative market. NASA, the Internal Revenue Service, the Census Bureau, the U.S. Geological Survey, OSHA, and the Navy and Coast Guard are just a few of the government agencies that already offer or plan to offer information on CD-ROM.

- **Business and Professional**—This market is already in full swing, with banks, insurance companies, law and engineering firms, hospitals and medical professionals quickly realizing the benefits of CD-ROM.

Because Philips has played such a prominent position in the development of optical technology, their assistance was sought during the writing of this book. The remainder of this chapter, which explains the basics of CD-ROM technology, is reprinted with permission of Philips and Du Pont Optical from their brochure, *CD-ROM Technology*.

CD-ROM MANUFACTURING

There are five basic steps in the manufacturing of CD-ROMs.

- **Data Generation**—Data generation is the process of setting up information for maximum speed and accessibility. This step is usually carried out by the customer or information provider (IP). In this initial step, all material is recorded on magnetic tape and is organized so that it can be easily accessed. During this process, a developer organizes a list of key words subject to search and retrieval procedures.

- **Data Preparation**—This step requires that material be organized in logical files that describe the disc layout. The data is then copied onto magnetic tapes, which are used in the next step.

- **Pre-Mastering**—This step consists of adding control codes for synchronization, address/mode indication, error detection, and correction. These codes are combined into individual CD-ROM format sectors. When sectoring is complete, the master disc can be produced.

- **Mastering**—This step begins by encoding information into the final CD-ROM format. Information is then recorded optically on the photo-chemical-coated surface of a glass disc. Following successful developing, the disc passes through an evaporation stage where it receives a thin silver coating. The disc master, carrying all the data in the form of billions of microsized pits, is then ready to make stampers and discs.

- **Replication**—Replication is a four-stage process. By a galvanic method, the disc master is transferred onto a nickel stamper or "mother." Using the same process, a number of positives or "daughters" are produced. From each of these, several stampers are made. Using injection molding techniques, these stampers are then used to replicate the desired number of CD-ROM discs. Finally, each disc is given a reflective metal coating that is then covered by a protective layer of lacquer. The label is added to the lacquered side of the disc.

THE BASICS OF CD-ROM

This section describes CD-ROM technology and the five steps discussed

3

above in greater and more technical detail. The information described in this section is not required reading for all who wish to make use of the technology but is presented here for those with a more technical background.

Physical Structure

A distinctive feature of CD-ROM is the form in which data are stored. Figure 1-1 illustrates the storage method. Data are impressed into the substrate as a series of pits of variable length along a spiral of constant pitch (1.6 μm). The substrate is given a reflective layer that is coated with a protective material.

Laser light passes through the substrate and is focused onto the reflective layer. In the area where there is not a pit (called "land"), light is reflected. Light in a pit is largely scattered. Thus, a change in the level of the reflected light signals a transition from a pit to land or the reverse (see Fig. 1-2).

For various reasons (which are detailed later in this section), binary 1's and 0's in the data are not simply represented by pits or lands. Instead, the transition from a pit to land or land to pit is a 1 and the path length between transitions to either pit or land represents a certain number of 0's. However, due to the fact that data are modulated, these 1's and 0's are not the same as their end-user equivalents.

CD-ROMs' use of optical technology has three major advantages over magnetic mass storage:

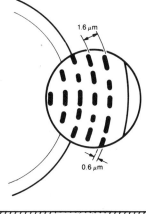

Fig. 1-1. Data are impressed into the substrate as a series of pits of variable length and are read by laser through the transparent substrate. Courtesy Philips and Du Pont Optical.

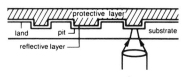

Fig. 1-2. A binary 1 is represented by a land/pit or pit/land transition; the number of 0's is determined by the path length between transitions. Courtesy Philips and Du Pont Optical.

- The high linear data density, which is 1.66 data bits/μm or 42 Kbits/inch. Given a track of 1.6 μm, these figures work out to 6 × 10^8 bits/in^2 or 10^6 bits/mm^2, a figure that is an order of magnitude higher than for magnetic materials.

- The long path over which the reflected light can travel and still be accurately detected. This allows the optical reading head to be maintained at a distance of more than 1mm from the surface of the substrate, thereby eliminating the possibility of head crashes.

- The protection of data, which is literally built in. Data are represented in a simple, mechanical manner—pits or lands. And the information side of the substrate is fully protected by a plastic coating. Moreover, CD-ROM is relatively insensitive to dust or scratches on the read-out surface, because they are out of focus and thus only cause a marginal loss of light. The overall result is trouble-free storage for many years.

Recording Format

Data on the CD-ROM are modulated in order to meet four basic criteria:

1. To achieve a high density without incurring problems of resolution.
2. To make the data self-clocking.
3. To minimize error propagation.
4. To facilitate the servo system by minimizing spectral power (use of low frequency power).

Taking these points in order:

1. The resolution of the optical system is determined by the wavelength (780nm) of the laser light and the numerical aperture of the objective lens (0.45). This produces a resolution of approximately 1 μm (0.6 × λ/NA). Any attempt to read data with a bit density above this figure will produce intersymbol interference; therefore, the only method to increase bit sensitivity beyond this point is to modulate the data. This imposes a minimal run-length limitation on the modulation scheme. In other words, transitions must not occur too close to each other. Otherwise, problems of resolution will occur.
2. Clock pulses must be regenerated from the data stream after it has been read from disc. This self-clocking facility also imposes a restriction on run length, but this time it is the maximum distance between transitions that is the limitation. In other words, if the run length is too long, there are not enough transitions for reliable regeneration of the clock.
3. The error correction system is based on 8-bit symbols. The modulation method should not split up these 8-bit symbols over more than one modulation symbol. Otherwise, errors will be propagated. The encoding method should map one 8-bit data symbol onto one modulation symbol.
4. In order to give a low (ideally zero) dc level for the servos (see Fig. 1-3), the length of pits and land should be equal over the disc.

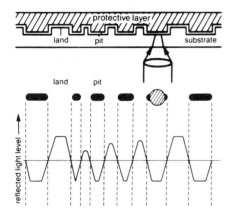

Fig. 1-3. The optical system receives low light levels from the pits (scattering) and high levels from the lands (reflecting). Courtesy Philips and Du Pont Optical.

Data Readout

In order to ensure accurate, high-speed readout of data from the disc, the optical system must maintain focus on the track, stay on track, and maintain a constant data rate. Figures 1-3 and 1-4 illustrate how the first conditions are met.

The laser light is focused through the transparent substrate onto the reflective layer. In Figure 1-3, this light is shown in the ideal position, centered on the track. (Note: One revolution of the spiral is considered, for convenience, to be a track.) This same position is indicated by the light path B of Fig. 1-4. The reflected light passes through a prism, which causes it to be deflected by 90 degrees. It then passes through an optical wedge, which splits the light beam into two equal halves, each of which is subsequently focused onto a pair of photodiodes.

When the beam is in the correct position (B; see top of Fig. 1-4), which is focused on the track (the solid line), the two beams are focused on the center of each diode pair (positions B1) and therefore the diodes receive equal amounts

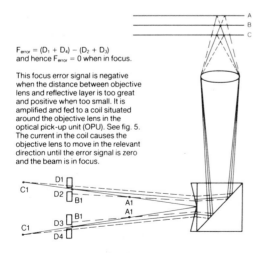

$F_{error} = (D_1 + D_4) - (D_2 + D_3)$
and hence $F_{error} = 0$ when in focus.

This focus error signal is negative when the distance between objective lens and reflective layer is too great and positive when too small. It is amplified and fed to a coil situated around the objective lens in the optical pick-up unit (OPU). See fig. 5. The current in the coil causes the objective lens to move in the relevant direction until the error signal is zero and the beam is in focus.

Fig. 1-4. The principle of focus control. Courtesy Philips and Du Pont Optical.

of light. If, however, the disc moves in such a way that the focused light falls short of the track (position C), the reflected beam (the -- line) is wider and the optical wedge causes the split beams to focus behind the diodes in position C. As a result, the inner diodes D_2 and D_3 receive less light than the outer diodes. The reverse is true when the disc moves in the opposite direction to position A (the -⋅- light path).

TECHNICAL HIGHLIGHTS OF PHYSICAL STRUCTURE

The most critical parameter for achieving high information densities in the CD system is the diameter of the focused laser beam when it hits the reflective surface. This spot diameter (defined as diameter of spotwith down to half of maximum intensity) is given by:

$$d = 0.5\ \lambda/NA$$

where λ is the laser wavelength and NA is the numerical aperture on the image side (see Fig. 1-5). As we want to minimize d, we can either minimize the wavelength or maximize the NA. Because of length-of-life requirements (5,000 + hours), we cannot use the (solid state) lasers operating below 700nm, but will be operating at, about 800nm. In maximizing NA, however, the manufacturing tolerance of the optical light path rapidly becomes smaller. For example, the tolerance in local skew of the disc relative to the optical axis is proportional to NA^{-3}, the tolerance for disc thickness to NA^{-4}, and depth of focus to NA^{-2}. Considering these factors, an NA of 0.45 has been chosen, which gives $d \approx 1\mu m$.

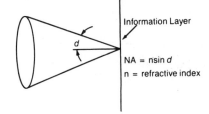

Fig. 1-5. Calculating the diameter of a focused laser beam. Courtesy Philips and Du Pont Optical.

TECHNICAL HIGHLIGHTS OF RECORDING FORMAT

In CD-ROM, the first two of the four basic modulation criteria previously mentioned are met by setting the minimal run length to 3 channel bits and the maximum to 11 channel bits. The third is achieved by selecting the minimum number of bits that can map 8-bit symbols with the above limitations on run length. This is a 14-bit modulation symbol.

The modulation scheme is designated Eight-to-Fourteen Modulation (EFM). Each information symbol of 8 bits is mapped in 14 "channel" bits, with the previously described constraints. There are 267 different 14-bit symbols that meet these two constraints. Consequently, 11 of the maximum run-length symbols are deleted, leaving 256, which matches the 28 possibilities of 8-bit wide data.

A one-to-one correspondence can therefore be established between the original 8-bit and the encoded 14-bit modulation symbol, using a conversion look-up table (CLUT) stored in a read-only memory (ROM). Part of this table is shown in Table 1-1.

Taking, for example, decimal 8 as represented in binary by **00001000**, the EFM equivalent is **01001001000000**. The constraints are clear: there is a minimal 3-channel-bit run length between transitions. (Note: A run length is a 1 and then two or more 0's until the next transition to a 1.) Thus, **100** is before the next 1. And, in this case, the longest run length is seven (one 1 followed by six 0's). Figure 1-6 shows this represented on the disc.

The 14-bit modulation symbols generated in this way, however, cannot be concatenated without the possibility of violating the constraint of at least two 0's between 1's; i.e., a 1 at the end of one block could concatenate with a 1 at the beginning of the text. For this reason, additional merging bits are inserted between successive symbols after modulation. In actual practice, three such bits are employed, although two would suffice.

	data bits	channel bits
0	00000000	01001000100000
1	00000001	10000100000000
2	00000010	10010000100000
3	00000011	10001000100000
4	00000100	01000100000000
5	00000101	00000100010000
6	00000110	00010000100000
7	00000111	00100100000000
8	00001000	01001001000000
9	00001001	10000001000000
10	00001010	10010001000000

Table 1-1. Part of the 8-to-14 Code Conversion Table. Courtesy Philips and Du Pont Optical.

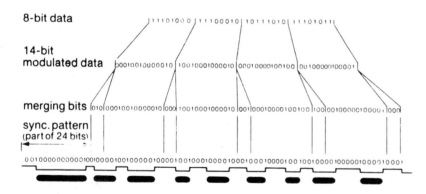

Fig. 1-6. A binary 1 is represented by the transition from a land to a pit or a pit to a land. A binary 0 is represented by the run length between transitions, i.e., length of a pit or land. Courtesy Philips and Du Pont Optical.

Error Correction

The compact disc has a very powerful error-correction capability that compensates for the influence of:

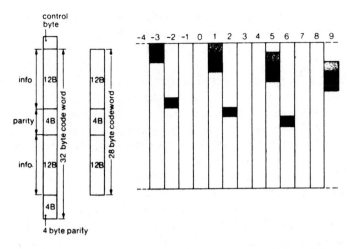

Fig. 1-7. The first parity group corrects single-symbol errors and flags multiple-symbol errors. The second parity group can correct a two-symbol error and flag uncorrectable errors. Further error correction is possible by EDC/ECC in the reserve capacity of a CD-ROM sector. CD frames and their parity groups are spread over adjacent frames. The first byte of frame 1, plus the second byte of frame 5, plus the third byte of frame 9, and so on, form the first three bytes of a codeword, which uses the second parity group. Courtesy Philips and Du Pont Optical.

- Minute imperfections in the production materials and those introduced during the production process.
- User-caused damage caused by scratches and fingerprints.
- Dust and other particles on the surface of the disc.
- Possible degradation in longtime storage.

The system has been designed to compensate for "burst" errors that can arise from these influences and can also extend over several frames. This is done by employing a Reed-Solomon code with interleaving of data frames in order to extend error correction capabilities over a number of adjacent frames. This is known as the Cross Interleaved Reed-Solomon Code (CIRC). See Fig. 1-7.

After demodulation, CD frames are split into the control and display part (one symbol) and a data part (32 symbols). The former goes to the control and display circuitry, and the data part to the error-correction circuitry. The 32 symbols (bytes) of the data part are made up from 24 bytes of information plus two groups of 4-byte parity symbols. The first parity group is used to correct single-symbol errors. Although one parity group is sufficient to correct up to two symbol errors, this capability is used instead to increase the ability to detect and locate multiple errors. Thus, the first group (a) corrects single errors, and the second (b) flags CD frames that contain multiple errors when they occur.

At this stage, a CD frame comprises 24 user-bytes and the second of the two 4-byte parities, that can therefore correct up to two symbol errors, because the position of those errors has already been flagged by the first parity group. At this stage, any remaining errors are flagged in the output. An example of the interleaving technique is given in Fig. 1-8.

9

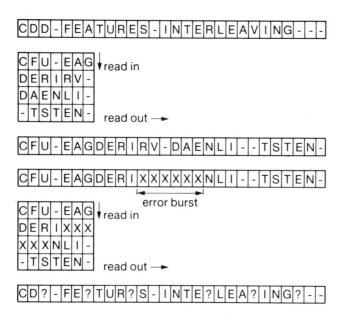

Fig. 1-8. Interleaving spreads an error burst over several frames. This is equivalent to reading data into the columns of a RAM and then reading the data out from the rows. Thus, a six-symbol dropout is spread throughout the data stream, enabling it to be error-corrected. Courtesy Philips and Du Pont Optical.

Figure 1-8 shows how this technique enables a multiple burst, equivalent to 7 × 32 bytes, to be corrected. The symbols that form the code words are spread over many frames, which reduces the probability of two or more errors falling in the same code word.

The code symbols are interleaved as follows: symbol 1 of frame 1 is in the same code word as symbol 2 of frame 5, with symbol 3 of frame 9, and so on, with jumps of four frames until symbol 28. With this technique, errors extending over seven frames can be corrected.

Scrambling/Control

The 2,336 bytes of user data are scrambled to reduce the DSV of the servo control circuitry that can arise due to the occurrence of a systematic data pattern. As data are not random sequences of symbols, certain sequences can occur in which the third merging bit cannot be selected for DSV reduction. Scrambling the data, however, gives it a more random character.

Data Layout

The data on a CD-ROM are organized along a spiral, written with constant linear density. The data along the spiral are divided into blocks of 2,352 bytes; each block has an absolute address expressed in minutes (0-74), seconds (0-60) and 75ths of seconds or blocks (0-74). See Fig. 1-9.

A simple time/position algorithm ensures fast access under microprocessor

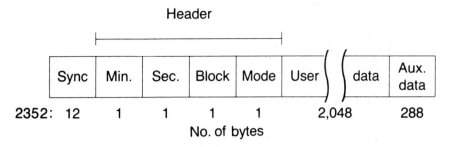

Fig. 1-9. CD-ROM data block system. Courtesy Philips and Du Pont Optical.

control. Sync bytes 1 and 12 are all 0's; bytes 2 through 11 are all 1's. The mode byte defines usage and the content of user and auxiliary data:

• Mode 0 means all user data and auxiliary data bytes = 0.
• Mode 1 means user data available to user, auxiliary data according to error detection code (EDC), error correction code (ECC) specification.
• Mode 2 means user data and auxiliary data available for user.

The disc starts with a lead-in area where the blocks have specially defined headers. Next is a program area that can be divided (by the help of subcodes) into 99 tracks. Finally, there is a lead-out area.

As shown earlier, the user data in the blocks are subdivided into frames consisting of:

• A 24-channel bits sync pattern
• 24 data bytes
• 8 error corrections and parity bytes
• 1 control and display byte

The sync pattern is 12 bits high-level (logic 1) and 12 bits low-level (logic 0). The data bytes are controlled by the user. The error corrections and parity contain values as given by the Reed-Solomon encoding scheme used.

The control and display byte contains eight bits designated P, Q, R, S, T, U, V, W. Each bit forms, together with corresponding bits in other frames, a subcode channel with a capacity of 98 (frames per block) × 75 (blocks per sec), which gives a transmission rate of 7.35 kHz.

The P-channel is used for identification of track starts. A flag is set for a minimum of 2 seconds; when the flag goes to logic 0, the data starts. The Q-channel is used for more sophisticated control. It has information on type of track, copy allowed/prohibited, track number, running time within track, running time on disk and table of contents (during lead-in track). The channels R, S, T, U, V and W are logic 0. These are write-protected channels.

Radial Tracking

In most cases when error signals have to be generated, the high frequency

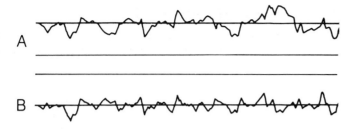

Fig. 1-10. Symbol-by-symbol minimizing of the DSV is depicted in A. Four-symbol minimizing of the DSV is depicted in B. Courtesy Philips and Du Pont Optical.

content of the detector signal is not of interest. The light distribution is detected with a low-pass filter such that the high frequency variations due to the pits or holes are suppressed. Optically, one could say that the pits are rushing along so fast that we are only able to see a track due to its average gray level and individual pits or holes are no longer visible.

This has a consequence for the coding scheme used. There should be an effort to get the difference of lands and pits as close to zero as possible (minimize the DSV), as this difference represents the undesirable DC or low frequency. Figure 1-10A shows a symbol-by-symbol minimizing of the DSV. Figure 1-10B shows the same, but for four symbols, which achieves a 10 dB enhancement with respect to Fig. 1-10A.

Error Sources

Some of the effects to consider in mastering and replication of a CD disc are:

- **Crosstalk**—variations in the reflected beam due to adjacent tracks. Factors influencing crosstalk are scanning spot quality and track spacing.
- **Intersymbol Interference**—crosstalk in the track direction. The optically detected position of a transition should not deviate more than ± 0.5 of a clock pulse length (± 0.6 μm). Offsets in the transition moments are mainly due to the finite extent of the scanning spot in the track direction. The position of a detected transition in a data stream thus depends on the digital data that precede and follow the actual signal.
- **Signal-to-Noise Ratio (SNR)**—The total power is the sum of a number of contributions:

  - Photon Shot noise (stochastic)
  - Microroughness of the optical disc
  - Irregularities of the recorded effects

The photon shot noise gives a physical limitation to the SNR; irregularities of the recorded effects do not affect the system as much as photon shot noise or micro-roughness of the optical disc.

DATA PREPARATION/PREMASTERING

The CD-ROM premastering process extends the customer's "disc image" by adding a CD-ROM level of addressing and error detection/correction. It is identical for all CD-ROMs and is the only "data preparation" step defined by the Philips/Sony CD-ROM specification.

The CD-ROM input or "disc image" contains all application programs, data files and index files, as well as all disc directory and file structure information desired by the customer. The "disc image" contains hundreds of thousands of 2,048-byte CD-ROM sectors.

The CD-ROM premastering process expands each sector to 2,352-byte CD-ROM sectors by adding the following information to each sector (see Fig. 1-9):

12	bytes of CD-ROM synchronization (fixed value)	
4	bytes of CD-ROM header (address and mode)	
2,048	bytes of CD-ROM user data (from the input file)	
288	bytes of CD-ROM auxiliary data (EDC/ECC)	
2,352	bytes total	

The CD-ROM premastering output is a data stream that consists of fully encoded CD-ROM (2,352-byte sectors) and contains the exact same number of CD-ROM sectors that were used in the input. This output is fed to the laser-beam recorder.

LASERBEAM RECORDING

Having processed the digital information to yield a bitstream on the CD-ROM, we let this information modulate the intensity of an argon-ion laser ($\lambda \approx 457.0$ nm) when writing on a flat glass substrate coated first with an adhesive and then a thin (0.12 μm) layer of photosensitive material (resist) that has been baked for stability.

In the exposed area, light is absorbed, which has the effect of locally changing the solubility. The height structure then appears in the development stage, when an alkaline solution is made to flow over the resist layer and dissolves the photoresist in the exposed areas.

Although the principles of exposure and development of photoresist on masters resembles well-known techniques in optical microlithography used in the mass production of integrated circuits, there are some considerable differences. One such difference is the small size and the high optical quality of the light spot necessary to produce pits only about 0.6 μm wide. This is only possible with diffraction-limited optics and a recording objective of high numerical aperture up to 0.8. When an argon-ion laser with a wavelength of 447.9 nm is used as a light source, a recording spot can be obtained with a full width at half maximum (FWHM) of only 0.30 μm. For general purposes, however, a somewhat lower NA of 0.65 is used, resulting in a diffraction-limited spot with FWHM-0.35 μm.

To get a well-defined pit structure, the development is monitored by a HeNe laser which gives information on how the development is progressing and can indicate when to stop it. Normally, the whole development cycle is 20 to 30 seconds.

STAMPER MAKING

After inspection, the master leaves the mastering process and a nickel shell is electroplated onto the silvered surface of the master. When the nickel copy is separated from the master, the information in the relatively soft resist on the master is destroyed.

The nickel copy, which contains the negative of the master surface structure, is called a father. The father can be used for low-volume reproduction or it can be used in the generation of a family of nickel stampers. In the latter case, after a chemical modification of the nickel surface of the father, several mother positives are grown by electroplating. By the same process from each of the mothers, several sons are produced. These negative masters are used as stampers in mass replication.

Moulding

Derived from technologies well-known in the record-pressing business (pressing and injection moulding), it had to be customized to the fine specification of the CD. Established raw material did not meet these demands either.

While the LP system tolerates a warp of, for example, 1.5 mm, the CD must not bend more than 0.4 mm even at temperatures of 55 degrees Celcius and at relative humidity between 0 and 95 percent. The material must not contain bubbles or inclusions bigger than 1/10 or 2/10 of a millimeter, respectively, and it has to be highly transparent and homogenous for optical readout.

Disc moulding is done automatically under pressure and heat, again in a clean-air environment. The 12 cm disc that results must be as clean and as accurate as optical glasses, its surface showing mirror-like smoothness. In contrast to the LP, a CD surface has to be optically flat. Orange peel structure and waviness must not exceed 1/1000 mm.

Metalizing

Metalizing is the next step. The moulded disc, coming out of the automatic moulding machine, must be protected against dust and electrostatic charging. In a vacuum, the side carrying all the tiny pits (200,000 per square mm) is coated with aluminum to build a reflecting layer 60 μm to 70 μm thick. Again, microscopic irregularities might ruin the disc.

Lacquering

After metalizing, lacquering with protective varnish takes place by dripping the lacquer on the rotating disc, onto the aluminum. This first protective layer must not bend, crack, nor tear the disc, and it must be compatible with the aluminum layer below and the label coating above.

Now, the centerhole has to be punched with utmost accuracy, expressed in fractions of a millimeter. The correct position of the centerhole is determined optoelectronically according to the tracks on the disc. This is another totally new process.

Label Printing

Printing of the label directly onto the protective lacquer proceeds similarly to the LP. In the case of the CD, however, the label may serve as a protective layer too. The record is now finished—inspection and packing follow. The total flow is shown schematically in Fig. 1-11.

Apart from random quality tests at different manufacturing stages, there are playing controls as well as visual control at the end before all CDs leave the factory. Finally, remember that malfunction can occur if the laser beam is deflected by dirt or damage. Multiple greasy fingerprints on the surface can also cause distortions in the playback. But once wiped off, the disc will play like new. Nevertheless, the consumer must learn that similar to glasses, this optical product has to be handled carefully. Both package and player design have taken this into account.

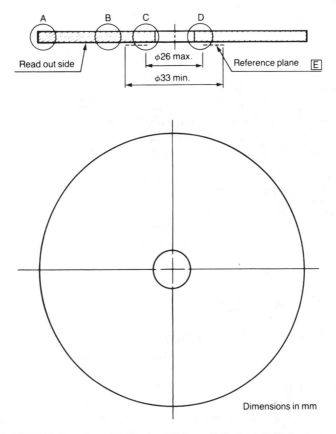

Fig. 1-11. CD-ROM disc schematic. Courtesy Philips and Du Pont Optical.

CD-ROM MEDIA SPECIFICATION

This specification defines those parameters of compact discs that affect their interchangeability. It is offered as a reference for those who intend to make discs or players compatible within the optical system described in this standard.

System Description

The optical digital CD-ROM disk system functions as follows. The information carrier is a disk consisting of a transparent substrate of which one surface contains the information covered with a reflective coating over which a protective layer is applied. The information on the disc is stored in one spiral-shaped track of successive shallow depressions (pits), starting at the inside at a fixed diameter and moving to the outside. The digitally encoded data is stored in the lengths of these pits and in the distances between them, which only take discrete values.

The information is read out by a beam of light that passes through the transparent substrate and is reflected by the encoded surface. The reflected beam is modulated by the information encoded in the surface. The information is followed by means of servo systems for tracking and focusing.

Data Specification

- The *Information Area* is the recordable part of the disc. This area is divided into three parts: the lead-in area, the program area, and the lead-out area.
- The *Program Area* is divided into a maximum 99 information tracks, each having a minimum length of 4 seconds, not including the pause length preceding this track. Each information track can be a data track or an audio track.
- A *Data Track* is a track with information encoded as 8-bits-wide symbols (bytes) organized in blocks of 2,352 bytes.

Requirements for Measurements

Atmospheric Conditions. Measurements and mechanical checks can be carried out at any combination of temperature, humidity, and air pressure within the following limits unless otherwise specified:

- Ambient temperature: 15°C to 35°C
- Relative humidity: 45% to 75%
- Air pressure: 86kPa to 106kPa

Requirements for the Measuring Pickup. The optical pickup to be used for disc measurement must comply to the following requirements:

- Wavelength: 780 ± 10 nm
- NA: 0.45 ± 0.01
- Intensity at the rim of the pupil of the objective lens: 50% of the maximum intensity value

- Diffraction limited performance of the optical system: within the Marechal criterion

GENERAL SPECIFICATION OF CHARACTERISTICS

Readout System

- Readout mode: in reflection, through transparent disc
- Track shape: one spiral, no track interruption in information areas

Outer Diameter

- Outer diameter of disc: 120 ± 0.3 mm, measured at $23 \pm 2°C$ and $50 \pm 5\%$ RH
- Eccentricity: ± 0.2 mm, relative to center hole (largest inner circle)
- Edge shape: free from burrs; chamfer or radius permitted
- Disc weight: 14 to 33 gr

Center Hole

- Diameter: $15 + 0.1$ mm, measured at $23 \pm 2°C$ and $50 \pm 5\%$ RH
- Shape of center hole: cylindrical
- Edge shape: chamfer or radius permitted; burrs at the information side of the disc are permitted

Thickness

- Thickness of disc: $1.2 \, ^{+0.3}_{-0.1}$ mm (see Figs. 12 and 13), including protective layer and label

Clamping Area

- Clamping area on both sides of the disc: 26 to 33 mm, both surfaces flat; see Figure 12
- Thickness of clamping area: $1.2 \, ^{+0.3}_{-0.1}$ mm, including protective layer and label
- Height of reference plane: equal to front surface in information area

Deflection. Disc fixed between two concentric rings ($\phi_{min} = 29$mm, $\phi_{max} = 31$mm), with a clamping force between 1N and 2N,

- Maximum deflection: ± 0.4 mm
- Deflection, averaged over one revolution: ± 0.3 mm
- Maximum angular deviation of the beam incident surface from the reference plane: $\pm 0.6°$
- Maximum angular deviation of the reflected beam in the radial direction, from the normal line of the reference plane (including unparallelism of disc substrate): $\pm 1.6°$

All within information area (45 mm to max. 118 mm diameter).

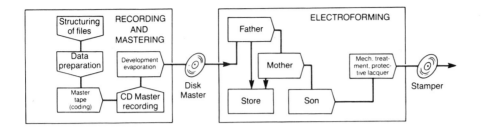

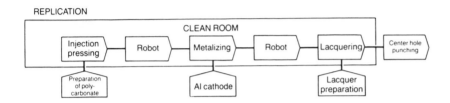

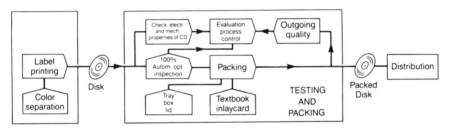

Fig. 1-12. Stages in the development of a packaged disc. Courtesy Philips and Du Pont Optical.

Label

- Inner and outer diameter: must not exceed dimensions of the disc, see Figure 13.
- On which side of the disc; see Figure 13.
- Label information:
- The total label requirements are outlined in the Art Specifications/PDO 0003.

Optical Requirements. Within information area (45 mm to maximum 118 mm diameter):

- Thickness of transparent disc's substrate 1.2 ± 0.1 mm, excluding reflective layer, protective layer, and label
- Refractive index of transparent substrate: 1.55 ± 0.1

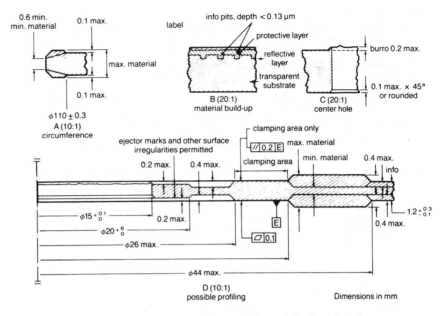

Fig. 1-13. Disc thickness measurements. Courtesy Philips and Du Pont Optical.

- Maximum birefringence of the transparent substrate: 100 nm, double pass
- Reflectivity: 70%
- Maximum variation of reflectivity: 3%

Recorded Area

- Starting diameter of program area: $10 \, {}^{+0}_{-0.4}$ mm, measured at $23 \pm 2°C$ and $50 \pm 5\%$ RH
- Maximum diameter of program area: 116 mm, measured at $23 \pm 2°C$ and $50 \pm 5\%$ RH
- Maximum starting diameter of lead-in area: 46 mm, measured at $23 \pm 2°C$ and $50 \pm 5\%$ RH
- Minimum outer diameter of lead-out area: outer diameter of program plus 1 mm

Track Pitch

- Track pitch: $1.6 \pm 0.1 \, \mu m$, in program area and lead-in/lead-out areas

Rotation

- Sense of rotation: counterclockwise, seen from readout side
- Scanning velocity: 1.20-1.40 m/s
- Maximum velocity variation on one disc: ± 0.01 m/s

Vertical Deviations of the Information Layer. As observed by the optical stylus, also included are tolerances on thickness, refractive index, and deflection. Disc fixed between two concentric rings (θ_{min} = 29mm, θ_{max} = 31mm), with a clamping force between 1 N and 2 N.

- For frequencies below 500 Hz:

  - Maximum vertical deviation from nominal value (1.2 mm above reference plane at refractive index of 1.55): $\pm$ 0.5 mm
  - Maximum rms value: 0.4 mm
  - Maximum vertical acceleration: 10 m/s^2, disc rotating at scanning velocity

- For frequencies above 500 Hz: maximum vertical deviation: $+1\mu$m

Radial Deviations of the Track

- For frequencies below 500 Hz:

  - Maximum eccentricity of track radius: $+70$ μm, relative to center hole (largest inner circle)
  - Maximum radial acceleration (exc. and unroundness): 0.4 m/s^2, disk rotating at scanning velocity

- For frequencies above 500 Hz:

Environment. The following operating conditions for the media have to be taken into account:

- Temperature: $-40°$ C to $70°$ C
- Relative humidity: 10% to 95%
- Absolute humidity: 0.1 to 60 gm^{-3}
- Maximum temperature transition: $-50°$ C/hour
- Maximum humidity transition: 30% RH

2
The Multimedia CD-ROM
for Integrated Systems

Many CD-ROMs currently available are conversions of online databases or print information that require only the addition of search and retrieval software. This type of implementation, however, is fairly straightforward. Newer CD-ROMs are now being produced that combine graphics and audio with text, a process that requires the use of more sophisticated techniques.

One company that first made its mark in videodisc and is now actively involved in integrating images and text is Online Computer Systems, Inc., in Germantown, Maryland. Online has developed highly sophisticated image compression and decompression hardware and a series of controller cards that allow for playback of digitally encoded audio from CD-ROM. Because they are pioneering multimedia applications of CD-ROM, Online's President, William H. Ford, was asked to contribute to this book. His paper on integration of text and image is presented here with his permission.

Publishing Integrated Text and Image Databases on CD-ROM by William H. Ford

This paper focuses on the issues of combining images and text into an integrated CD-ROM delivery system. The examples used are from a parts catalog application. Techniques for dealing with half-tone images are also examined. Use of a local area network for resource sharing is reviewed. The concepts and techniques presented here are in actual use on several systems for government and industry clients.

System Requirements

For a CD-ROM-based information system employing images to be successful, it has to meet the following mandatory requirements:

- The system must support databases up to 250,000 records, of which each record can consist of 2,000 characters of information, coupled with an image ranging from ¼ page to greater than one full 8 ½ × 11 page of graphic information.
- A base information system must provide a minimum of two key-access methods. The first would be a structured hierarchical access method to allow an individual to start at the top of a major category and walk his/her way down to a specific part. A typical example would be the selection of a class of automobile, the front fender of an automobile, the wheel of the automobile, explosion of the wheel area, the disk brake view, and the part number for that item. This type of access would be primarily used by novice customers requiring information on a specific item. The second access method required is by keyword search to allow queries to be made against the database when the user does not know a specific part exists. A typical example of this requirement would be the search for a mechanical part in a large database. For instance, if the user desires to locate a screw that is 2 inches in length with brass-plated hexagonal head and ¼ inch in diameter, the system would re-trieve all occurrences of screws meeting that search specification and display the various thread types and shank sizes available.
- The system must be capable of supporting images larger than 8½ × 11 in a technical manual; typically, these would be fold-out pages.
- The system must provide a highly visual-oriented interface whereby the user does not have to use complex syntax to search and/or navigate through the parts information system.

It is highly desirable that such a system be capable of supporting the following types of extended functionality:

- It should be capable of supporting half-tone images and limited color capability where appropriate. An example might be detailed views of parts locations inside an automobile engine.
- To deal with large images greater than 8½ × 11, it is necessary to provide a multi-level pan and zoom capability.
- There are no standard screen display formats at this time, and the cost of high-resolution displays greater than 1000 points by 1000 points is quite expensive. It is highly desirable that the system be capable of operating on lower resolution displays, the minimum being 640 × 400 black and white.

Large Databases (Greater than 250,000 Parts/Records)

One of the major problems in capturing and storing large image-related databases is the size of the files created from straight digitizing. Therefore, during this project, consideration was given to a combination of either digitizing and OCRing the text, keyboard the text and digitizing the images, or a combined technique to achieve the maximum space compression possible. Other data reduction techniques were considered for reducing the image space requirements.

To illustrate the space requirements for a large image database, Fig. 2-1 shows the number of 8½ × 11 pages per disc that were scanned at 300 dots per inch (dpi) and compressed using CCITT Group 4 compression. We have illustrated that one disc using digitizing only at 300 dpi will allow 5,000 to 8,000 pages; whereas if 75 percent of the space on each 8½ × 11 page is text, and it is OCR'd or keyboarded and the remaining 25 percent of image space is digitized, 20,000 to 32,000 pages can be accommodated on a single disc. Clearly, where possible, one should try to store text as ASCII strings and only digitize images. For this project, it was decided that all text would be stored in ASCII form and all drawings would be digitized and stored in compressed raster form.

300 dpi Group 4 Compression

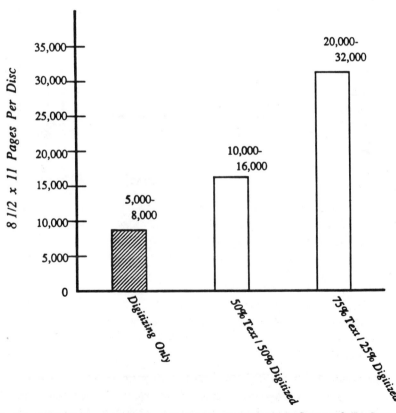

Fig. 2-1. CD-ROM storage capabilities with various scanning methods. Courtesy Online Computer Systems, Inc., Germantown, MD.

Text Database Sizing

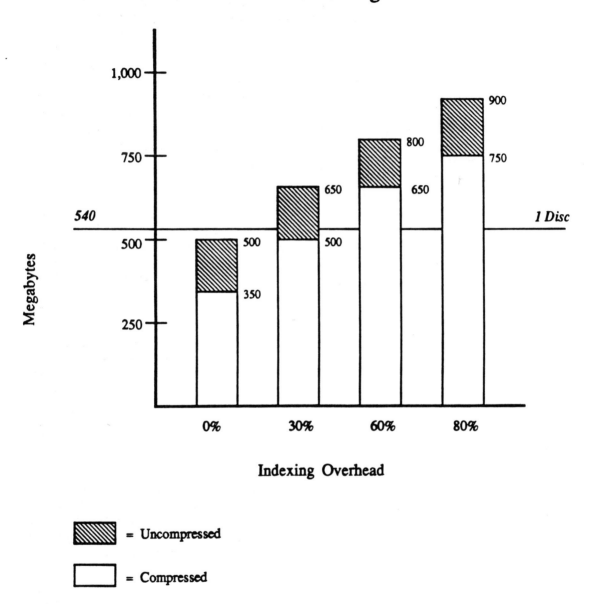

Fig. 2-2. Text database sizing. Courtesy Online Computer Systems, Inc., Germantown, MD.

Figure 2-2 depicts the text database size for a 250,000 parts catalog where each record consists of 2,000 characters of textual information for several values of indexing overhead. Two values, uncompressed and compressed, depict the file size when the ASCII text has been compressed using a modified Huffman code or equivalent or no compression at all. Disc capacity has been set at 540 megabytes, although as much as 600 megabytes should be possible. As indicated in Fig. 2-2, with a 30 percent overhead and no compression, the entire text file cannot fit on a single disc. If a more realistic full text indexing overhead of 60 percent is assumed, the 600-megabyte capacity of the extended disc is exceeded.

In order to provide a full keyboard access capability coupled with a hierarchically structured index over the top of all parts, a major decision was made to place the text and index structures on one disc and images on separate and distinct discs organized by major classification codes. This allows the delivery of a complete parts information system on a two-drive system, having text and indexes mounted in one drive and the currently viewable images on the second.

Hierarchical and Keyword Search

Two techniques were considered for indexing the file. One was human indexing through actual review of the printed material; the second was an automated indexing approach based on the actual structure of the printed document. Due to the inconsistency of this structure, it was decided that a combination of human-supported indexing directed by the structure of the document be employed.

Supporting Images Greater than 8½ × 11

There were two techniques considered for digitizing images greater than 8½ × 11 inches. The first was a high-resolution, motion-control system that would allow 1/1000 of an inch repeatable positioning in both X and Y direction to allow a scanner to segment images larger than 8½ × 11. A second approach considered was the photo reduction of an image and subsequent digitizing at a resolution sufficient for reproduction on displays and hardcopy. It was decided that a combination of image reduction and motion control transfer would be well-suited for this project. Figure 2-3 depicts the process of placing an image greater than 8½ × 11 on a large platen. Movement of the platen is controlled by a computer which also commands the camera to capture that specific view. A grid is programmed into the computer that is retraced for each image of that size. The ability to program two-dimensional motion transfer sequences provides significant reduction in the transfer cost of large images.

Highly Visual-Oriented Interface

Figure 2-4 depicts a simple example of a hierarchical search where the user wishes to locate a power transformer through the hierarchical method. The user would select electronic at the top level, passive at the second level and associate the keyword transformer. At the third level, the user would see only the nodes of "electronic" that contain the word "transformer" or some form of "transformer."

Figure 2-5 depicts the capability to search the database using a predefined template. Once the user has defined the subject category,

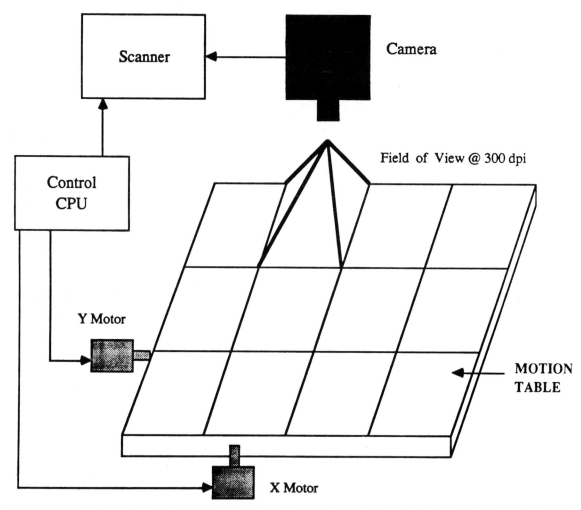

Fig. 2-3. Placing an image larger than 8.5 by 11 on a large platen. Courtesy Online Computer Systems, Inc., Germantown, MD.

he/she must enter the necessary parameters to find the power transformer of choice. The system being implemented provides, for each component and classification type, a unique template that allows parameters to be entered and qualifying records to be browsed. The example presented is one in which the user enters a primary voltage of 115, cycle equal to 60, secondary voltage of 12 with a rating of 2 to 4 amperes, a test voltage equal to or greater than 1500 and a height less than 3 inches. In this example, two transformers qualified. (Note that both have a height less than 3 inches and comply with the other search parameters.) Also note that in the image availability column, there is an image available so that the user can see the physical characteristics of this part.

Support of Half-Tone Images and Optionally Limited Color

For half-tone images, there are two basic techniques for approaching

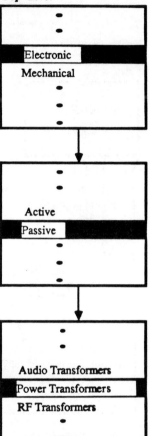

Fig. 2-4. A hierarchical search example. Courtesy Online Computer Systems, Inc., Germantown, MD.

image capture and display. The ideal approach is to provide a multi-bit-per-pixel digitizing process, typically 6 to 8 bits per pixel, to allow for high quality gray-scale playback on both display and hardcopy devices. The second approach is a technique for dithering high resolution bits on a 300 dpi format to allow the display of pseudo half-tone images through appropriate bit combinations. For this project, the dither technique was selected and color imagery was not included. Color imagery was excluded due to the large capacity requirements and lack of cost-effective display technology.

Provide a Multilevel Zoom and Pan Capability

There are two approaches to providing pan and zoom functionality to the user. One is the software approach, which is extremely processor-intensive; the second is a combination of a hardware assist and software

Part #	Primary Volts/Cycles	Secondary Volts/Amps	Test Volts	Size H x W x D	Weight Pounds	Image Available
	115 / 60	12 / 2-4	≥ 1500	< 3/ /		

Number Qualified :   2

F-218	115 / 50-60	12 / 2	1500	2 / 3 1/4 / 1 7/8	1.1	1
F-219	115 / 50-60	12 / 4	1500	2 9/16 / 4 / 2 1/4	2.3	1

Fig. 2-5. A predefined search template. Courtesy Online Computer Systems, Inc., Germantown, MD.

control. Due to the complexity of the images being processed, this project demanded the hardware assist capability. Figure 2-6 depicts an 8½ × 11 image digitized at 300 dpi overlaid by a 640 × 400 pixel IBM PC view, a typical Genesis display of 800 × 1000 pixels and a high-resolution 1600 × 2400 pixel display such as the Princeton unit. As can be seen by the relationships, the lower resolution devices provide only a peephole into the full-resolution image. To make these lower resolution devices more effective, Online developed a hardware decompression card with a 2, 3, 4, 5, 8 and 16X pixel compression capability to allow near real time pan and zoom across images equal to or greater than 8½ × 11 at 300 dpi. This hardware capability also provides edge detection feature to prevent the loss of critical information at the higher pixel compression factors. Through the use of a hardware assist, the effectiveness of a low resolution 640 × 400 display becomes much more acceptable. It is important to note that the laser printer output always operates at 300 dpi.

PROTOTYPE FUNCTIONALITY

To test the concepts and techniques developed for this project, a prototype system is being assembled that consists of a series of IBM PC-AT-based processors, driving a number of displays having resolutions from 640 × 400 pixels to 1600 × 2400 pixels and operating on a local area network from a shared disc file server containing up to eight CD-ROM drives. This system will handle in excess of 150,000 parts online per eight-drive unit. The system is capable of supporting up to four such drive sets; thus, the total capacity is in excess of 500,000 parts online. Figure 2-7 depicts the base unit with a CD-ROM file server host connected to a single eight-drive optical storage unit with an auxiliary laser printer for hardcopy output. Multiple user stations are configured to allow simultaneous access to both text and image data. The overall objective of this prototype effort is to determine the functional requirements of the system in an operational setting. The two user classes to be served are the end user desiring a specific part for a specific device and an engineering or research

Display Views @ 1:1 for 8 1/2 x 11 @ 300 dpi

Group 4 Hardware Decompression
with 2, 3, 4, 5, 8, 16x Pixel Compression
o Near Real Time Pan
o Horizontal Edge Detection

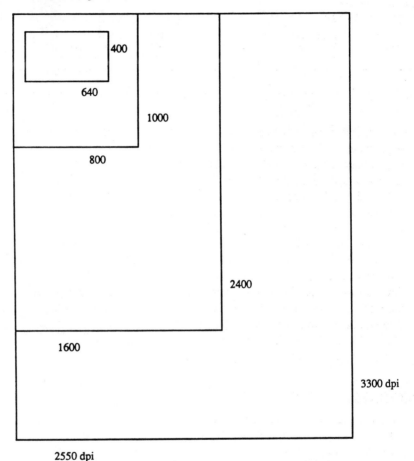

Fig. 2-6. A 300dpi image that has been overlayed by three other display formats. Courtesy Online Computer Systems, Inc., Germantown, MD.

person wishing to search a complex parts information system for a part that meets his/her specific requirements.

Based on progress to date, it is clear that CD-ROM technology can support an integrated multi-user environment with near real-time pan and zoom capabilities on multiple display device types and that a highly interactive visual interface is possible that will reduce the complexity of user interactions necessary to search for visually oriented information. Finally, the architecture

Prototype Configuration

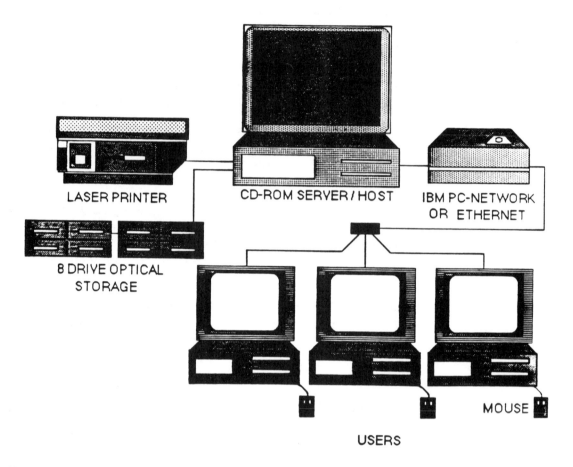

LASER PRINTER

CD-ROM SERVER / HOST

IBM PC-NETWORK
OR ETHERNET

8 DRIVE OPTICAL
STORAGE

MOUSE

USERS

Fig. 2-7. A base unit prototype with a CD-ROM server host. Courtesy Online Computer Systems, Inc., Germantown, MD.

presented provides a significant growth capability as new hardware technology emerges.

DIGITAL AUDIO

Digital audio, the process of adding voices, music and/or sound effects in combination with text on compact disc, is finding application in both CD-ROM and the newer CD-1. One company that recently announced the availability of multi-media CD design and production services is Earth View Inc., in Seattle, Washington, under the name Interactive AudioMation (IAM). IAM productions will specialize in a blend of audio with text, graphics and input functions in any interactive computer program.

Interactive AudioMation uses high-quality prerecorded audio—voices, music and sound effects—to add an increased level of realism, drama and impact to both business and consumer applications. A single CD holds an hour or more of sound segments that can be accessed in about one second and played back under program control.

Interactive AudioMation can be implemented in various hardware configurations:

- Personal computer with a CD-ROM driver and an audio playback board.
- Personal computer with a combination CD-audio/CD-ROM drive.
- CD-1 player with built-in computer (scheduled for availability in 1988).

Bryan Brewer, president of Earth View, was asked for his perspective on digital audio, and his comments are presented here with his permission.

Sound Advice
by Bryan Brewer

To many people today, "digital audio" is extremely simple. All you do is put the CD in the player and press "play." The same will be true of digital audio tape (DAT) when it reaches the consumer market. But you need to know more to understand the role digital audio can play in a CD-ROM multi-media application.

Digital audio may be a new subject to many computer users and developers, because storing audio digitally requires a lot of data—so much, in fact, that it has not been practical to record much audio on floppy discs. What was needed was a mass storage medium that could hold hundreds of megabytes—hence, the invention of the compact disc. Today's music CDs use about 150K worth of storage for one second of stereo sound.

The most common method of converting sound into kilobytes involves a process called pulse code modulation (PCM), where the sound to be digitized is picked up by a microphone, which creates an analog electrical signal. This signal, which can be displayed graphically as a sound waveform, is a direct representation of the original sound's sound waves.

Sound wave vibration rate, or frequency, is measured in Hertz (Hz), or cycles per second. The range of human hearing extends from about 20Hz (a very low, barely audible hum, such as a diesel engine in the distance) to about 20,000Hz, or 20kHz (a high-pitched hiss, such as escaping compressed air). Most sounds we hear are combinations of many frequencies, forming complex waveforms that constantly vary over time.

Sound also varies in loudness, reflected by the height, or amplitude, of the waveform. The larger the separation between the peaks and valleys, the louder the sound.

In analogy audio, frequency is recorded as physical or magnetic variations that represent the waveform. The squiggles in a record groove or the fluctuations in the magnetic particles on an audio tape are "analogs" of the sound waveform. The fidelity with which the sound is reproduced depends in part on the analog representation's accuracy.

Digital audio, on the other hand, uses techniques to measure the waveform's frequency and loudness and to store these measurements as numeric, or digital, data. In pulse code modulation (PCM), a circuit called an analog-to-digital converted (ADC) measures, or samples, the amplitude of the waveform—not continuously, but at discrete points at regular intervals (Fig. 2-8). The rate at which an ADC samples sound—its sampling rate—is also expressed in Hz or kHz.

Pulse Code Modulation

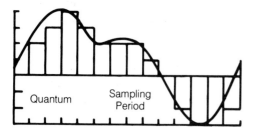

Quantum   Sampling Period

Fig. 2-8. In pulse code modulation, an analog-to-digital converter samples the amplitude waveform at discrete points and at regular intervals. Courtesy Bryan Brewer, President of Earth View, Inc., Seattle, WA.

The sample rate must be at least twice the frequency of the highest sound to be reproduced by the system. The CD-Audio (CD-A) standard—the so-called Philips/Sony Red Book—reproduces sounds in a frequency range up to 20kHz using a sampling rate of 44.1kHz.

In addition to sampling rate, quantization level is the other parameter of a PCM system (Fig. 2-9). This refers to the number of bits used to store the waveform amplitude's value for each sample. CD-A uses 16-bit quantization, which yields a range of 65,535 equal increments (2 to the 16th power minus 1) to express the value of a sample.

The quantization level determines the recorded sound's signal-to-noise (S/N) ratio. More bits means a finer approximation of each sample's value, resulting in less system noise. The 16-bit quantization of CD-A reproduces sound with a S/N ratio of about 98 decibels (dB). The decibel is a meas-

Sampling Rate and Quantization

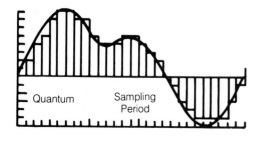

Quantum   Sampling Period

Fig. 2-9. Sampling rate and quantization are the two prime determinants of the reproduced sound's overall quality. Courtesy Bryan Brewer, President of Earth View, Inc., Seattle, WA.

ure of relative loudness between two sounds—in this case, it's the difference between the CD system's noise and the loudest signal it can produce without distortion. By contrast, the S/N ratio on tapes and LPs is usually in the 50 to 60dB range, which results in more system noise.

For a digital audio system, sampling rate and quantization are the prime determinants of the reproduced sound's overall fidelity. They can be compared, up to a point, to the resolution and color depth specifications for graphic images. The audio sample's amplitude value and a pixel's color value are represented by a specific number of bits. The number of samples per seconds, or pixels per image, is multiplied by the number of bits per sample or pixel to determine the total amount of data required for audio or image storage.

In both cases, increasing the number of samples or pixels, or the number of bits per sample or pixel, generally results in a truer sound or picture. But the trade-off for increased fidelity is increased data storage. And despite CD-ROM's massive capacity, the storage/fidelity trade-off can become a crucial issue in some multi-media applications.

The CD-A standard, fixed at 16-bit quantization and 44.1kHz sampling rate, yields a maximum of about 74 minutes of stereo playing time on a CD. When the audio is played from a disc, a circuit in the player called a digital-to-analog converter (DAC) converts the digital stream back into an analog electrical signal, which can then be amplified and played back through speakers or headphones.

You can store this level of "red book" audio along with other data such as text, images and programs on a CD-ROM disc. If the CD-ROM data takes up 100MB, you still have up to an hour of stereo audio playing time. This combination is particularly suited for use in a "dual-mode" CD-ROM drive, such as the Amdek LaserDrive 1 now on the market. It can send CD-ROM data to the computer or it can play "red book" audio—under software control—through its own built-in DAC and audio output connectors.

This approach, however, has some drawbacks. First is the 74-minute limitation in audio playing time, which is further diminished by any CD-ROM data stored on the disc. Second, a dual-mode drive cannot simultaneously access CD-ROM data and play audio. In some applications, this may not be a limitation, especially if text and images can be buffered effectively in the computer's memory before an audio segment plays.

A way around these limitations is to store audio as CD-ROM data encoded at a different standard, and play it back through a digital-to-analog converter on a computer's expansion board. For lack of a standard term, let's call this "CD-ROM audio." And it's not only the terminology that lacks standards; no widely accepted encoding standards exist for mid- and lower-fidelity CD-ROM audio.

The situation is not surprising because there hasn't been much audio action in the PC arena. A few audio playback boards are available, but they use varying and often incompatible audio encoding methods.

One standard that has found compatibility is the 12kHz, 8-bit PCM encoding used for the Facts on File Visual Dictionary CD-ROM prototype disc. The audio reproduces frequencies up to 6kHz (quite adequate for spoken word recording) at a S/N ratio of about 50dB. The disc contains more than an hour's worth of English and French terms. It sounds acceptable at this playback level and is compatible with DAC hardware for the IBM PC, Apple Macintosh and Apple IIe. A disc encoded in this standard can play about 12 hours of monophonic sound.

The general lack of audio standards was recognized by Microsoft's Bill Gates in his keynote speech at the CD-ROM conference in May 1987. He urged the CD-ROM industry to pursue an agreement.

The issue of audio standards may well be settled by technology that is emerging from another format, CD-I. The CD-I audio standard includes regular ''red book'' audio as well as three new lower-fidelity levels that use an encoding technique known as adaptive delta pulse code modulation, or ADPCM. Adding ''adaptive delta'' to the PCM encoding process reduces the number of bits required to reproduce a given sound fidelity level, effectively resulting in data compression of the digital audio information.

CD-I's three audio levels are designated A, B and C (Fig. 2-10). Level A is the highest fidelity, with a 17kHz frequency range at 90dB S/N ratio. This level sounds very nearly as good as ''red book'' audio, but it uses only eight bits per sample due to the ADPCM compression. Level B keeps the same frequency range, but uses only four bits per sample, which reduces the S/N ratio to about 60 dB. At this level, you begin to hear some of the system noise, but music still sounds quite good. Level C uses the same four-bit ADPCM encoding, but halves the sampling rate, yielding a frequency range of 8.5kHz. This level loses some of the upper frequencies needed for good music reproduction, but speech sounds very good.

CD-I's three sound levels give the approximate audio fidelity heard on an LP, FM broadcast, and AM radio, respectively. Each decrease in level halves the storage requirements, thus doubling the playing time. And

CD Audio Standards

	CD Digital Audio	CD-1 'A' Hi-Fi Music	CD-1 'B' Mid-Fi Music	CD-I 'C' Speech
Sampling Rate	44.1 kHz	37.8 kHz	37.8 kHz	18.9 kHz
Freq Range	20 kHz	17 kHz	17 kHz	8.5 kHz
Encoding	16-bit PCM	8-bit ADPCM	4-bit ADPCM	4-bit ADPCM
S/N Ratio	98 dB	90 dB	60 dB	60 dB
Max Playing Time	74 min stereo	2.4 hr stereo 4.8 hr mono	4.8 hr stereo 9.6 hr mono	9.6 hr stereo 19.2 hr mono
Approximate Fidelity Equivalent	CD	mono LP	mono FM	mono AM

Fig. 2-10. The CD-I audio standard includes CD audio plus three new lower fidelity levels. Courtesy Bryan Brewer, President of Earth View, Inc., Seattle, WA.

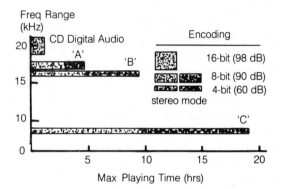

Fig. 2-11. The lower quality sound levels result in a storage/fidelity tradeoff. Less space on the disc for a given amount of sound means it can be encoded at a lower level. Courtesy Bryan Brewer, President of Earth View, Inc., Seattle, WA.

you can choose monophonic instead of stereo, which further halves the storage need. At the extreme, you could fill a disc with more than 19 hours of C level mono sound.

The main reason for these lower-quality sound levels is to address the storage/fidelity trade-off issue (Fig. 2-11). If you have less space on the disc for a given amount of sound, then you can encode it at a lower level. This will often be the case for multimedia CD-I applications that have a lot of pictures and graphics on the disc.

Can CD-I audio standards be used in the CD-ROM environment? There is certainly no technical barrier. It's simply a matter of time before CD-I audio encoding hardware appears in recording studies and CD-I decoding chips become available on the market.

Whether or not Philips and Sony will license CD-I audio technology apart from a complete CD-I system is another question. They might keep their ADPCM tricks inside a CD-I machine for a while to give that product a competitive advantage.

At the same time, CD-ROM could greatly benefit from the de facto incorporation of CD-I audio standards for multi-media applications. The addition of CD-I audio decoding chips to dual-mode CD-ROM drives and audio playback boards would simplify disc compatibilities and add an increased capability level to multi-media CD-ROM applications that use audio.

3
CD-ROM
Companion Technologies

Although the primary emphasis in this book is on CD-ROM, there are a number of other optical technologies that warrant discussion. This chapter discusses CD-I, DVI and WORM, three companion technologies that are fast making themselves known.

COMPACT DISC-INTERACTIVE (CD-I)

In February 1986 at the Microsoft CD-ROM Conference, Philips and Sony announced CD-I, and the fledgling CD-ROM industry's participants were stunned, to say the least. Here were Philips and Sony announcing a newer, and in some ways, better technology at a time when developers were launching full-scale projects using CD-ROM technology and assuring their customers that the market was stable.

As the dust settled and clearer heads prevailed, it became evident that CD-I would be a companion technology that would enhance rather than detract from CD-ROM and that the two would not even be competing for the same market share. This, combined with the fact that CD-ROM is available now while CD-I is not expected to be available until mid- or late-1988, means that those involved with CD-ROM development projects can breathe a sigh of relief.

CD-I uses the same technology as CD-ROM, but differs in a number of very important areas. First, CD-I is being targeted toward the consumer market, not the business market. Second, a CD-I player will be a stand-alone device, much like a VCR, that can be attached to a television or stereo and can be controlled by means of a keyboard or mouse device. It will allow for interactive games, educational programs, graphics accompaniment to music and will be similar to a computer in that it has its own microprocessor (Motorola 68000) and ROM-based operating system (CD-RTOS, which stands for compact disc real-time operating system). It will allow for a CD audio player to be "piggybacked" as an enticement to those who now own them. Philips has developed a separate standard for CD-I (the Green Book) to ensure compatibility among players and discs, and the standard includes formats for audio, graphics, and text.

The interesting thing about CD-I is that plans are for the players to have the capability of reading CD-ROM data as well, which gives CD-ROM developers, who until now have been targeting their services toward the professional market, an opening into the consumer market. So the two technologies, rather than competing against one another can and probably will complement each other, with CD-I being the catalyst the optical technology industry needs to bring it to the attention of a larger segment of the population.

DIGITAL VIDEO INTERACTIVE (DVI)

With the announcement of DVI, additional confusion was generated. However, DVI is yet another companion technology that allows for full motion video, something that neither CD-ROM nor CD-I are capable of. The following is reprinted with permission of David Sarnoff Research Center, which has developed its first prototype DVI product and continues research into this technology.

Digital Video Interactive Technology
David Sarnoff Research Center

During the 1960s and 1970s, advances in digital technology were largely responsible for the growth of large-scale computer systems in business, government agencies and universities. The effect on consumers was large, but indirect.

Over the past decade, however, the consumer has increasingly felt the impact of digital technology, both at home and at work. White collar workers today schedule projects and prepare budgets using personal computers, while blue collar workers supervise digitally controlled robots on automated assembly lines. At home, digital technology has made a wealth of new products possible, including pocket calculators, digital watches, video games, home computers and the compact disc audio player. In addition, many existing products have been drastically improved through digital technology, including home appliances, cameras, heating and air conditioning control systems, automobiles, televisions and VCRs.

The driving force behind the growing importance of digital technology has been in the extremely rapid advances in digital integrated circuits. The complexity of digital integrated circuits has quadrupled every three years for the past two decades. Today, very large-scale integrated (VLSI) circuits contain more than one million transistors. As a result, only a handful of VLSI chips are now required to implement the electronics of sophisticated products such as personal computers. Because the cost of such products is heavily influenced by the number of VLSI chips they contain, these products are relatively inexpensive.

Because of the inherent complexity of processing video signals, video-based products have been among the most difficult to design using digital VLSI technology. However, VLSI technology has advanced to the point where consumers will soon have the opportunity to buy all-digital television receivers and VCRs. The transition from analog to digital technology in television products will not only result in improved picture quality but will also add new product features such as the ability to show a second channel in a small window in a corner of the television screen.

Over the past five years, a number of companies have attempted to develop highly interactive systems centered on low-cost, high-capacity mass memories—specifically, the analog videodisc player and digital CD audio players. Interactive Video Disc (IVD) was the first attempt to merge the realism of motion video and audio with the interactivity of personal computers. This was accomplished by providing a laser videodisc player with a computer interface. In a typical IVD system, an application running on a personal computer controls the sequencing of still-frame and motion video and audio in response to a user's inputs. A 12-inch videodisc can store up to 54,000 still frames of video or up to 30 minutes of full-motion video and audio or an appropriately scaled combination of still and motion video.

IVD systems have been marketed for several years, and they range in price from $1,000 to $10,000 per system. They are used as training tools in medical and industrial sectors, learning stations in universities, and in point-of-information terminals. According to a study in *Videodisc Monitor*, the videodisc market in the United States will reach $1.6 billion by 1990. IVD has achieved relatively low market penetration to date, partially because its analog video signal hampers interactivity. Because it often needs a sophisticated graphics display subsystem to fully meet application requirements, IVD is also expensive.

Introduced in the early 1980s, CD-ROM is a computer peripheral cousin of the mass-marketed CD audio player. The CD-ROM drive mechanism is basically the same as that for the CD audio player and hence is relatively inexpensive. CD-ROM drives use a beam of laser light to follow data tracks on the CD. The laser reads the markings on the CD and sends corresponding digital binary signals to the computer.

One advantage of CD-ROM is that it can store as much as 540 megabytes of data, equivalent to 150,000 printed pages on a single CD. The CD-ROM disc can store a thousand times more data than a floppy disc and approximately 25 times more data than a 20-megabyte hard disk drive. This large storage capacity makes it particularly suitable for large databases, such as encyclopedias.

Although CD-ROM is used mostly for storing large, infrequently changing text databases, there are no restrictions on how the data stored on a CD may be used. A number of applications use the CD to store graphics as well as text. Applications featuring digital audio and still-frame video have also been proposed.

The first commercial CD-ROM products, including CD-ROM drives and databases, appeared on the market in 1985. DiskTrend Inc., a market research firm in Los Altos, California, estimates approximately 30,000 CD-ROM players were sold worldwide in 1986, up from 8,300 in 1985. Sales of CD-ROM media are expected to reach $937 million by 1991, according to estimates from Input, a market research firm in Mountain View, California.

CD-I is another variant of the CD audio player. Unlike CD-ROM drives, which typically have an interface with a personal computer, CD-I players are intended to be stand-alone products. Sony and Philips of the Netherlands announced a preliminary set of specifications for CD-I in March 1986. When they become available, CD-I players will have the ability to play back text, graphics, CD-quality audio, and still-frame video from a single CD-I disc. The primary focus of CD-I is on entertainment and educational applications in the mass consumer market.

Although each of these systems provides the user access to a variety of media, each is limited in its capabilities. IVD is expensive, has only a low level of video interactivity and often requires a separate, expensive graphics display system. CD-ROM currently offers little more than interactive access to a large amount of text and graphics, and CD-I is not yet available in a product.

Work on the merging of digital technology and video technology has been ongoing over the past four years at the David Sarnoff Research Center in Princeton, New Jersey. This center, which is a subsidiary of SRI International, was formerly GE/RCA Laboratories, and GE is continuing to fund this research under contract. Scientists at the center have developed a proprietary approach called DVI Technology which takes advantage of the digital storage capacity and data rate of the standard CD-ROM drive to provide features that are well beyond the capabilities of IVD and CD-I.

Digital Video Interactive (DVI) technology combines the interactivity of the graphics capabilities in personal computers with the realism of high-quality motion video and multitrack audio in an all-digital integrated system. DVI has the ability to display one hour of motion video from compressed digital data stored on a single, standard CD-ROM disc. DVI's motion video can be combined with foreground video objects, text, dynamic graphics, and multitrack audio, all under the user's control.

Because of its varied and flexible display and sound capabilities, DVI technology will create new market opportunities for application developers in the areas of realistic simulations, education, training and video paint, animation, editing, and special effects. It will also open opportunities in presentation preparation and display, sales tools, and scientific imaging.

At the heart of DVI is its ability to produce one hour of full-screen, full-motion video from digital data stored on a standard CD-ROM disc. Producing digital video is by no means a new concept. In television studios, digital video enables editors to make changes to a tape without diminishing its video quality. Producing digital-based video, however, is a complex process that requires large amounts of data. When a standard screen of analog video measuring 512 × 400 pixels is converted into digital form, the information takes about 600 kilobytes of data per image or frame.

In television, about 30 frames of video must be displayed each second in order to portray full-motion effects, which results in 18,000 kilobytes of data required each second. Although CD-ROM holds about 540 megabytes of data, it can store only about 30 seconds of digital video. In addition, because CD-ROM reads data out at a rate of 150 kilobytes per second, it is not fast enough to show video at its real-time speed. For example, it would take more than one hour to show 30 seconds of digital video.

The solution to the problem of too much image data and not enough storage capacity is the Research Center's compression-decompression scheme. In DVI technology, before a master is made of the CD, the digital video and audio are compressed so that fewer bits are required to represent each second of video and audio. The compression process requires large amounts of computing power. However, because compression is done only once and need not be done in real time, larger commercially available computers can be used.

When CD-ROM video and audio is played back, the compressed data must then be enlarged or decompressed in order to recapture video and audio qualities. Whereas compression is done only once and not in real time, decompression must occur in real time each time the CD is played.

In DVI, the David Sarnoff Research Center uses a proprietary, very large-scale integration (VLSI) chip set to perform the decompression processing and display capabilities that result in real-time video. The Video Display Processor (VDP) developed at the Center, is a two-chip set that consists of a pixel processor and an output display processor. The pixel processor, called VDP1, is the processing engine that runs the decompression algorithms in software. VDP1 is designed to process 12.5 million instructions per second (MIPS—a standard measure of microprocessor speed).

The instruction set features several special video/graphic instructions that can perform several operations in parallel. This results in a substantial increase in video and graphics processing power for VDP1 compared to other video display processors. It is this engine that allows DVI to combine full-motion video with video overlays, text and dynamic graphics all in the same video frame.

The output display processor, VDP2, gives DVI technology its resolution modes and pixel formats. VDP2's resolution ranges from 256 to

768 pixels horizontally and up to 512 pixels vertically. The VDP2 can select any one of the 16 million colors available in each pixel. This amount of color selection is one of the things that permits DVI to bring television-quality pictures to the computer screen for the first time. The VDP includes a computer bus interface that allows the chip set to be used in a variety of system architectures, including the IBM PC AT.

Development and Status

DVI was developed at the David Sarnoff Research Center, a pioneer center in numerous electronic technologies, including the television system used today. Their broad skills in television, display processor design, computer science and VLSI technology were essential in developing DVI.

Research into the project began more than three years ago after Larry Ryan conceived the idea of using a customized VLSI chip set to combine non-real-time compression of video frames with real-time decompression.

The hardware being used to develop system software and application software is a prototype pair of personal computer boards. The VDP chip set is designed into one board, and an off-the-shelf digital signal processor chip is used to implement multitrack digital audio on the second board. The final version of both boards, which will be completed by the end of 1987, will fit into an IBM PC AT.

Potential Markets and Applications

The David Sarnoff Research Center is the first to introduce a technology that integrates software programs, text, graphics, sound and full-motion video on a personal computer. DVI lets application developers incorporate a variety of media in their programs—from motion video to still images, to graphics or text and audio on one storage medium. As a result, DVI technology will spur the development of a range of products that will serve and expand existing markets as well as create new ones.

Many of today's computerized industrial training programs are interactive simulation application programs that lead users through interactive step-by-step procedures and sequences of events. To be effective, training systems must be realistic and provide students with a high degree of interactivity. Often, graphics-based simulation systems are inadequate for the real-life sessions needed in medicine, aviation and maintenance training, for example. Because of its ability to integrate video images, video textures and real audio, DVI is particularly suited to these training simulation applications.

Educational markets have long understood that visual aids can help a child's learning process. For many years, videotape has been a popular method of supplementing lectures and lessons. Although education is in need of an interactive video teaching tool, interactive videodiscs have proven to be too expensive. The need for these tools, combined with a skrinking teaching population, is putting pressure on educational institutions to establish learning laboratories where students can independently learn their designated curriculum. DVI's combination of motion video, digital audio, photographic stills and computer graphics has tremendous potential in this market area, particularly once the technology becomes less expensive. The Center believes DVI technology will first be applied in higher education and will make its way to elementary and second schools by the 1990s.

Retail stores are also a potential market for DVI. Increasingly, they are using in-store marketing systems to help boost sales. According to Touche-Ross, the installed base of in-store marketing systems will grow from 1,200 to 50,000 by 1990. Although some stores are using interactive videodisc systems, their $10,000 price tag has limited their penetration.

Retail applications that require buyers to "configure" or design their purchases are ideal for a system using DVI technology. DVI's video texturing, full-motion video and computer graphics capabilities could be used in systems for designers, landscapers and automotive showrooms. DVI gives buyers the ability to realistically try out different products on a computer without the help of a salesperson.

If packaged into a player, DVI could also affect consumer applications. By 1990, the Center expects the low price of DVI technology to bring it into home applications—including games, personal education packages and home maintenance applications.

The market for DVI technology will grow as systems developers begin to recognize the potential for a sophisticated interactive integrated medium. Market research indicates that the potential for existing limited technologies is great; GE and the Center believe the possibilities for an integrated medium are even greater.

According to Disk/Trend, sales of optical storage devices, including CD-ROM will be approximately $1.3 billion by 1989. Frost & Sullivan, a research group in New York, predicts the market for all optical products could reach $2.5 billion to $4.5 billion by 1990. Analysts are also expecting that the market will continue to grow as technology evolves, prices drop and products proliferate. DVI technology will be a significant contributor to this market growth. GE and the Center have invited companies and individuals to join with them in developing the full potential of DVI technology.

Design & Decorate: A Prototype Application for DVI Technology

Design & Decorate (Fig. 3-1) is a prototype application developed by the Center using DVI technology. Co-developed with Videodisc Publishing, Inc. of New York City, it is one of a number of pilot DVI applications in development at the Center.

Design & Decorate offers the interior designer, retailer or manufacturer a tool that is tailored to their needs. It is possible for customers and clients to see room designs filled with photo-realistic furnishing and

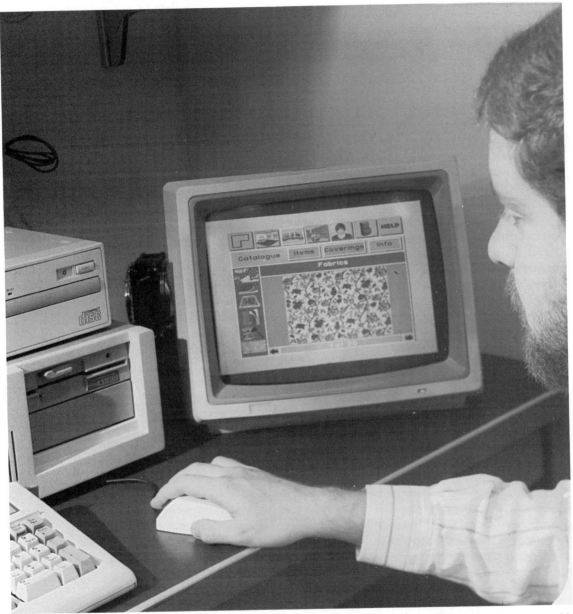

Fig. 3-1. Design and Decorate is a prototype CD-ROM-based system that offers the designer, retailer, or manufacturer a specialized development tool. Courtesy David Sarnoff Research Center, Princeton, NJ.

fabric textures and make design changes instantly. The capacity of CD-ROM allows volumes of manufacturer's catalogs to be stored on disc and instantly accessed. Everything from fabrics to wood finishes and sofas to area rugs are displayed on a video screen with photographic clarity and complete product information. Design & Decorate can help professionals experiment with different design ideas and communicate those ideas effectively to their customers.

The primary activities of the prototype program are:

- Plan - Select a basic room shape, dimensions and orientation; arrange furniture and select a view for seeing the room in Elevation.
- Elevation - View the room, complete with selected furniture, coverings and arrangement.
- Catalogue - Search instantly for furnishings and coverings.
- Storeroom - Create collections of favorite items for comparisons and future use.
- File - Save room designs and storerooms.
- Help - Learn through general instructions or get on-the-spot assistance, all with the personal touch audio narration provides.

Technical Elements

An item is a piece of furniture or accessory which is represented in the DVI system both in photographic form in Catalogue and as a three-dimensional object in Elevation. A texture is a photograph of a fabric, a wood finish, painted surface or any flat surface. These photographs are stored in digital form on the DVI system, where the Design & Decorate user can browse through them in the Catalogue. When a texture is applied to an item—for example, the user requests that a particular chair be upholstered in a selected fabric—the DVI 3-D system software automatically scales it and rotates it in perspective to fit the various surfaces of the object.

To achieve a high level of realism when drawing 3-D objects, the DVI software can simulate multiple light sources of varying intensity. Each time a surface is drawn, the angle and brightness of the various light sources is taken into account to draw a realistically lit image. DVI also provides "smooth shading," a method of smoothing the changes in brightness across neighboring surfaces. This technique visually combines the multiple parts, composing a 3-D item into a single smoothly curved surface. The hierarchical nature of the system allows complicated 3-D objects to be "assembled" out of less complicated structures. The assembled object can then be manipulated by the system as a single unit.

WORM TECHNOLOGY

Yet another companion technology is WORM (Write Once, Read Many times), which is finding application in government and industry. Timothy J. Green, President of N/Hance Systems, a specialty marketer of mass storage peripherals for PCs, supermicros and minicomputers, was asked to discuss WORM technology. His comments are reprinted here with his permission.

WORM Optical Discs
by Timothy J. Green

Optical data storage, particularly the new WORM (Write Once, Read Many) optical disc, is changing the way many people think about data storage. Optical technology's high capacity, low cost per megabyte, compact size, and security make it an important supplement to virtually every personal computer with a hard disc.

Optical technology is a well-understood, proven method of data storage. Its development began more than a decade ago, and a stream of products including videodisc players, laser discs, high fidelity compact audio discs, and now data storage systems have been brought to the market. Today, there are hundreds of thousands of optical devices in use.

Optical data storage systems have two characteristics that make them ideal for applications ranging from office automation to scientific computation. Their extremely high storage capacity is typically 10 to 20 times that of a standard PC hard disc and their cost per megabyte of storage is one-fifth that of hard discs.

The standard, 5.25-inch, doubled-sided WORM optical disc holds more than 200 megabytes of data, compared with 360 kilobytes for a 5.25-inch floppy disk, or 10 to 20 megabytes for Winchester disks. Soon to be released are larger capacity WORM discs that hold up to 500 megabytes per side for a total of 1.1 gigabyte. Two hundred megabytes is equivalent in capacity to 600 floppy discs, about 100,000 sheets of paper or eight full, four-drawer file cabinets. While a WORM optical disc costs more than a Winchester disc or floppy disc drive, it is by far the most economical in terms of cost per megabyte of storage capacity, as shown in Table 3-1.

The WORM optical disc provides 115 megabytes of storage per side. Once written, data are permanently stored and accessible, giving users a way to track historical data. This is an important consideration for archiving information and maintaining audit trails. Data stored on a hard or floppy disk can be written over or inadvertently erased. Optical discs store data randomly, so the information is available much more quickly than it is on tape, which stores data sequentially.

Write-once data storage is built on a simple concept. A laser burns a hole in the disc's surface, making the data permanent and secure. The data cannot be erased or overwritten and short of destroying the disc car-

Table 3-1. Storage Media Capacity, Total Cost, and Cost per Megabyte. Courtesy Timothy J. Green, President of N/Hance Systems, Dedham, MA.

TYPE OF DISC	CAPACITY	PRICE	Price/Mb
5.25″ N/Hance 525 Optical	240Mb	$2,750	$11.00
5.25″ Winchester	20Mb	$795	$39.75
Bernoulli Box	20Mb	$2,349	$117.00
5.25″ floppy disc drive	360Kb	$110	$367.00

tridge, cannot be lost. The removable cartridge is only slightly larger than a 5.25-inch diskette and is much less volatile. It can be shipped easily or stored safely without some of the concerns encountered when storing or shipping magnetic media. For example, because data are written optically, it cannot be lost through accidental exposure to magnetic fields. Also, head crashes are impossible because the optical disc system has no read/write heads that come in contact with the disc surface. This, plus the fact that optical disc systems operate under a range of environmental conditions and tolerate dust and other contaminants better than magnetic media, makes them quite rugged.

CD-ROM is the only other optical technology currently available. Users cannot write data to a CD-ROM, and the data stored are permanent and unalterable. The discs hold up to 600 megabytes of data, which is about three times that of current WORM optical systems. Part of the reason for this greater capacity on CD-ROM is that the discs are produced under ideal data mastering conditions and the data are formatted as a continual string along a spiral groove.

Through developments in the software device drivers necessary to integrate the WORM system on a PC, the user can use a WORM disc system just as a hard disc. The only difference is that the data is retained permanently. These device drivers are completely transparent, both to DOS and the user, and update only the changed portion of the file being appended. Furthermore, it does not impinge the WORM's data access performance significantly. Additionally, this new device driver has a utility that allows the user to follow and file's audit trail back to initial creation. Thus, the WORM is ideally suited for many applications.

WORM optical discs, as previously mentioned, differ from CD-ROM in the way the data are formatted. Instead of grooves, a WORM disc uses an embedded servo, a very reliable way to assure accurate laser head-to-track alignment. When formatting a WORM disc, a laser burns a pair of pits that act like guardrails on a narrow road along both sides of the track. The servo path guides the read/write head between the pits with great precision. The embedded servo also helps assure that discs can be interchanged among any of the supplier's drives.

WORM optical disc systems also use sophisticated error-correction algorithms to ensure data reliability. The combination of the embedded servo and error correction codes allows WORM optical drives to spin faster than CD-ROM drives, giving WORM drives a higher data transfer rate between the disc and the PC.

Although the WORM can now be used just as a hard disc, the user should still consider how it is used to avoid a frivolous waste of space performing tasks that would normally be relegated to a scratch disc. In combination with a hard disc, the optical media can provide its user with the storage capacity to handle all needs, the ability to track every version of a file, all on a permanent, portable, secure media.

By appending existing files, the user creates a readily followed audit trail that allows a user to trace data alterations back through any number of revisions. This is especially important in terms of financial and operational applications in which historical data must be retained or in engineering applications, where a series of changes must be saved.

As an example, a large accounting firm's legal department uses WORM discs in its litigation support systems. The firm stores information on a high capacity WORM disc as a case progresses, allowing their attorneys easy access. It is even possible to enter entire case references to the disc. By using digital scanners, copies of evidence presented in the case can also be stored. Neither of these processes can be cost-effectively accomplished using magnetic storage.

As another example, a major magazine publisher is planning to tie a WORM system into its central text editing system. As a manuscript progresses through writing and editing stages, a ''snapshot'' of each set of revisions will be stored for historical purposes so that a writer or editor can trace the manuscript back through the various stages at any time.

Sometimes, finding a use for a new technology is easy. Other times, it's not. The ease of pinpointing a new application for optical disc systems depends on how badly an individual needs high volume, low cost, unalterable storage. Uses for optical discs—CD-ROM or WORM—abound in every office.

4
CD-ROM Drives

The electro-mechanical devices that read and sometimes write CD-ROM optical discs can be referred to as drives, following the magnetic disc drive idiom in the computer field. However, CD-ROM technology is still highly geared toward the original video disc and devices that read these optical media are more often called *players*.

In any event, the technology that surrounds the devices that produce video images on our television receivers is the same technology that allows CD-ROM drives to deliver their data. Naturally, this is an optical technology that has been integrated with an electronic system. This combination is often referred to as Opto-Electronic.

The CD-ROM drive is used, basically, to read the stored information on the CD-ROM discs by means of an opto-electronic system that usually incorporates a laser diode with a solid state photodiode or photo-detector. The first video players used gas lasers in place of the laser diode, but this former technology has now reached its well-deserved obsolescence in favor of the reliable, simple, one-piece laser diode. Just as the transistor has replaced the vacuum tube, the solid state laser diode has replaced the more mechanically complex alternate forms of laser generation.

Figure 4-1 outlines a pictorial diagram of the basic CD-ROM reading device or, more specifically, of the laser optical pickup. This is the section that converts the data stored on the CD-ROM disc to electrical impulses. Following this stage, the electronic circuitry is, for our purposes, identical to the more

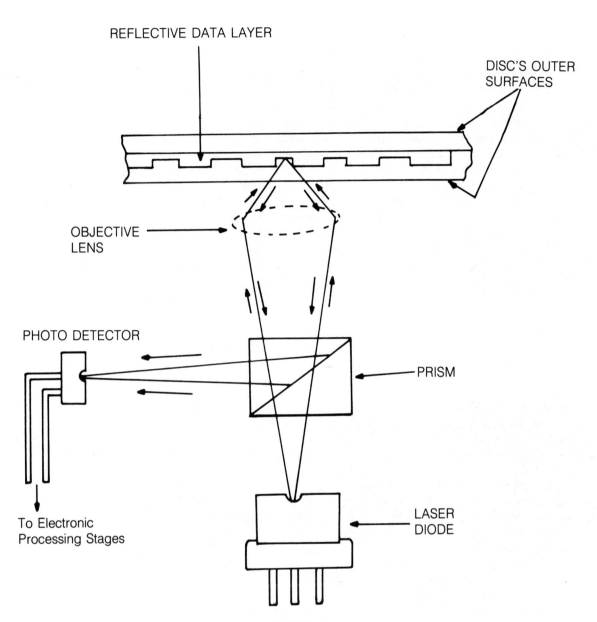

REFLECTIVE DATA LAYER

DISC'S OUTER SURFACES

OBJECTIVE LENS

PHOTO DETECTOR

PRISM

To Electronic Processing Stages

LASER DIODE

Fig. 4-1. The operation of the optical read section of a CD-ROM drive.

standard magnetic disc drives found on most microcomputers today. These latter devices contain a magnetic reading section (called disc heads, magnetic pickup devices or, simply, heads) to convert the magnetic data stored on floppy discs to digital electronic pulses. The CD-ROM drive uses the optical pickup stage to convert optically stored data into digital electronic pulses. The electronic circuitry used for processing these retrieved digital signals can be identical. Only the initial retrieval modes are different.

Referring to the pictorial diagram, the laser diode projects its concentrated light beam through a prism and then through an objective lens which focuses the beam on the reflective layer within the disc. This layer lies below the disc surface, so the portion containing the stored data is relatively free from distortion or erasure due to handling scratches on the outer surfaces of the disc. Quite simply, the scratches and fingerprints that can easily accumulate on the disc surface are "out of focus" within this precise optical reading system.

The reflecting layer within the disc returns the light from the laser diode. The objective lens again concentrates this scattered light and passes it back to the prism. However, from this angle, the prism does not pass the light as with the original strike from the laser diode. Rather, it redirects this beam to another opto-electronic device—the photodiode or photo-detector. This solid state device allows changing light levels to modulate an electric current. In other words, a change in light intensity at the optical input of the photodiode produces a like change in electric current at the diode output. The optically stored data contained on the CD-ROM disc has been effectively read and converted to its electrical equivalent.

Again, from this point on, the electrical signals can be processed, altered, converted, etc., just as if they came from a magnetic storage device or, for that matter, any other type of data storage medium. All that is necessary now is to decode the data and deliver it to its intended destination. This is usually done by the random access memory (RAM) section of the microcomputer, which is used to act upon the collected data. Alternately, retrieved information can be delivered to a modulator for display on a television receiver.

COMMERCIAL CD-ROM DRIVES

Commercial CD-ROM drives are made by a host of companies, many of which have been supplying the computer market place with other memory storage products for years. These CD-ROM drives closely resemble the more standard hard disc drives and the wide-faced floppy disc drives standard with more personal computers today. Indeed, they must (as most are designed to) be used in conjunction with or as replacements for some of these magnetic media devices. Many CD-ROM drives can be mounted in the computer within the slot originally reserved for a magnetic disc drive.

In researching this text, I obtained a Toshiba XM-2100A CD-ROM drive and used it with an IBM PC-XT. My experiences should be typical of installations using other makes of CD-ROM drives and interfacing them with other types of computer systems.

The Toshiba drive tested was a stand-alone unit to be mounted outside of the computer system unit. Another model is also available from Toshiba that will mount in one of the two disc drive slots contained in the system unit chassis.

Installation of my unit was quite straight-forward. Before doing anything, it was first necessary to de-crate the drive and remove a screw from the bottom panel. This screw is used to make the optical head stationary during shipping. When reshipping the drive, it was necessary to move the optical head to the initial position and to re-insert and tighten the set screw.

The CD-ROM drive controller was quickly inserted in one of the slots within the IBM PC-XT chassis and the interface cable was connected between this card and the drive. The entire installation took less than seven minutes.

Figure 4-2 shows a drawing of the front panel of this CD-ROM drive. The CD-ROM discs are inserted and removed at the disc tray. The tray is automatically opened or closed by either a command from the host computer or via the open/close button on the front panel. To prevent unintentional operation of the disc tray, this button must be pressed for approximately 3 seconds before operation results. Also, this open/close operation can be locked out via a command from the computer.

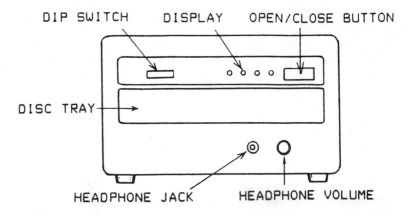

Fig. 4-2. Front panel of a Toshiba CD-ROM drive. Courtesy Toshiba Corp.

Figure 4-3 shows a block diagram of the Toshiba CD-ROM drive. This unit is equipped with a SCSI interface controller; I/O connectors that allow daisy chain connections (connection of two or more CD-ROM drives to be operated as a single unit); a digital audio reproduction function; high speed access with a linear motor; and high-efficiency data transfer with a high capacity data buffer memory that is 16 KB standard and expandable to 64 KB.

This particular unit has a maximum data capacity of 683 MB with a maximum data transfer speed of 1.4 MB per second. Normal access time is 400 ms with maximum access times of less than 700 ms. This stand-alone unit operates from 100 to 240 Vac.

Figure 4-4 shows another CD-ROM drive unit from Reference Technology, Inc. The Clasix Series 500 is designed specifically for information distribution involving large amounts of text, numeric, image, or mixed media data. The Clasix series of CD-ROM drives connect externally or internally to a personal computer and provide either IBM parallel or SCSI interfaces. They are available in full- and half-height models.

The series 500 model is a high capacity unit capable of storing over 250,000 pages of text or up to 40,000 pages of images. As is the case with many sup-

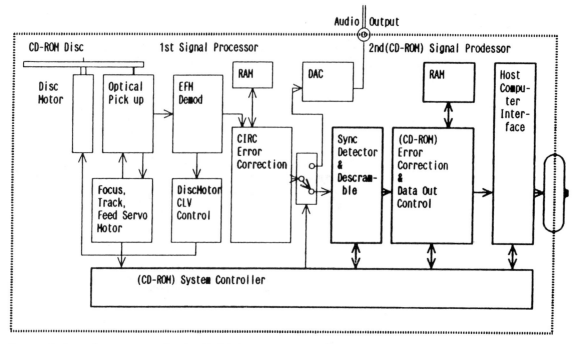

Fig. 4-3. Basic configuration of the Toshiba CD-ROM system. Courtesy Toshiba Corp.

pliers of CD-ROM drives today, Reference Technology offers these devices as a part of a complete solution approach that includes project management, application development, hardware, software, data capture, data conversion, data merging of images and text, data preparation, systems integration, maintenance, and support. The company works with customers to define effective information distribution solutions, design the systems, and implement them via the CD-ROM storage devices.

Storage capacity of the Series 500 drives is at least 550 MB in a format of 2048-byte blocks. Average seek time is less than 800 ms with the average total access time of less than 900 ms. Disc rotational speed is 220 to 480 RPM.

Figure 4-5 shows Reference Technology's Series 2000 model. This is an extremely high capacity drive that can be attached to mini, micro, and personal computers. It utilizes a 12-inch read-only optical medium with the trade name of Clasix DataPlate to deliver the large amounts of storage. The model 2000 is fully compatible with the entire IBM PC line and most work alike. The host computer interface is made via the PC DataDrive adapter, a proprietary item from Reference Technology. This unit provides high-speed data access, high data rates, and high data reliability for single or multi-user systems. The data access speed is a rapid 125 ms with a disc rotational speed of 1800 RPM.

SONY CORPORATION

As these words are being written, Sony Corporation of America, Compo-

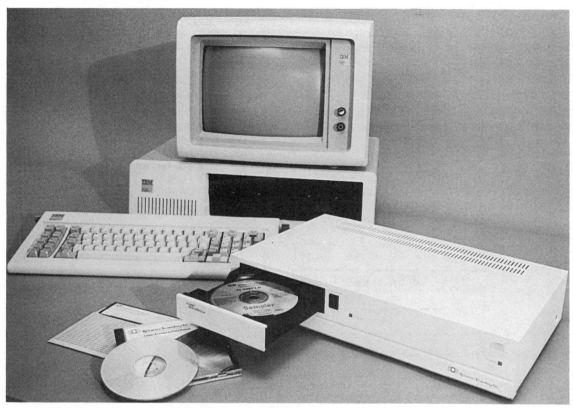

Fig. 4-4. The Clasix Model 500 DataDrive Series. Courtesy Reference Technology, Inc.

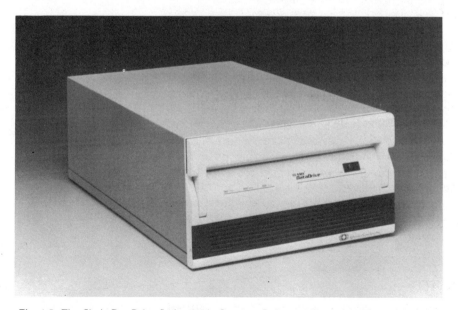

Fig. 4-5. The Clasix DataDrive Series 2000. Courtesy Reference Technology, Inc.

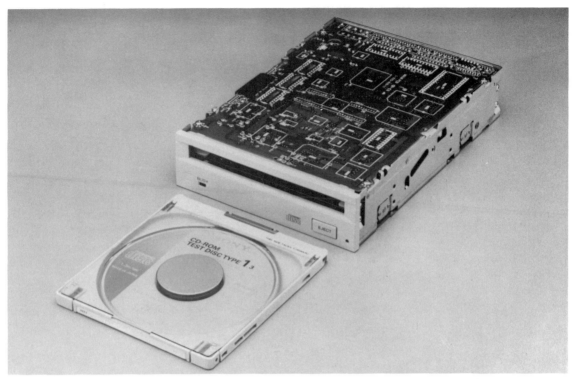

Fig. 4-6. Sony Half-Height Internal CD-ROM Drive, Model CDU-510. Courtesy Sony Corporation of America.

nent Products Division, has just announced two new CD-ROM drives. The CDU-510, shown in Fig. 4-6, is an internal half-height CD-ROM drive equipped with an IBM PC, XT, and AT interface. It uses the standard Sony CD-ROM cartridge.

Sony also offers a family of stand-alone CD-ROM drives that includes the Model CDU-6111 shown in Fig. 4-7. This is a high-end drive that features a built-in power supply, SCSI interface, and full audio capabilities. All use the Sony standard CD-ROM cartridge.

Offering high-reliability and performance, both types of CD-ROM drives are ideal for applications that require large data storage capabilities and quick data retrieval. Production quantities of both of these product lines should be available by the time you read these words.

Sony Corporation advertises that it is the co-inventor of the CD-ROM drive and has ''led a foray into a new technology that will revolutionize drive performance. As one of the first manufacturers to provide this product, Sony intends to be a leading CD-ROM drive manufacturer providing both internal half-height and stand-alone models.''

HITACHI

Hitachi Sales Corporation has recently introduced a complete line of CD-ROM drives, each of which provides 552 megabytes of on-line storage. The

SPECIFICATIONS

PERFORMANCE

Capacity:	552 MBytes
Transfer rate:	153 KBytes/sec (sequential)
Access time:	0.8 sec* (typical)
Seek time:	1.2 msec (track to track)
Average latency:	70 msec (inner)/150 msec (outer)
Speed:	200 to 535 rpm (CLV)

Calculated from performing random access 200 times.

DISC

Diameter:	12 cm
Recorded side:	single side

POWER REQUIREMENTS

12 V DC power:	0.25 A (average), 1.3 A (maximum)
5 V DC power:	0.45 A (average), 0.7 A (maximum)

AUDIO SPECIFICATION

No. of channels:	2
Frequency response:	20 to 20,000 Hz ±3 dB
Distortion:	0.1 % or less (at 1 kHz)
Output level:	
Headphones:	0.55 V rms typical (maximum volume level) (100 Ω load)
Line:	0.8 V rms typical (47 kΩ load)
Output terminal:	
Headphones:	3.5 mm dia. minijack
Line:	4-pin terminal (2.5 mm pitch)

INTERFACE SPECIFICATION

Interface:	40-pin parallel interface (TTL level)
Applicable connector:	40-pin header type

OPERATING CONDITIONS

Ambient temperature:	5 to 40°C
Relative humidity:	20 to 80 % Rh
Vibrations:	0.1 G (30 to 300 Hz, in x, y, and z directions)
Impact:	2 G

STORAGE CONDITIONS

Ambient temperature:	−20 to +55°C
Relative humidity:	15 to 80 % Rh

RELIABILITY SPECIFICATION

MTBF:	10,000 hours
Soft read error (recoverable):	10^{-9} or less
Hard read error (non-recoverable):	10^{-12} or less (When the disc's symbol error rate is less than 10^{-3})
Seek error:	10^{-6}

DIMENSIONS

CDR-3500 (WxHxD):	146 x 41.3 x 205 mm (excluding the front panel)
Disc cartridge (WxHxT):	124.6 x 135 x 8 mm
Weight:	
CDR-3500:	about 1.5 kg
Disc cartridge:	about 75 g

Table 4-1. CDR-3500 Drive Specifications. Courtesy Hitachi Sales Corporation.

Fig. 4-7. Sony stand-alone CD-ROM drive, Model CDU 6111. Courtesy Sony Corporation of America.

CDR-3500 shown in Fig. 4-8 is a second-generation CD-ROM drive that provides wide flexibility and wider compatibility. This is the smallest drive in Hitachi's CD-ROM line-up and allows 552 megabytes of on-line memory to be built directly into a small, laptop computer. Miniaturized optoelectronic technology and attention to application allow this unit to be used in both horizontal and/or vertical mounting configurations.

This is a half-height CD-ROM drive that can directly replace a current computer's second floppy disc drive for use as a data base. An audio circuit is included that enables the drive to also be used in computer-aided instruction (CAI). Supply voltages are identical to those of floppy disc drives used in IBM PC compatible machines. This makes installation and start-up very simple. Figure 4-9 shows the location of various major components and the dimensions of the CDR-3500. Figure 4-10 provides a complete set of operational specifications.

Figure 4-11 shows the Hitachi CDR 2500S full height CD-ROM drive unit. This is a stand-alone drive and contains its own power supply that operates from the 115- or 220-volt AC line. The model CDR 2500 is designed for installation within the system unit of an IBM PC or compatible. This unit directly replaces a full height floppy drive. The CD-IF25A interface card is available for proper connection of these drives to a PC/XT/AT and can be plugged directly into an expansion slot. Other interfaces are available for connecting these drives to computers that use the SCSI standard. Figure 4-12 provides dimensions and specifications for these units.

Hitachi also offers another stand-alone unit that conforms with the

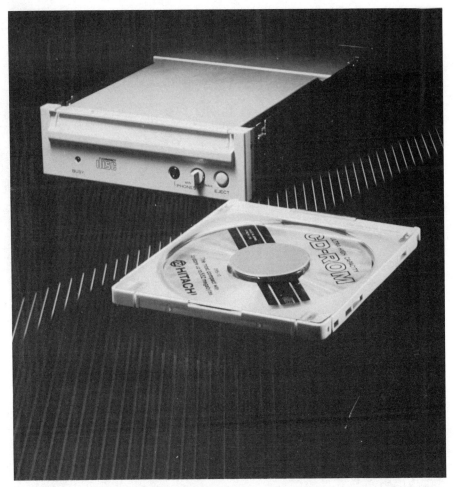

Fig. 4-8. Hitachi CDR-3500 Slimline CD-ROM Drive. Courtesy Hitachi Sales Corporation.

Fig. 4-9. Dimensions of the CDR-3500 drive. Courtesy Hitachi Sales Corporation.

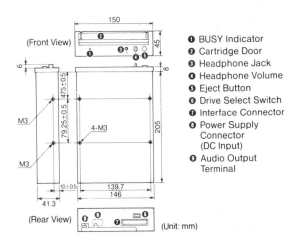

❶ BUSY Indicator
❷ Cartridge Door
❸ Headphone Jack
❹ Headphone Volume
❺ Eject Button
❻ Drive Select Switch
❼ Interface Connector
❽ Power Supply
  Connector
  (DC Input)
❾ Audio Output
  Terminal

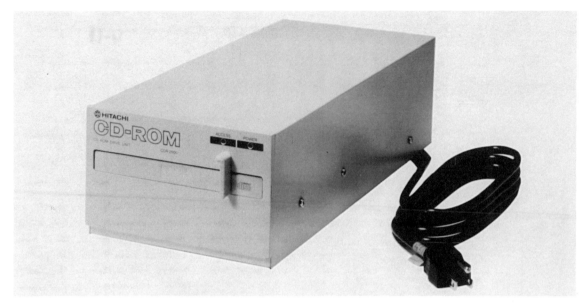

Fig. 4-10. Hitachi CDR-2500S stand-alone CD-ROM drive. Courtesy Hitachi Sales Corporation.

"packaging" seen from most suppliers of CD-ROM drives today. The CDR-1503S is powered from the standard 120-volt house main supply and is shown in Fig. 4-13. While the packaging presents a slim, almost delicate appearance, the unit features a reinforced body and is quite rugged. It is especially designed to be used in a stacked configuration between the computer system unit and the monitor. The monitor rests atop the drive, which in turn is seated on the system unit. An interface card is available for PC/XT/AT computers and plugs into one of the expansion slots. Figure 4-14 shows dimensional measurements and Fig. 4-15 provides operation specifications.

SANYO

Sanyo Business Systems Corporation has also entered the CD-ROM market with two basic units that are available in built-in as well as stand-alone configurations. The ROM-2500U series is the same size as a half-height floppy drive and offers 540-megabyte storage capability on each CD-ROM disc. Average seek time is 0.3 seconds and this unit incorporates a linear motor laser pickup, 32-kilobyte RAM buffer and custom LSI (large-scale integrated circuit). The ROM-3000U series are full height counterparts.

Again, both basic models are available as built-in or stand-alone units. Additionally, each is available with a Sanyo standard interface or with the SCSI interface.

SUMMARY

And the list goes on! More and more of the present leaders in the electronic marketplace (and the future leaders as well) are introducing newer and

DIMENSIONS
CDR-2500

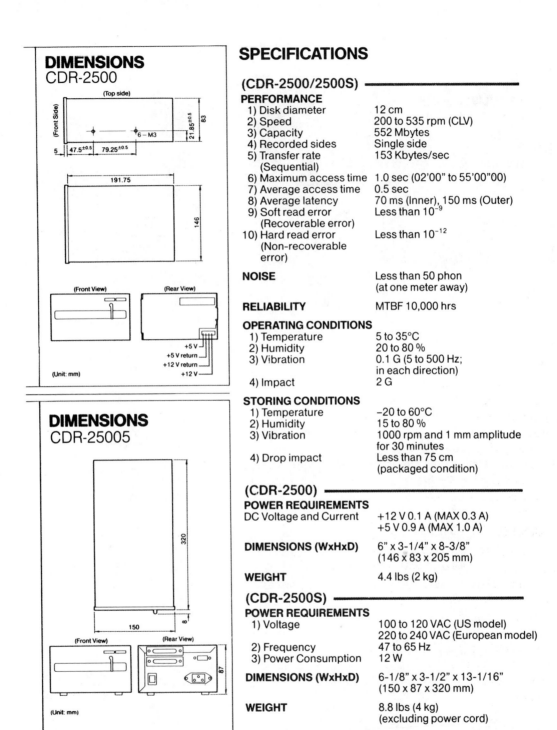

SPECIFICATIONS

(CDR-2500/2500S)

PERFORMANCE
1) Disk diameter	12 cm
2) Speed	200 to 535 rpm (CLV)
3) Capacity	552 Mbytes
4) Recorded sides	Single side
5) Transfer rate (Sequential)	153 Kbytes/sec
6) Maximum access time	1.0 sec (02'00" to 55'00"00)
7) Average access time	0.5 sec
8) Average latency	70 ms (Inner), 150 ms (Outer)
9) Soft read error (Recoverable error)	Less than 10^{-9}
10) Hard read error (Non-recoverable error)	Less than 10^{-12}

NOISE
Less than 50 phon (at one meter away)

RELIABILITY
MTBF 10,000 hrs

OPERATING CONDITIONS
1) Temperature	5 to 35°C
2) Humidity	20 to 80 %
3) Vibration	0.1 G (5 to 500 Hz; in each direction)
4) Impact	2 G

STORING CONDITIONS
1) Temperature	−20 to 60°C
2) Humidity	15 to 80 %
3) Vibration	1000 rpm and 1 mm amplitude for 30 minutes
4) Drop impact	Less than 75 cm (packaged condition)

(CDR-2500)

POWER REQUIREMENTS
DC Voltage and Current +12 V 0.1 A (MAX 0.3 A)
+5 V 0.9 A (MAX 1.0 A)

DIMENSIONS (WxHxD)
6" x 3-1/4" x 8-3/8"
(146 x 83 x 205 mm)

WEIGHT
4.4 lbs (2 kg)

(CDR-2500S)

POWER REQUIREMENTS
1) Voltage	100 to 120 VAC (US model) 220 to 240 VAC (European model)
2) Frequency	47 to 65 Hz
3) Power Consumption	12 W

DIMENSIONS (WxHxD)
6-1/8" x 3-1/2" x 13-1/16"
(150 x 87 x 320 mm)

WEIGHT
8.8 lbs (4 kg)
(excluding power cord)

Fig. 4-11. Dimensions and specifications of Hitachi CDR-2500 drive line. Courtesy Hitachi Sales Corporation.

SPECIFICATIONS

PERFORMANCE
1) Disc diameter: 12 cm
2) Rotation speed: 200 - 535 rpm (CLV)
3) Capacity: 552 MBytes
4) Recorded sides: Single side
5) Transfer rate: 153 KBytes/sec (sequential)
6) Seek time: 1 msec (track to track)
7) Access time: 0.8* sec (typical)
8) Average latency: 70 msec (inner) 150 msec (outer)
9) Soft read errors (recoverable): less than 10^{-9}
10) Hard read errors (non-recoverable): less than 10^{-12}

*Calculated from performing random access 200 times.

DIMENSIONS
1) Width: 370 mm (14-9/16 inches)
2) Depth: 330 mm (13 inches)
3) Height: 76 mm (3 inches)
4) Weight: 4.2 Kg(9.3 lb)

OPERATING CONDITIONS
1) Temperature: 5 to 35°C
2) Humidity: 20 to 80% Rh
3) Vibrations: 0.1 G (5 - 500 Hz, in each direction)
4) Impact: 2 G

STORAGE CONDITIONS
1) Temperature: -20 to 60° C
2) Humidity: 15 to 80% Rh
3) Vibrations: 1000 rpm, 1 mm amplitude
4) Drop impact: less than 70 cm (when packaged)

AUDIO PERFORMANCE
1) Number of channels: 2
2) Frequency response: 20 - 20,000 Hz ±2 dB
3) Dynamic range: 75 dB (IHF A, 1 kHz)
4) Signal-to-noise ratio: 75 dB (IHF A, 1 kHz)
5) Distortion: 0.1% (1kHz)
6) Channel separation: 60 dB (1 kHz)
7) Output level Line out: 0.8 V rms (typical) (RL = 47 kΩ)
   Headphone out: 0.55 V rms (typical) (RL = 100 Ω)
8) Output jacks Line out: RCA type pin jack
   Headphone out: 3.5 mm dia.

ACOUSTIC NOISE less than 50 dB A (measured one meter from drive) (without head access)

POWER REQUIREMENTS
US Model
1) Voltage: AC 120 V
2) Current: 0.2 A
3) Frequency: 60 Hz
Europe Models
1) Voltage: AC 220 V or AC 240 V
2) Current: 0.1 A
3) Frequency: 50 Hz

Table 4-2. Operating Specifications for Hitachi CDR-1503S. Courtesy Hitachi Sales Corporation.

Fig. 4-12. Hitachi 1503S "stacked design" CD-ROM is placed between the computer system unit and the monitor. Courtesy Hitachi Sales Corporation.

better CD-ROM drives. Those presented in this chapter are representative of what the market *had* to offer as these words were being written. Undoubtedly, even newer models have been introduced by the time you read these words.

The computer manufacturers are starting to respond to the CD-ROM movement. IBM presently offers a CD-ROM option for its line of Personal System 2 computers. Other top microcomputer companies are doing likewise. It can be theorized that the first of the 5th generation computers could contain their own, internal operational data bases with many, many megabytes of information contained on CD-ROM discs.

DIMENSIONS

Fig. 4-13. Dimensions of the Hitachi CDR-1503S. Courtesy Hitachi Sales Corporation.

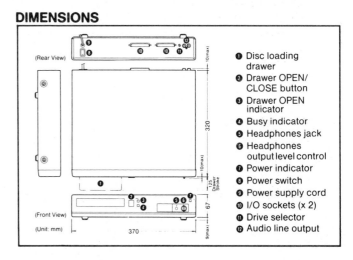

❶ Disc loading drawer
❷ Drawer OPEN/ CLOSE button
❸ Drawer OPEN indicator
❹ Busy indicator
❺ Headphones jack
❻ Headphones output level control
❼ Power indicator
❽ Power switch
❾ Power supply cord
❿ I/O sockets (x 2)
⓫ Drive selector
⓬ Audio line output

CD-ROM drive units for microcomputers are presently in a state of very advanced evolution. The technologies that allow access to more data more quickly are changing weekly. Perhaps this evolutionary process will somewhat parallel that of the hard disc drive, starting at the stepper-motor beginning and proceeding on through voice coil upgrade equivalencies. In any event, the CD-ROM drive has made its presence felt in even the smallest of popular microcomputers. This will be a continuing trend as more and more users take advantage of and come to expect the vast data access possible using CD-ROM storage.

5
Systems Integrators

Systems integrators serve a real need in the CD-ROM industry—they are essentially one-stop providers of everything from the initial consultation to delivery of the compact discs themselves. Some systems integrators, upon delivery of the final product, allow the owner of the information to market the product; others are, in effect, the publisher and marketer as well.

The majority of systems integrators also offer their version of retrieval software, and to them, this is what makes their product unique. This is also where the greatest competition is taking place for obvious reasons. With all data being placed on compact disc having to comply with the same standards, the competition is the various ways the data can be manipulated and retrieved.

The information in this chapter is compiled from information provided by the companies themselves and is not intended to promote one company over another.

KNOWLEDGE ACCESS INTERNATIONAL

Knowledge Access International in Mountain View, California, has been involved in CD-ROM almost since its inception and, in fact, designed one of the industry's first stand-alone databases on CD-ROM in 1982. The company is organized into three major divisions to respond to the varying needs in the marketplace—Electronic Publishing Division, Government Contracts Division, and the Service Bureau Division. Staff members work to meet customer specifications from product design through data preparation, data installation, product integration, documentation, packaging, field testing, marketing, sales, distribution, and customer support.

Knowledge Access' software is the KAware Retrieval System and is, according to the company, the only retrieval software system to combine retrieval and post-retrieval functions for bibliographic, full text, directory, numeric and graphic database products. The system has been developed as a software library, with optional features to simplify custom design and maximize cost effectiveness for specific industry applications. The company has produced many stand-alone databases on CD-ROM and is one of the first companies to produce multiple databases in optical disc format, including CD-ROM, WORM, and Optical Read-Write.

KAware Retrieval System

The KAware Retrieval System components have been engineered as separate modules with optional features to help keep down the cost of custom designs. The size of the database and fields is only limited by the storage capability of the disc. Multi CD-ROM disc access linkage is possible through the use of multiple drives.

The KAware User Interface features easy-to-understand menus that guide a user through a search. The Program Overview feature is a text presentation of the program to help the first-time user. Dynamic on-screen help is context-specific and is available at the touch of a function key. Dual access modes allow the user to search the database through a special lock-out system. Keyboard or mouse capability is available, and custom user interfaces can also be implemented.

The KAware Retrieval Engine provides search and retrieval in as little as 0 to 3 seconds. The user can edit and refine each search by referring to the "summary table" for number of hits. The scan mode creates a window into the database for browsing through records. Automatic scroll at user-selectable speeds is available. Restricted field indexing allows searches by specific, fully menued items, such as city, state, product, company, author, title, abstract, numeric range, or value. Full-text indexing allows searches by keyword, thesaurus vocabulary, or permuted multiple words. All products include proximity searching with user-defined adjacency, negation, truncation, Boolean operations, hierarchical, parallel, and group sets. The Explode feature allows the user to find all related information for a specific word search. The Subset feature permits the user to search through selected data on the disc. The Summary Option creates a list of all documents searched during the session, allowing the user to backtrack to create new combinations. Retrieved records can be saved in ASCII, DIF, MailMerge, or other formats and reloaded for use with word processors, spreadsheets, or personal database managers. Information can be displayed on the screen or output to a printer. The print option includes mailing labels, order forms, telemarketing cards and full reports. Powerful post-processor functions allow manipulation of separate elements in the database. Numeric fields can be designed for ranking and tabulation or bivariate analysis utilizing an electronic calculator. Text fields can be designed for alphabetization or added through use of the electronic notepad.

The KAware Graphic Retrieval System is designed to access databases that are graphic only or combine both text and graphics. The graphic system has three levels of magnification for display and supports both monochrome and color images (32,000 colors). Bit-map and CIITT Group 3 and 4 image support makes the KAware Graphic Retrieval System appropriate for databases that contain photographs, full color charts, schematics, technical drawings and graphs. Text and accompanying images can be seen on the screen simultaneously or individually through the use of separate windows.

The KAware Retrieval System has been engineered in C programming language for portability with some assembly language routines. The product line supports the IBM PC and compatibles operating with MS-DOS 2.0 and higher and Microsoft Windows and all CD-ROM drives currently available from Philips, Hitachi, and Sony. KAware graphics utilizes the Hercules Graphics Card from Hercules Computer Technology. Custom products also operate on the Apple II series of computers.

Knowledge Access states that their retrieval system can be customized for industry-specific application in as little as 30 days. The company can joint venture a product or assume full publishing responsibility for creating and marketing a database. Their clients include Harris Information Services, Market Statistics, Pergamon Press, Database Services, The Oryx Press, The College Board, Times Mirror Press, Dun and Bradstreet, CINAHL American Society of Hospital Pharmacists, and others.

RETEACO

Reteaco Inc., established in 1984, is a full-service supplier. Its services include user needs analysis, project management, database indexing, screen/report format design, implementation of FindIT, its search and retrieval software, and mastering and replication of the compact discs.

FindIT

FindIT is Reteaco's search and retrieval software system. It currently runs on IBM PC or compatible devices under MS-DOS. Search commands are entered through a standard keyboard using cursor control keys. FindIT can operate efficiently with 512K of main memory. Other options such as a PC AT, larger memory, etc., can be used with further improvement of performance. FindIT can operate on Philips, Sony, and Hitachi CD-ROM readers, and the company is adding software as required to use other readers. More than one CD-ROM reader can be attached to a single microcomputer. The current limit is eight readers, allowing for more than four gigabytes of data to be accessed. Although color displays enhance its use, the system will operate with a monochrome monitor.

FindIT system operation is intuitively obvious. The user is presented with a consistent screen display from function to function, is able to move freely to any desired function screen, is not locked to rigid paths and can exit at any time.

The user may type letters to locate a specific word. Only those characters need be typed to establish the uniqueness of the word selected. If, for example, the user types "cha" the highlighted word to appear on the word list might be "chablis." Add an "r" and the highlighted word might be "character." This high-speed system allows the user to select the specific word and any derivations of the word that might also be required in the search.

Words are selected by using the right arrow key, and there is an automatic "OR" to allow the user to add plurals or other versions of the same thought. This "define and select" method is used throughout the system.

The FindIT word list method (referred to by the company as "word wheels") is a unique approach to assisting the user. The lists can be browsed using the up and down arrow keys or the page up and page down keys. Reteaco states that it has produced a single word wheel with as many as seven million unique records that can be retrieved.

By touching a function key at any time, the user can get detailed instructions on what actions can be taken in the specific screen in use at the time. Help screens can also be written specifically for the particular database to give additional useful information.

FindIT is responsive to user entry. User entry of an incorrect character, such as an alpha character in a numeric field or a misspelling, is identified immediately.

The system allows the user to search for any word in any specific field or in any record, unless specified as non-searchable at database definition time. The high speed of FindIT allows users to search a database, find records, change the selection criteria easily, and quickly and perform another search. Those experienced in online searching will also find that the system is responsive to sophisticated search requests.

FindIT allows the user to browse whether or not a search question has been entered. It is equally easy to browse multiple databases on a single disc, browse through the fields, the indexes, or individual records. If a user knows the sequence number of a specific record, it is possible to go directly to the record, bypassing all the intermediate selection screens.

Selected records can be examined, and from any selected record, it is possible to browse forward or background to check a reference. At any time, it is possible to go to any function screen, enter or change a search query, and do a new search.

The system also allows for easy full text searching. Even in a database with many fields, the user has the option of searching the entire database as though there were no fields. The system sets no restrictions on the number of fields or the length of fields. A single search query can include a search across a number of specified fields.

FindIT provides a fully automatic approach to using Boolean logic to define a search query. Simply selecting words can automatically build the query connected by AND, OR or NOT Boolean operators. Parentheses are also added automatically and displayed for clarity as the Boolean expression is being created.

At every step, from the time the user turns the system on until the search is completed, prompts can be available to assist in making the search effective and fast. Prompts disappear as soon as the user touches a key. The search may be restricted to the contents of any predefined field in the database. The user may ask for the occurrences of a word anywhere in the database or only in the selected field. When records are found, they are displayed on the screen using selection arrow keys.

FindIT provides for split-window display. Selection choices are consistently displayed on the left-hand side of the screen. User entries and help screens appear on the right. These multiple windows and split screens are used throughout the various functions.

Reteaco's FindIT system is fast. The average speed for a Boolean operation or retrieval of a record is less than two seconds. Complex Boolean statements across a large number of records can take longer, but any specific record can be retrieved in less than two seconds.

Most times, the objective of a search is not just to find the information, but also to put it to use. For this purpose, FindIT allows for rapid transfer of selected records to diskette or hard disc. From there, it can be edited, moved to a word processor, spreadsheet or any MS-DOS program suitable for the data. Records can also be printed directly from the CD-ROM, up to the limit set by the publisher for each session.

While traditional types of inverted database structures can take as much as double the space of the original data to create the index capability, the FindIT system uses a very small amount of overhead to accomplish the same objectives. For this reason, Reteaco normally leaves in words that are often taken out of the search capability. The typical FindIT CD-ROM uses less than 25 percent of the space on the disc for software, indexes, and other overhead. This means that there is space available for more than 450 megabytes of original data.

Each Reteaco FindIT CD-ROM is delivered with an access diskette and cannot be read without it. This provides access control to any or all sections of the CD-ROM. Various encryption techniques are also available. The customer has the option of having a completely open disc meeting logical file format standards or a closed disc with controlled access. The choice is up to the publisher of the data. Reteaco is also able to provide advice on the storage and retrieval of various types of graphic and picture data.

Reteaco has also developed a language selection option for all of their CD-ROM databases. Initially available in English/French, the system can easily be adapted to offer any combination of English, French, Spanish, German or Italian. With language selection, a single access diskette enables the user to select the language of preference with a single keystroke. The chosen language is then used for all on-screen prompts, function key definitions and help windows for the FindIT search and retrieval software and user interface. This feature is of particular value in multilingual environments, because switching back and forth from one language to another is fast and does not involve changing either the access diskette or compact disc.

Reteaco has produced more than 100 database titles incorporating FindIT. Their customers include government departments and agencies, educational institutions, publishers and corporations in a variety of industries. Applications have included operations and parts manuals, catalogs, telephone and business directories, dictionaries, bibliographic data, newspapers, and magazines.

SILVERPLATTER INFORMATION SERVICES

SilverPlatter provides complete services needed by publishers and/or information providers to enable production of CD-ROMs. These services include specific product design, data preparation, creation of indices, and disc production. The company provides search and retrieval software and the necessary hardware, and SilverPlatter offers full marketing services as well.

To use their products, an IBM PC or compatible with 512K of memory is needed, although 640K is recommended for improved performance. The computer should have a standard keyboard, monitor (either color or monochrome) and at least one floppy disc drive. SilverPlatter software can be used on a 5¼-inch floppy or a 3½-inch cartridge. No fixed drive is required for the SilverPlatter Information Retrieval System. In addition, the subscriber must provide a copy of MS-DOS or PC-DOS, Version 2.1 or greater. This is used to prepare a software diskette for accessing the CD-ROM according to documentation.

The SilverPlatter Search Retrieval software has been specifically developed to optimize access to information. It enables users to perform all of the search tasks now possible with major online systems and give rapid response time. Key features of the software are:

- Complete help information, allowing first-time users to effectively conduct their own searches.
- Boolean search capability using AND, OR and NOT.
- Right-hand word truncation, enabling searches for all words with a common base index.
- Ability to restrict a search to specific sections of a record.
- Proximity searching, permitting searching for certain words that are adjacent or near one another.
- Ability to display or print records to defined sections.
- Browse the dictionary of indexed words in the glossary.

KNOWLEDGESET CORPORATION

KnowledgeSet is a pioneer in the field of optical media, being the first to store an encyclopedia both on videodisc and CD-ROM—the Grolier's Encyclopedia both on videodisc and CD-ROM—the Grolier's Encyclopedia. The company offers products and services for the commercial and consumer segments of the optical disc marketplace.

KnowledgeSet has developed its own software that includes the Text Knowledge Retrieval System (KRS), the Graphic Knowledge Retrieval System (KRS), as well as data preparation software for the new CD-I optical recording standard. The Text Knowledge Retrieval system requires 256K on an IBM PC or compatible using any standard monochrome monitor; the Graphic Knowledge Retrieval System requires 640K, a mouse, and a graphic display monitor and interface card.

Knowledge Retrieval System

Shared features of the Text and Graphic Knowledge Retrieval Systems include:

- Full Text Word Searching - Search for specific words and phrases in the database (except stopwords).
- Topical (Browse) Searching - Browse randomly through articles/documents.
- Boolean Search Specifications - Operators include multiple word search (AND), alternate word search (OR), and exclusive word search (NOT).
- Adjacency Search - Search for words that occur next to each other as in a phrase or proper name.
- Association - Search for words that are referenced together within a specific span of text.
- Intermediate Sorts - Search for groups of words that have variable intermediate words. You can search for John F. Kennedy and John Fitzgerald Kennedy simultaneously using an ambiguous placeholder (a period) in the search specification.
- Proximity Searching - The search specification can be narrowed by indicating that the searched words must appear in exact order or within a specified number of words apart (from 1 to 999).
- Restricted Field Searches - A search can be restricted to a single field of data type such as footnotes or bibliographies.
- Input Methods - In the Text KRS, the user issues all commands using functions keys; in the Graphic KRS, the user issues all commands using a mouse.
- Right Truncation - Provides word searching with ambiguous suffixes. A question mark specifies a search for both singular and plural occurrences of a word. An asterisk specifies a search for all occurrences of a word with all possible suffixes such as–ed,–ing,–s,–ism,–es.
- Spill File Storage - Provides a temporary storage area on magnetic disc for large complex searches where the search information "spills" over from or fills the computer's random access memory.
- Query Storage - The user can save a search specification to a magnetic disc file for later use.
- Printer and Disc File Output - Information retrieved from a CD-ROM database can be printed or saved in a magnetic disc file for later use.
- Word Lookup - Allows the user to view the complete word list of the CD-ROM database. This can be useful to find out if a specific word exists in the database.
- Screen Display Format Options - Specify single- or double-spaced lines of text, line length in number of characters, right justification of text and hyphenation.

- Text Viewing Features - Scroll text forward and back, by line or by page, view next and preceding article/document, view outline to access articles/documents by headings and subheadings.

Features exclusive to the Graphic Knowledge Retrieval System include:

- User interface based on graphic icons, drop-down menus, windows and the mouse.
- Bookmarks - Place holders in the text manually or let the KRS do it automatically.
- User Level - Select beginner, intermediate or expert functionality.

Both the Text KRS and the Graphic KRS may incorporate optional features, listed below. Certain features are available in both the text and graphics versions, while others are exclusive to one or the other. KnowledgeSet states that not all options are covered in the standard software licensing fee and that certain features require substantial engineering work to implement and must be paid for outside the standard fee. Note that certain features are only available if the data to be searched and retrieved supports the use of that feature.

- Vector Graphics with Zoom and Pan Capability - Graphics must be in vector format; otherwise, they must be converted to vector format. (GraphicsKRS only, included in standard license).
- Bit-Mapped Graphics with Pan Capability - Graphics must be in bit-format; otherwise, they must be converted to bit-mapped format. (Graphic KRS only, included in standard license)
- Field Specific Searching - Enables the user to search exclusively with specific fields of data. (Text and Graphic KRS, additional engineering required, not included in standard license)
- Online Help System - Publisher is given standard online help to modify according to publisher's requirements and applications. KnowledgeSet provides technical writing and editing services for a nominal fee. (Text and Graphic KRS, included in standard license)
- Gold Key - Allows instant access to another software application, such as a word processor; returns the user to the same place in the KRS that is left to use the other application. (Text KRS only, not included in standard license)
- Hot Links - Also called Dynamic Cross-references or Hypertext, provides direct access (links) to related articles/documents. Database must be prepared using KnowledgeSet's data preparation system. (Text and Graphic KRS, included in standard license)
- Custom Screen Design - Screens can be designed to publisher specifications limited by the type of display hardware to be used. (Text and Graphic KRS, not included in standard license)
- Output Templates - Defines specific format for data printed or saved to a disc file. (Text and Graphic KRS, not included in standard license)
- Citations - Lists article titles in the database that refer, through cross-

references, to the article currently being viewed. Article citations must exist in the original database. (Text and Graphic KRS, included in standard license)

- References - Lists article titles in the database that the article currently viewing refers to through cross-references. Article references must exist in the original database. (Text and Graphic KRS, included in standard license)
- Expert View - Through the use of a KnowledgeSet-designed heuristic, Expert View provides a list of article titles that are most closely related contextually to the currently viewed article. Articles in the database are selected by the KRS based on weighted or relative interconnectivity to the currently viewed article. Both citations and references must exist in the original database. (Text and Graphic KRS, included in standard license)
- Outlines - Provides access to articles by headings and subheadings. (Text and Graphic KRS, included in standard license)
- Database Selection - Enables the user to select one database from several available databases stored discretely on the CD-ROM. (Text and Graphic KRS, included in standard license)

Typical commercial users of KnowledgeSet services and software products are companies and agencies with large data access requirements such as catalogs, encyclopedia, technical references and research materials. In the consumer market, KnowledgeSet has developed the Electronic Encyclopedia on both videodisc and CD-ROM. These products were developed for the Grolier Electronic Publishing Company, publishers of the 20-volume (9 million word) Academic American Encyclopedia. All 20 volumes occupy only one-fifth of a CD-ROM disc. The Electronic Encyclopedia is a good example of a CD-ROM application created to serve the consumer and educational markets.

ONLINE COMPUTER SYSTEMS

Online, while certainly active in CD-ROM, has been prominent in the videodisc industry since its inception and continues to be a major player in this field. Along with a full complement of CD-ROM services, Online is unique in that they offer a wide range of hardware products and are active in developing image compression and decompression techniques. I had an opportunity to visit this company in Germantown, Maryland, and their facilities are most impressive. Online's services and products include development tools, database build, CD-ROM premastering, CD-ROM driers, retrieval engine and retrieval system.

Development Tools

Online has developed a series of tools that provide capabilities for solving complex database problems, including:

- Audio Editor - allows for digitizing, editing and storing digital audio. This system allows a user to create a complete sound library or database.
- Graphics Editor - allows for creating, editing and storing graphics.
- Simple Indexing - allows for indexing and accessing either audio or graphic data on CD-ROM.

- Numerical Indexing - allows for accessing extremely large numerical databases numbering in the millions of records.
- Record Manager(s) - allows for storage and management of complex data structures including, but not limited to, repeating fields, hierarchical data and mixed data.
- Field Indexing - allows for indexing and searching field-oriented data.
- Word Indexing - allows for indexing and searching text-oriented data.

Database Build

Online currently supports several CD-ROM formats, including the Microsoft extensions and High Sierra formats. The extensions overcome the 32 MB full size limitation in MS-DOS and allow access to the entire 550 to 600 MB CD-ROM disc. Online also offers a database build service that will support applications in clusters of eight drives, up to a maximum of 32 drives per PC for a larger address space of 17 gigabytes. A level of security can be provided at the software and/or hardware level. Online offers a family of CD-ROM controllers that have an encryption capability on-board.

CD-ROM Premastering

Online offers a direct premastering service to those clients that want to create either MS-DOS, Xenix or CP/M-86 compatible CD-ROM drives. The client supplies the images on floppy disc, selected streamer tape, or nine-track tape for premastering. Online will organize all the directories on the CD-ROM (including mixing operating system formats on the same disc) as part of its service.

CD-ROM Drivers

Online has developed a family of CD-ROM drivers designed to operate exactly the same across multiple operating systems. This technology allows a user to be totally independent of the CD-ROM drive hardware.

Retrieval Engine

Online has developed a series of software libraries for searching and retrieving data from CD-ROM. These libraries also allow access via Topical Index or Structured Table of Contents. The libraries are designed primarily for those who wish to customize the user interface for a specific application and support multiple database access, keyword access, Boolean operators, word proximity, word truncation, field-restricted search, search in paragraph and/or sentence, numerical range searching and multiple disc databases.

Retrieval System

Online has developed a general-purpose User Interface to its Retrieval Engine libraries for those users that do not require custom capabilities. Significant features include multi-window capability, image display (full page), management of search sets, data extraction for word processing input, communication with remote systems, access via local area networks and structured search menus including hierarchical subject thesauri.

Local Area Networks

Online offers its OPTI-NET Local Area Network support for CD-ROM. OPTI-NET currently operates with the IBM PC network and Ethernet protocols. The IBM PC network will support up to 32 simultaneous users and the Ethernet system is capable of supporting up to 128 simultaneous users.

Hardware

Online offers both individual CD-ROM components and integrated systems for electronic publishing, public access, and training applications. Their hardware offerings include:

- Online CD-ROM Controller - a family of IBM PC cards that control the CD-ROM drive and access data from the disc. These intelligent controllers are compatible with Sony, Hitachi, and Philips drives and provide full MS-DOS, Xenix and CP/M-86 compatibility, which enables the drive to act as a fully functional device totally transparent to the user. Up to four controller cards can be installed in a single PC and up to eight CD-ROM drives can be controlled by each card. Online's CD-ROM controller in a multi-disc environment provides overlap seeks for up to eight drives. This function provides high performance and large growth potential. The Online Optical Storage Unit is stackable and was designed to house from two to four drives. Online's controller supports multiple users over a local area network as well. Options available for the cards include on-board encryption, 256K on-board memory and on-board digital audio playback capability. The company is currently developing controller interfaces for other computers, including Multibus and Micro-VAX.
- Digital Sound Adapter - a series of cards designed specifically for audio applications using CD-ROM. One series of cards allows for digitizing voice, which is then stored on the disc, and decoding and playing back of audio. A lower cost card provides playback capability only. Up to 19 hours of audio can be stored on a single CD-ROM. The CD-ROM can also be used as an audio source for multiple units via a local area network.
- CD-ROM Drives - Online offers CD-ROM drives for resale or integration into a turnkey system.

A typical CD-ROM system includes an IBM PC or compatible with 512K memory, RS-232 communications, floppy disc drive, monitor, CD-ROM drive, CD-ROM controller, printer, and retrieval software license. Hard disc systems are available in capacities of 10 MB, 20 MB, 72 MB or greater. Online also offers upgrade kits for those who currently own an IBM PC or compatible. Upgrade kits include a CD-ROM drive, CD-ROM controller and retrieval software license.

Online's client list is impressive and include R. R. Bowker (Books in Print and Ulrich's Periodicals), government agencies, and major financial and business information organizations. Online is also the developer of numerous award-winning videodisc products.

TIME MANAGEMENT SOFTWARE (TMS)

TMS is widely regarded as an industry leader in optical disc technology, having demonstrated a system for storing and retrieving text from laser discs as early as 1982. They offer a full range of development services. Their software, RESEARCH, is made up of two products, RESEARCH Database Preparation Software and RESEARCH Retrieval Software.

Research Database Preparation software is the portion of the system that converts marked, formatted, input data into an organized and indexed database. This software, which runs in the VAX/VMS environment, begins with an input data file that conforms to TMS's RESEARCH Standard Form definition. RESEARCH Standard Form is an SGML-like language that provides for the definition of both the format and the logical structure of the database text. Any textual data can be converted into Standard Form, including both record-oriented and stream-oriented (markup) formats. Because database owners define the components of the Standard Form file, they control the overall appearance and functionality of the resulting database.

The software verifies the Standard Form file for correctness and creates a series of support files. These files include the directories and indices that the retrieval software uses to access the Standard Form file. The directories and indices support the end user's research activities with the database.

RESEARCH Retrieval is the portion of the system that gives the end user access to the database. The end user can perform a wide range of research activities that encompass the activities associated with more traditional forms of research. RESEARCH supports essentially two types of investigative activities:

- Searching - allows the user to retrieve text that contains a keyword or group of words. In addition to allowing control of the search domain, the software recognizes search connectors (AND and OR) and proximity indicators, so the user can also apply other sophisticated search criteria.
- Browsing - allows the user to retrieve a section of text without performing a keyword search. The beginning point for browsing is specified either by selecting an entry from the hierarchical Database Table of Contents or by specifying a Key Value.

Once the specified text is on screen, the user can scroll the database in either direction as desired. Because the software retrieves the text in context, the user always has a book-like view of the entire database. In addition, RESEARCH allows the user to:

- Perform a sideways search. While reading the database, a user may encounter a term or phrase to use as the basis for a new search. The software supports such sideways searches by allowing the user to simply move the cursor to the term or phrase that will be used as the new search expression.

- Perform a point-to-point browse. This is a way of moving around within the database in a non-hierarchical fashion, jumping from reference to reference. This feature allows the user to retrieve text that is logically related to the research topic but does not necessarily contain the search term.
- Save sections of text and copy it into the software's Notepad. The user may also add notes to the Notepad and even write the Notepad to a file that can be edited with a word processor.
- Reopen the database to a text passage that has already been located through previous activity. The software automatically records the previous retrieval activities as an Activity History.

RESEARCH Retrieval runs on an IBM PC or compatible under MS-DOS version 2.0 or later. The PC must have at least 384K of memory and a hard disc drive.

TMS also offers LaserDOS Origination software, which converts data files from magnetic tape or disc into a form suitable for input to a CD-ROM mastering system. The current version of software creates CD-ROM disc images that conform to the High Sierra format. LaserDOS operates in the VAX/VMX environment, thus providing the user with a wide range of price and performance operations. Among its features, LaserDOS:

- Allows interactive specification of the subdirectory hierarchy of the target disc.
- Allows full control over directory and file naming.
- Automatically creates a VTOC and file directory.
- Supports interactive disc content verification before the disc is mastered by allowing a PC to access the disc image on the VAX as if it were a CD-ROM.
- Creates a disc image compatible with Microsoft's MS-DOS CD-ROM extensions.
- Formats output tapes conforming to the input specifications of major mastering facilities.

Although LaserDOS Origination is targeted for CD-ROM discs, the underlying file system is appropriate for any read-only medium or any medium that will be used as such. Thus LV-ROM discs (videodiscs containing digital data), WORM discs and other media could be candidates for the CD-ROM file system with its attendant benefits. LaserDOS Origination is available for licensing or as a service to customers who choose not to acquire a license to the software.

Another software-based product from TMS is TMSFAX, a facsimile compression and decompression system that offers CCITT Group 3 and Group 4 Facsimile Image Compression and Decompression capabilities to PC users. TMSFAX products are designed for those who want to add image compression and decompression capabilities to their existing or future product lines.

TMSFAX is a software product that can decompress a Group 3 or Group 4 image within 10 to 45 seconds, depending on the content of the image and microcomputer processing power. TMSFAX features independent horizontal and vertical scaling parameters and a linkable applications program interface for Lattice C and Microsoft C. It also allows for user-definable windows that can display alphanumeric characters, decompressed images or both.

Because monitor and printer drivers are loadable, TMSFAX is source and destination device independent, which enables support of virtually any monitor or printer in the marketplace. TMS provides device driver specifications so clients can develop custom drivers for any monitor or printer. In select cases, TMS will write device drivers for customers as part of their service.

TMSFAX decompresses fascimile images from standard MS-DOS files. Thus, compressed image input may come from a wide variety of sources, including CD-ROMs, modems, networks, floppy discs, Winchester discs, DRAW discs and WORM discs. TMSFAX can compress images from scanners, Winchester disks, floppy discs, networks, or paint packages. TMSFAX compressed images can be stored as standard files on floppy disc, Winchester disc, magnetic tape or CD-ROM, or other optical storage media.

TMS also offers two libraries of facsimile functions to simplify development of applications software using TMSFAX. The TMSFAX Decompression Applications Library keeps track of all display device parameters, thereby making it easier for a developer to write a fascimile applications that are monitor and printer independent. The TMSFAX Compression Applications Library manages all compressed image file functions, yet allows the applications developer to pass image headers and raw image data.

REFERENCE TECHNOLOGY

Reference Technology is a full-service developer and offers a broad range of products and applications services, including both hardware and software. Their services include developing applications, customizing software, receiving data in raw form and completing any necessary data capture, converting data from any unique formats, indexing the data, putting the data in the format for file manager access, and producing the compact discs. Their software, CLA-SIX, is a family of software products that includes:

- CLASIX Standard File Manager and CLASIX Custom File Manager - permits access to the industry standard for data formatting and eliminates the need to master different optical discs for different systems. The Custom File Manager improves performance when accessing a large number of files, and both file managers allow the application program to access very large files by eliminating the 32 million byte size restriction of IBM PC DOS and expanding the file capacity to mainframe levels. They provide a directory that contains an entry for each data file on the CLASIX DataPlate or CLASIX CD-ROM DataPlate.

- CLASIX Key Record Manager - an access method that allows retrieval of information by multiple keys. The package is designed to speed up applications programming by means of effective indexing.

76

- CLASIX Query Plus - incorporates the functionality of the CLASIX Key Record Manager and provides Boolean search capability to query fields based on logical combinations of words and numeric values within the key fields.
- CLASIX Full Text Manager - text retrieval software package that allows users to perform free-text or structured searches. Text files are searched based upon indexes for every word (other than predefined stopwords) that occurs in any document in the database.

Reference Technology also offers DOCUSYSTEM, a CD-ROM document delivery and management system that allows a user to capture, store, retrieve, print and distribute images along with text. This is accomplished through a series of hardware and software products, including:

- CLASIX DOCUCAPTURE Service - allows for capturing of 8½ × 11 images at 200 or 300 dots per inch. The company compresses, indexes, formats and stores the images on CD-ROM.
- CLASIX DOCUSTATION - allows a client to retrieve and display images stored using the above service. The system consists of an IBM PC, XT, AT or compatible, a high-resolution display, a laser printer that produces eight pages of images and text per minute, a CLASIX Image Management Controller card, and a CD-ROM drive.
- CLASIX DOCUTRIEVE Software - supports full zoom and pan of documents and words with other CLASIX software.

INFORMATION DIMENSIONS

Information Dimensions, Inc., (IDI) is a for-profit organization formed in early 1986 from Battelle's Software Products Center as a separate entity from Battelle's contract research and development environment. IDI has been prominent in the development of database management systems using BASIS, a textual and bibliographic data management system used in technical libraries and other specialized markets. They have now developed MicroBASIS, retrieval software for CD-ROM applications and offer full development services. Clients can elect to build applications in-house using BASIS on a DEC VAX or Micro-VAX or have IDI handle the complete process.

BASIS provides advanced capabilities for loading and maintaining extremely large databases once the data is prepared in machine-readable form. BASIS' loading module accepts a variety of data input formats, including fixed and free. Database loading using the full BASIS system is performed on the DEC VAX, the BASIS-compatible machine most similar to the IBM PC in its required formats. More than 20 indexing options provide BASIS database administrators flexibility for organizing complex textual and numeric data. Fields can be indexed in a variety of ways, and BASIS maintains vocabulary control through a thesaurus that supports 13 relationships.

MicroBASIS offers easy-to-use interaction facilities. Window, menu, and free-form query interfaces can be developed for a wide variety of applications. The retrieval system supports phrase, single, and multiple term, range and word proximity searching within defined context areas. Searches can be performed on word prefix, suffix and embedded character strings. Boolean operators can be nested in command statements for narrowing the scope of searches. Query retrieval aids such as adjacent index term display, index, and thesaurus browsing and previously retrieved document set listings assist users in finding information.

In command language and menu modes, MicroBASIS enables users to store online query sessions for re-execution with its Profile facility. Search statements, output requests, and other repetitive input can be saved and reactivated via menus and prompts. A context-sensitive Help facility provides user assistance at an interaction point.

MicroBASIS' Window facility enables novice users to be productive without training. Function keys activate help and option functions via pop-up windows. The numeric keypad, tab, and spacebar are used for navigation. The Extract function allows users to cut and paste information and add their own commentary and annotations. The extracts are written to MS-DOS files for further manipulation by word processing and spreadsheet programs.

Hardware requirements include an IBM PC, XT, AT or compatible, 640K memory, a hard disc drive, a CD-ROM drive, and a graphic adapter, all of which can be supplied by IDI if desired.

AMTEC INFORMATION SERVICES

AMTEC offers a full range of optical media services and their own retrieval software, OPTI/Search. They offer full integration of text, tabular and line art, and digitized graphics and has developed specialized scanning equipment as well. This company, unfortunately, did not provide specific information about OPTI/Search's features, although a representative of their company did contribute a piece on their position in delivering electronic information, which is presented in Chapter 7.

6
CD-ROM Titles

This chapter describes some of the CD-ROM titles currently available or expected to be available by the first quarter of 1988 and has been compiled based on information provided by the companies themselves. Some are marketed by both the developer of the product and the information provider, although the majority are marketed by the IP only.

To use most of the products described here, you need an IBM PC or compatible with at least 512K RAM (640K is recommended for manipulation of data) and a CD-ROM drive. Most of the time, a subscription agreement is entered into, and most companies allow you to either purchase or lease the CD-ROM drive and sometimes the computer hardware as well. If a company does not provide this service, they can refer you to a vendor who can. A subscription usually includes updates, the search and retrieval software (included on the compact disc or on a floppy disc), documentation, and telephone support. Contact each company individually for more specific information and refer to Appendix B for a complete listing of CD-ROM titles.

Disc Title: ERIC
Available from: SilverPlatter Information, Inc.
                       or
           ORI, Inc. Information Systems Division

The Educational Resources Information Center (ERIC) database is the national U.S. bibliographic database covering the literature of education. It is comprised of two separate files: (1) Resources in Education (RIE), handling the document and reporting "fugitive" literature and (2) Current Index to Journals in Education (CIJE), handling the published journal article literature, as contained in over 775 major education-related serials/periodicals.

The ERIC database is available on one or more archival discs that do not require updating, i.e., 1966-1975 and 1976-1982. Data from 1983 to the current year is contained on a separate disc and is updated on a quarterly basis. Each disc is totally independent, containing all the records, indexes and software necessary for full use. The RIE and CIJE retrospective files are on separate discs, while the current disc contains both RIE and CIJE records.

Disc Title: PsycLIT
Available from: SilverPlatter Information, Inc.
   or
   Psychological Abstracts Information Services

The PsycLIT database provides summaries of the international literature in psychology and related fields compiled from Psychological Abstracts, a major resource for information in psychology and the behavioral sciences cumulated since 1974. It covers more than 1,300 journals and monographic series from approximately 45 countries in more than two dozen languages.

Disc Title: NTIS Bibliographic Database
Available from: SilverPlatter Information, Inc.

The National Technical Information Service (NTIS) Bibliographic Database is comprised of documents from three major agencies: (1) U.S. Department of Energy (DOE); (2) U.S. Department of Defense (DOD); (3) National Aeronautics and Space Administration (NASA); plus other Federal, non-Federal and foreign agencies and sources. The NTIS database is one of the world's leading sources of information on products and services for the achievement of U.S. productivity and industrial innovation.

The NTIS database consists of citations of government-sponsored research, development and engineering reports, as well as other analyses prepared by government agencies, their contractors, or grantees. Formerly, NTIS was primarily focused on the physical sciences: physics, chemistry, materials and electrotechnology. Today, NTIS reflects the expanded and diversified areas covered by the Federal agencies. The NTIS database is comprised of reports that cover nearly every topic of practical importance. These reports document information on such topics as business and finance, engineering, environment, communications, robotics, biotechnology, and transportation.

The research for NTIS reports is often conducted by U.S. corporations and universities under contract to government agencies. Approximately 400,000 reports in the collection are produced by foreign government agencies, academic institutions and other foreign organizations. Some 70,000 completed reports are funneled into NTIS annually from these sources. Approximately 30,000 of the 1,160,000 documents acquired by NTIS from the various agencies are fully processed by NTIS. This includes descriptive cataloging, subject classification and indexing, and abstracting. The remaining documents acquired by NTIS have been cataloged and indexed by subject specialists at the originating agencies.

Disc Title: COMPU-INFO
Available from: SilverPlatter Information, Inc.

COMPU-INFO contains 12,000 computer product listings from 1,500 companies worldwide. Microcomputer Review, COMPU-INFO's print counterpart, was formerly a private file used by the U.S. government and other large corporations. COMPU-INFO contains data on prices, operating systems, hardware and communications and is organized to allow easy access to a wide range of information. A user can quickly reference information by company name, model, price or by any of 300 features. Information about speed, capacity, connectivity, product age and price allow for comparison of similar products from diverse vendors. COMPU-INFO provides full address, area code and phone number for each company. this information can be used for conducting surveys, writing proposals or bids, generating leads for DEM products and services or research.

Disc Title: LISA
Available from: SilverPlatter Information, Inc.
                    or
                    Library Association Publishing Ltd.

Library & Information Science Abstracts (LISA), published by Library Association Publishing Ltd., is the world's leading international abstracting service for Librarianship Information Science and related disciplines. The LISA database covers librarianship, information science, plus related disciplines; includes references on library management and materials; and provides exceptional depth of coverage in such new technology areas as teleconferencing, videotext, databases, online systems, telecommunications, and electronic publishing. The database contains over 81,000 citations from 550 periodicals. These periodicals are from 100 countries and are published in over 30 languages. In addition to abstracts from the leading journals, LISA also includes non-serial publications such as reports, monographs and conference proceedings.

Disc Title: AGRICOLA
Available from: SilverPlatter Information, Inc.

The AGRICOLA database contains bibliographic records of materials acquired by the National Agricultural Library (NAL) and cooperating institutions in the agricultural and related sciences. Ninety percent of the records describe journal articles and book chapters, and the remaining ten percent describe monographs, series, microforms, audiovisuals, maps, and other types of materials.

The database consists of records for literature citation of journal articles, monographs, theses, patents, software, audiovisual materials, and technical reports relating to aspects of agriculture. In addition, AGRICOLA also contains a number of subfields of related bibliographic citations that have been prepared by specialized sources, e.g., the Food and Nutrition Information Center (FNIC) and the American Agricultural Economics Documentation Center (AAEDC). This combination of NAL records and records contributed by other information centers and cooperators make AGRICOLA the largest database of agricultural information.

Disc Title:	Ca-CD
Available from:	SilverPlatter Information, Inc.
	or
	Elsevier Science Publishers
	or
	Year Book Medical Publishers

Ca-CD has been compiled from Year Book Medical Publishers and Elsevier Science Publishers and contains cancer-related bibliographic records from 1985 to the present. EMBASE, the database of Elsevier Science Publishers, provides approximately 30,000 cancer-related records per year from all disciplines in the entire EMBASE database. Ca-CD records from EMBASE are selected, classified, and indexed by medical information specialists.

Ca-CD also contains records from the Year Book of Cancer and cancer-related records from other Year Books published by Year Book Medical Publishers. Articles included in the Year Book are the result of a year-long search of the world literature on oncology conducted by a professional board of editors and advisors. Each Year Book on a Ca-CD includes a concise summary of the original journal article, plus commentaries by the editors and medical advisors.

SilverPlatter has merged into one reference record any records that are duplicated between the two files, while at the same time preserving the unique information provided by each publisher. This concept enables the researcher with a cancer-related need to retrieve records by drug trade name (from Elsevier). Records include an author abstract plus enhanced commentary (from Year Book). Ca-CD also contains records that are unique to each of the publishers' files.

Disc Title:	MEDLINE
Available from:	SilverPlatter Information, Inc.
	or
	Cambridge Scientific Abstracts

Produced by the National Library of Medicine (NLM), MEDLINE contains bibliographic citations and abstracts for biomedical literature. Considered the primary source of biomedical information, MEDLINE provides health professionals with access to information necessary for research, health care and education.

MEDLINE is international in scope, with approximately 75 percent of the citations published in the English language. It contains references to articles in over 3,000 major medical journals. MEDLINE's coverage is extensive; it includes such topics as microbiology, delivery of health care, nutrition, pharmacology, and environmental health. MEDLINE also includes Medical Subject Headings (MeSH), the controlled vocabulary maintained by NLM and assigned by the professional indexers to each record.

Disc Title: CHEM-BANK
Available from: SilverPlatter Information, Inc.

CHEM-BANK is a source of information on hazardous chemicals. It includes three major databases: RTECS (Registry of Toxic Effects of Chemical Substances from the National Institute for Occupational Safety and Health); CHRIS (Chemical Hazard Response Information System from U.S. Department of Transportation); and OHMTADS (Oil and Hazardous Materials-Technical Assistance Data System from the U.S. Environmental Protection Agency).

The Registry of Toxic Effects of Chemical Substances (RTECS) is a compendium of toxicity data extracted from scientific literature. Recognized worldwide as the leading source for basic acute and chronic toxic information, it contains identification, toxicity, and general information for over 87,000 chemicals and 310,000 compound names. Chemicals are identified by prime name, synonym, RTECS accession number, CAS registry number, molecular formula and weight, or Wiswesser line notation. Toxic effects data with accompanying bibliographic reference are present under five main categories: skin and eye irritation, mutation, reproductive effects, tumorigenic data, and toxicity data. Information covers type of effects, organ system affected, route of administration, animal species, and dose. Supporting information includes Toxicology and Cancer reviews (IARC, ACGIH TLV data and other), Standards and Regulations (OSHA, EPA, etc.); NIOSH Criteria Documents, and pertinent status reports from government agencies (NIOSH, NTP, NCI, EPA, OSHA).

The Chemical Hazard Response Information System contains detailed information to assist with emergency response, accident prevention, and safety procedure design in the transportation of hazardous chemicals. It covers over 1,000 key chemicals, with up to 94 data fields each, and is invaluable in preparing material safety data sheets and in safety program design and training.

The Oil and Hazardous Materials-Technical Assistance Data System contains numeric data and interpretive comments, facilitating rapid effective response to emergency spills. Extensive hazardous materials information (up to 120 data fields for each of 1,400 chemicals) offers broad support to environmental research and enforcement activities. Chemical identifiers include name, synonyms, trade names, Accession number, CAS registry number, SIC code, chemical formula, and composition. Data areas covered include physical and chemical properties, reactivity, transportation and storage, detection, fire protection and explosion, environmental fate and chemistry, toxicology, human contact and hazard information, response, and disposal advice.

Disc Title: OSH-ROM
Available from: SilverPlatter Information, Inc.

OSH-ROM contains three leading databases in occupational safety and health. The disc contains NIOSHTIC, the database of the National Institute for Occupational Safety and Health; HSELINE, the database of the Health and Safety Executive, a U.K. Government agency; and CISDOC, the database of the International Occupational Safety and Health Information Centre of the International Labor Organization.

Collectively, NIOSHTIC, HSELINE and CISDOC contain over 240,000 citations taken from over 500 journals and 100,000 monographs and technical reports. This information covers occupational safety and health literature from over 50 countries going back to 1960 and, in special cases, earlier. Subject areas include toxicology, epideminology, occupational medicine, pathology, physiology, metabolism, chemistry, industrial hygiene, health physics, control technology, engineering, behavioral sciences, ergonomics, safety, hazardous wastes, occupational safety and health programs, education, and training. Industries covered range from the primary through tertiary sectors, with particular emphasis on agriculture, mining, nuclear technology, manufacturing (particularly chemicals and explosives), engineering, and construction.

Disc Title: A-V ONLINE
Available from: SilverPlatter Information, Inc.
or
National Information Center for Educational Media

A-V ONLINE is an audiovisual materials database that covers videotapes, films, audiocassettes, filmstrips, and other media on any subject. A-V ONLINE incorporates cataloging from the Library of Congress, publishers' catalogs and library collections. Citations include annotations and subject descriptors, audience level, and name and address of commercial source. A-V ONLINE is the database of the National Information Center for Educational Media (NICEM).

The database contains documentary, instructional, information, and recreational programs. More than 300,000 items are described, supplemented each year with approximately 20,000 changes and additions. Coverage includes materials in English, Spanish, French, German, and other languages.

Disc Title: CIRR
Available from: SilverPlatter Information, Inc.
or
JA Micropublishing, Inc.

The Corporate and Industry Research Reports (CIRR) database is an index to research reports by Wall Street analysts and economists that are stored on microfiche. It is a cumulative index of over 75,000 company and industry reports that analyze more than 7,000 North American and 1,000 foreign companies, providing insight to economic, competitive, technical and political issues. CIRR on CD-ROM provides a microfiche reference number for each record, facilitating access to the full text of any report.

Disc Title: Sociofile
Available from: Sociological Abstracts

Sociofile presents in-depth abstracts of articles from the more than 1,500 serials published worldwide in sociology and its sister disciplines, along with enhanced bibliographic citations of relevant disserations. Sociofile user aids include the Sociological Abstracts User's Reference Manual, the Thesaurus of Sociological Indexing Terms. The database contains all abstracts of journal articles in the Sociological Abstracts database from 1974 onward and enhanced disseration citations beginning with 1986.

Disc Title: Books in Print Plus™
Available from: Bowker Electronic Publishing

Books in Print Plus™ is a database containing over 750,000 titles from the Books In Print volumes produced by R. R. Bowker. It also contains more than 602,000 titles cross-referenced under 63,500 Library of Congress headings from the Subject Guide to Books In Print, the Books in Print Supplement of over 40,000 titles, Forthcoming Books' 85,000 soon to be released titles with complete publisher and ordering information, and complete names and addresses of all book publishers. Electronic ordering is available in conjunction with Baker & Taylor, Blackwell, Brodart, Ingram and other distributors' ordering software.

Disc Title: Books in Print Plus with Book Reviews Plus™
Available from: Bowker Electronic Publishing

Books in Print Plus with Book Reviews Plus™ contains everything listed above, including electronic ordering capability, and an additional reference that lets the user know if reviews have been found for a particular title and then provides access to the review with the touch of a key. All reviews include publication and date of review, and 20,000 new reviews are added over the course of each year.

Disc Title: Ulrich's Plus™
Available from: Bowker Electronic Publishing

Ulrich's Plus™ contains Ulrich's International Periodicals directory of over 68,000 periodicals listed alphabetically by title in 557 subject categories; more than 36,000 titles from Irregular Serials and Annuals; an ISSN Index that lists more than 75,200 current and 13,800 former ISSN titles; Bowker's International Serials Database Updated with up-to-date information on new titles, title changes and cessations for over 6,000 titles each year; and complete names and addresses of all periodical publishers.

Disc Title: Books Out of Print Plus
Available from: Bowker Electronic Publishing

Books Out of Print Plus contains more than 300,000 titles declared out of print or out of stock by their publishers from 1979 to the present.

Disc Title: Personnet
Available from: Information Handling Services

Personnet is a combination of federal personnel full-text databases containing the Federal Personnel Manual plus related case decisions and other documents. A subscriber has several options in choosing the databases needed, including:

- The Federal Personnel Manual (FPM), which includes FPM chapters, supplements, letters, and bulletins
- Case Decisions, including:
  - Merit Systems Protection Board (MSPB)
  - Equal Employment Opportunity Commission (EEOC) Federal Sector
  - MSPB/EEOC Mixed Cases (decisions appealed to both MSPB and EEOC)
  - Federal Labor Relations Authority (FLRA)
  - Federal Service Impasses Panel (FSIP)
  - Administrative Law Judge (ALJ)
  - Comptroller General - Civilian Personnel
  - Associated Civil Court Cases
- Related Documents, including:
  - MSPB, FLRA, EEOC and OPM Regulations (From CFR Titles 5 and 29/Federal Register)
  - Civilian Personnel Law Manual
  - Equal Employment Opportunity Management Bulletins and Directives
  - Executive Orders (those pertaining to Federal personnel issues)
  - United States Code Title 5

Disc Title: CrossLink
Available from: Information Handling Services

CrossLink provides access to supply/logistics data from the federal cataloging system, plus related DOD and commercial data used to select alternate sources of supply and identify applicable specifications, standards, and manufacturers' catalogs. It includes sources such as:

- Master Cross Reference List (MCRL) 1, 2 and 3
- Management Data List-Consolidated (ML-C)
- Commercial and Government Entity (CAGE) Code (H4-8)
- Dun & Bradstreet's vendor profile
- Descriptive information from the federal cataloging system cross-referenced to vendor, specifications and standards information in related IHS microform services.

CrossLink also allows online access to the following logistics data:
- Technical characteristics of approved supply items
- Major Organizational Entity (MOE) Rule data
- Allowance Parts Lists (APLS)
- Complete references to military/federal standardization documents, vendor catalogs and industry standards
- Commerce Business Daily
- Additional business information and financial data from Dun & Bradstreet

CrossLink contains information on nearly 13 million items of supply in the federal cataloging system; software is provided on an accompanying floppy diskette.

Disc Title: GEOdiscs
Available from: Geovision, Inc.

Geovision publishes a series of highly accurate geographic CD-ROM databases. Data layers contained in the CD-ROM maps include roads, waterways, railroads, boundaries, elevation, land use and cover, census tract, and place and street names files. The USA Atlas CD-ROM gives a user the ability to go from an overview of the entire U.S. down to country level detail. Geovision's state series GEOdiscs provide a spectrum of geographic information from the state level down to city block level detail. Their Windows/On the World (WOW) applications program allows a user to create graphics, text or symbol overlays appropriate to the application and to link information from external databases to the map.

Disc Title: Hot Line
Available from: General Information, Inc.

General Information, a leader in directory and reference products in electronic and book form, has announced plans to release Hot Line, an expanded CD-ROM version of their National Directory of Addresses and Telephone Numbers. Hot Line, released in electronic form on floppy discs in December 1986, is receiving rave reviews, prompting the company to go ahead with plans for conversion to CD-ROM as well. General Information also plans to license the National Directory's database (which contains more than 150,000 listings of America's most important firms, government agencies, and institutions) to other publishers of CD-ROM reference products so that the directory can be available to users of a variety of CD-ROM applications.

General Information has also announced plans to release a CD-ROM version of the World Almanac that is included in Bookshelf Microsoft's reference compact disc for writers and office personnel. General Information owns the exclusive electronic rights to this product and licensed it to Microsoft for use in Bookshelf.

Disc Title: Life Sciences Collection
Available from: Cambridge Scientific Abstracts

Life Sciences Collection is a comprehensive database on the life sciences and contains abstracts and citations from more than 5,000 core journals, books, serial monographs, conference reports, international patents and statistical publications. It covers:

- Animal Behavior
- Bacteriology
- Biochemistry: Amino Acids, Peptides and Proteins
- Biochemistry: Biological Membranes
- Biochemistry: Nucleic Acids
- Biotechnology Research
- Calcified Tissues
- Chemoreception
- Ecology
- Endocrinology
- Entomology
- Genetics
- Immunology
- Industrial and Applied Microbiology
- Microbiology: Algology, Mycology and Protozoology
- Neurosciences
- Toxicology
- Virology

Disc Title: Aquatic Sciences and Fisheries Abstracts
Available from: Cambridge Scientific Abstracts

The Aquatic Sciences and Fisheries Abstracts database covers both English and foreign language publications based on information provided by the UN Department of International Economic and Social Affairs, the Food and Agriculture Organization of the UN, the Intergovernmental Oceanographic Commission, and leading research centers throughout the world. It includes a comprehensive review of worldwide publications and reports, monographs, dissertations, grey literature, and proceedings. Topics covered include:

- Acoustics and optics of aquatic environments
- Aquatic communities
- Biological and ecological aspects of marine, freshwater and brackish environments

- Fisheries, aquaculture and other living resources
- Legal, economic and sociological studies
- Limnology
- Marine meterology and climatology
- Marine technology and engineering
- Non-living resources
- Oceanography
- Pollution of aquatic environments
- Related offshore operations and services
- Selected descriptive works on the physical environment of aquatic organisms

Disc Title: Bookshelf
Available from: Microsoft Corporation

Bookshelf is a tool for writers and office personnel that contains ten frequently used reference works and is one of only a few "consumer" products available on CD-ROM. Bookshelf is unique among CD-ROM products because it is a memory-resident program, meaning it can run with other programs, such as a word processor. The references include:

- The 1987 World Almanac and Book of Facts
- The Chicago Manual of Style
- Bartlett's Familiar Quotations
- The American Heritage Dictionary
- Roget's II: Electronic Thesaurus
- Houghton Mifflin Spelling Verifier and Corrector
- Forms and Letters - a collection of forms, letters and outlines that can be customized to suit user needs
- U.S. ZIP Code Directory
- Houghton Mifflin Usage Alert
- Business Information Sources - a guide to sources of business information, including references from business journals, research reports and books on topics such as finance, economics, management and marketing.

Disc Title: Compustat PC Plus
Available from: Standard & Poor's Compustat Services, Inc.

PC Plus contains the COMPUSTAT financial database of over 10,000 companies and includes, for each company, up to:

- 15 years of annual data
- 5 years of quarterly data
- 10 years of Monthly Price-Dividends-Earnings data for companies and industry composites
- 7 years of Business Segment data
- 7 years of Geographic data including sales, operating income and identifiable assets of foreign subsidiaries

- 15 years of Annual data for inactive companies that have gone private, filed for bankruptcy, were acquired, liquidated, or no longer report.

Also included:

- 15 years and 20 quarters of Industry Aggregate data
- SIC codes
- Top company officers, company name, address with zip code, and telephone number.

Disc Title:	Magazine Index Plus
Available from:	Information Access Company

Magazine Index Plus is a database that contains indexes of articles appearing in over 400 magazines and indexing of articles in the New York Times as well. Coverage includes the current year cumulated with the previous three years of data from the Magazine Index and 2 months of index data from the New York Times. The product has been designed for use by library patrons and is extremely simple to use.

Disc Title:	Infomark Laser PC System
Available from:	National Decision Systems

National Decision Systems, a leading demographic and marketing information provider, has released a series of comprehensive national databases on CD-ROM that provide access to demographics, business, competitive and employment data, marketing information, survey research and product demand data, geo-demographic information, color mapping, and graphic capabilities. It includes:

- Demographic Database - includes 480 demographic items based on the 1980 census and provides current year estimates and five-year projections for selected key variables. The database is used to generate standard NDS demographic reports as well as information for color mapping.
- Business-Facts Database - includes detailed information on over 7 million businesses and 100 million employees.
- VISION Target Marketing System - a second-generation customer targeting and lifestyle segmentation tool that clusters neighborhoods with similar household lifestyles and classifies them into 48 geo-demographic market segments. Using VISION, a series of reports can be generated to identify, quantify and locate customers in terms of purchasing, financial and media behavior.
- Shopping Center Database - contains information on more than 7,500 shopping centers over 100,000 square feet identified by name, address and square footage.
- Consumer Expenditure Database - produces one-page reports with potential consumer expenditure data for ten major retail trade categories, shopping center square footage and a retail saturation index for each trade area.
- Color Mapping Database - contains over 100,000 current boundaries which are used by the PC color mapping system. PC mapping allows the user to

produce and analyze ZIP codes, census tracts/MCDs, counties and states.
- Site Locator System- features latitude/longitude coordinates for over 28,000 specific locations which makes it easy for a user to determine the latitude and longitude of any site in the U.S.

Disc Title: ENFLEX INFO
Available from: ERM Computer Services, Inc.

ENFLEX INFO provides access to the full text of current federal and state environment regulations and is designed to assist the environmental professional in managing the data and information needs associated with environmental regulatory requirements. This product provides the capability to:

- Identify new regulations
- List recordkeeping and reporting requirements for a hazardous waste generator
- Identify reporting requirements associated with an accidental spill
- Develop a comprehensive list of state and federal air, water and waste compliance requirements that apply to a particular situation
- Identify special compliance requirements
- Identify emergency planning regulations

Disc Title: Dissertation Abstracts Ondisc
Available from: University Microfilms International

Dissertation Abstracts Ondisc contains information on more than 900,000 doctoral dissertations and masters theses. It includes both bibliographic citations and 350-word abstracts for titles published since July 1980 just as they appear in UMI's printed Reference, Dissertation Abstracts International. In addition, bibliographic citations are included for dissertations prior to July 1980, dating as far back as 1861.

Disc Title: NewsBank Electronic Index
Available from: NewsBank, Inc.

The NewsBank Electronic Index provides access to over 700,000 newspapers articles from over 450 newspapers on issues, events, film and television, book reviews and authors, performing arts, art forms and exhibits, business and biographies from 1982 to the present. It is designed to be used as a companion to this company's NewsBank microfiche backfiles files in a library or other reference setting, with microfiche containing the full text of all articles referenced on the compact disc.

Disc Title: Conquest
Available from: Donnelley Marketing Information Services

Conquest is a demographic product that allows the user to identify emerging markets, select goods and services for existing and mature markets, evaluate retail sites, develop target market programs and create advertising strategies.

It includes:

- Demographic estimates and projections based on the largest household database (over 78 million individual households) available
- Over 100 million additional items of information
- Data on millions of businesses and sales potential for 20 types of retail stores
- Current detailed information on over 8,000 shopping centers (supplied by National Research Bureau)
- The only updated (1986) lifestyle segmentation system available, ClusterPlus
- More than a dozen database linkages including Nielsen, Simmons Market Research Bureau, Arbitron, Neodata, and Vals
- Completely integrated graphics and mapping capabilities

Disc Title: DeLorme's World Atlas
Available from: DeLorme Mapping Systems

World Atlas is a CD-ROM based geographical information system that has been completely developed by DeLorme, including software, and incorporates some of the best graphics currently available on CD-ROM. The system displays geographic information based on its level of importance. Features that are more significant such as country borders, interstate highways and large cities are displayed at less detailed, wider area scales. Less significant features such as secondary roads and small towns are displayed in more detailed, narrower area scales. Through this approach, the user can zoom down from a whole world view with only continents and oceans displayed to areas only one-half mile square with street names and buildings shown. The system controls data to better than one-meter resolution.

The user can access and display an area of interest from the map database by specifying the desired coordinates and scale. In approximately 10 seconds, the desired data is displayed at the chosen scale with the specified coordinates at screen center. The system provides a second means of access and display of data. This is the "fly-in" method, by which the user points with a mouse to the desired screen center and then specifies the display scale by indicating how many steps of zoom to fly in.

Disc Title: Million Dollar Directory
Available from: Dun's Marketing Service

The Million Dollar Directory, in the prototype phase of CD-ROM development at the time of this writing, is, in print form, a respected source for business professionals who need information on large U.S. companies. Listings on the top 160,000 public and private companies include location and phone number, officer names, SIC codes and line of business descriptions, size indicators, corporate family relations, DUNS numbers and other details. In addition to searching by company name or corporate family, the product allows for each by criteria, individually or in combination. Selection criteria include type of industry, geographical region, officer title, public/private indicator, employees (total and local), sales, and network.

7
Optical Disc Technology
The Past, Present and Future

The past, present and future of optical disc technology make for an interesting story. Who better to tell its story than those prominent in its creation, development, growth and implementation? This chapter presents comments from persons in such positions—creators, developers, and present and potential users of the technology. Their comments, which express viewpoints from quite different perspectives and positions, are reprinted with their permission.

AND NOW, THE MULTIMEDIA "INTERACTIVE" CD-ROM
by Dr. Jean-Pierre Isbouts
Manager, Applications Development
Philips and Du Pont Optical

Anyone who has followed the media industry must be impressed, and perhaps a bit puzzled, by new developments surrounding the compact disc—particularly so far as non-consumer, professional applications are concerned.

For developers and producers of instructional media, things used to be pretty well clear-cut. There is videotape, a fine tool but not capable of interactivity. There's the compact audio disc, an entertainment device really for music enjoyment at home or, perhaps, linear instruction in the classroom. And then there is the videodisc, the learning tool *par excellence* for its interactive dialogue, its simulation capability and unparalleled user-friendliness.

This understanding of the technology remained pretty much valid after the introduction of CD-ROM in 1985. CD-ROM is a high-volume database tool for local, PC-based retrieval. Well, our library people will have some use for that, we thought.

And then comes CD-I, introduced by Philips at the 1986 Microsoft Conference in Seattle, and the videodisc is no longer the only interactive medium. GE and RCA team up to present a technology called DVI (also presented in Seattle at the Microsoft Conference one year later), which proves that CD-ROM, given the proper data compression, can provide real-time, digital motion video.

And finally, Polygram introduces CD-V (Compact Disc-Video) at the June 1987 Consumer Electronics show in Chicago and proves that even analog video can fit on the very same, 5-inch "compact" disc.

Each Medium Has its Applications

Amidst the rise of new CD media, perhaps the biggest bone of contention (and quite undeservedly so) has been the polarization between CD-I and CD-ROM designers. CD-ROM developers claim, not without some truth, that the introduction of a "paper plane called CD-I" suspended some well-conceived CD-ROM projects.

The CD-I folks, on the other hand, tend to keep CD-ROM strictly within its bullpen where it found its first application: database publishing. This phenomenon has abated by now as most publishers and designers have come to understand the innate difference between the media: CD-ROM, a system designed for PC connectivity, versus CD-I, a stand-alone television player. But as a consequence, the perfectly legitimate multimedia capabilities of CD-ROM might have gotten the short end.

There is a simple answer to all this. No matter how you look at it, DVI and CD-I are specific applications of very straightforward CD-ROM technology, except CD-ROM, with all of its multimedia potential, exists today, whereas DVI and CD-I do not.

Does this mean that CD-ROM will also eliminate the videodisc from the range of instructional media? Of course not. Regardless of all the attention which compressed motion video has been getting, there is one important thing to remember: the videodisc will always remain the most efficient vehicle for delivering motion video for instructional, interactive purposes. Why? Because the videodisc is an analog video carrier without the need for expensive data conversion, compression, and re-acquisition—all costly factors that do not replace, but add to, the original production costs.

An application where CD-ROM (and possibly other future CD application media as well) could become a major alternative is in the category of instructional programs where motion video is *not* a prerequisite; where still-frame audio (SFA) or compressed audio-over-still is needed (without the expense for costly and incompatible decoder/encoder devices; where graphics or graphic animation must be used (without the need to choose from some 30 mostly incompatible graphics overlay cards); and where source materials may already exist in digital format, as in the case of most CBT programming.

The point, in short, is this: whereas the videodisc is the premier device for video, it is not an ideal carrier for digital audio, graphics, and data. Trying to include such media in laserdisc applications (known in the industry as level 3, 4 and 5 applications) will automatically limit the use and lifespan of an instructional program to the specific hardware configuration—and the cost associated therewith—whether the system is made by Sony, Pioneer, IBM, NCR, Visage, or several other turnkey system integrators.

Is CD-ROM An Interactive Medium?

For most media designers, the audiovisual presentation—particularly an interactive one—is essentially an exercise in video technology and video production techniques. Although this remains the case today, CD-ROM technology could become an important alternative, not in the least because of the lower cost threshold of program production that has often stymied creative videodisc efforts. At the same time, the CD-ROM production is a straightforward process—we could in fact coin the term "desktop production" versus the "studio production" usually associated with the videodisc, whereby CD-ROM, for one, can benefit from a wide range of available software and software tools on the market today.

The first time I saw a CD-ROM in action, the experience was truly—well, anticlimactic. In went this beautiful, thin, shiny disc with its sleek surface graphics (elements that cannot fail but impress the "old" videodisc generation, accustomed as it is to big 12" dishes in crumpled sleeves with dot-matrixed labels). The CD-ROM player whizzed, beeped and lights went off, and the result, lo and behold, was a string of text on the screen. "There!", my host said, with barely contained emotion.

The episode left a question: Is CD-ROM a data storage device, or can it truly become an audiovisual, interactive medium? The answer is yes, although not in a manner usually associated with "conventional" analog media, such as video, slide or film techniques.

Because of its vast resource of storage capacity, the CD-ROM has made possible the encapsulation of digital sources unheard of in the magnetic-only PC environment: sound, graphics, even photographic images. What's more, the CD-ROM offers a major advantage over analog carriers of audio-visual programming: each program element is a discrete file that can be matched with any other segment and played back at will, under control of the proper retrieval software.

For example, a given audio sequence can be retrieved at any time to support any image or graphics sequence. The inability of analog media to do the same has led, in the videodisc camp, to a wide and wild array of incompatible "compressed audio" devices which (for quite a bit of money in both production and hardware) promise to deliver a similar audio flexibility.

But it is clear that a free manipulation of audiovisual files—so often crucial in an interactive course—is a job done best in a digital environment. And no matter how you look at it, video, film, and other audiovisual media are analog—with fixed-position files.

The Man-Machine Interface

As far as the actual man-to-medium communications are concerned, here too we are faced with an environment determined by digital rather than analog properties. The analog videodisc—the first medium ever to introduce the concept of viewer interaction with audiovisual material—is essentially one of selective access to (mostly motion) material, driven by indexes or menus.

Because CD-ROM (and other similar digital media) are, by contrast, products of the computer industry, interaction comes down to the fine art of formulating and entering a qualified request. This query is matched with the contents of the database and will, most likely, result in a display of elements without any apparent relationship to one another—except for their common match with the user's search request.

The benefit of the videodisc model of interactive communications is that access is extremely rapid and that all elements are in place and on-screen, whether motion or still display, in a split-second. By contrast, the CD-ROM must process the request, search the database, upload the information into its digital memory, allocate discrete elements to their appropriate ports (audio, video, graphics etc.), provide synchronization utilities, and set the show in motion. Even in the best of times, with caching of indexes in RAM and hard disk and the fast-porting of 32-bit, multi-bus architecture, such access to audiovisuals is bound to be slower than we have come to expect from the videodisc.

On the other hand, whereas the available programmatic material (and access parameters) must be fixed in the production of a videodisc, this need is wholly absent when using CD-ROM. Given the availability of the material on the disc, the viewer is, in theory, free to sample the information at his leisure, make cross-references and so-called "sideways searches" of a complexity no designer could have possibly fathomed.

There is, of course, a happy medium between the two models. In fact, software producers are beginning to recognize that there is more under the sun than your typical Boolean or index-driven interactive system. This, obviously, is a major reason for the high public interest bestowed on the CD-I model—precisely because it promises to endow the digital optical medium with an interactive system so familiar to its older analog sister, the videodisc.

But intuitive rather than logical approaches to information retrieval are not the exclusive property of CD-I. Many software houses are working on user-friendly production and retrieval utilities for CD-ROM, including such advanced shops as Software Mart (Austin, TX), Macro Mind (Chicago, IL) and KnowledgeSet (Monterey, CA).

But then again, with the vast range of PC programming talent active today, nothing would deter the CD-ROM producer from doing what videodisc designers have done for years—develop a custom retrieval system from the ground up, uniquely geared to the requirements of the program.

The CD-ROM Production

So if the CD-ROM is a legitimate interactive audiovisual medium, how does one go about producing one? Simple: in eight easy pieces. Let's review them step by step.

STEP 1: *Determining the Requirements of the User*. One of the first and critical steps in developing a CD-ROM application is to formulate the unique requirements of its future user audience. What do we hope to achieve with the program? What are the expectations?

"Who will use the program?" is the second question. What is the profile of the future user? How does he or she expect to find the information required? Is the user computer-literate, or is a special (for example, simple, user-friendly) software environment required?

Next, try to determine how the program will be used. Will queries be entered by keyboard, mouse, touch-screen, or light pen? Will the program run as a stand-alone, PC-based software entity or will it form part of a larger (online or offline) database? With these three questions:

What is the program's objective?

Who will use the program?

How will the program be used?

we have, in effect, defined the unique user profile of this application. Each application (whether CD-ROM or videodisc based) thus entails its own individual user profile. Understanding the future user audience is of fundamental importance to analyze and develop all subsequent development steps.

STEP 2: *Media Selection*. Once we have a user's profile and we know the objectives of the program, we can take a look at the type of media that will be used to achieve these objectives. In the case of CD-ROM, this will invariably involve some type of database—either a pre-existing "data"-base or a traditional publication in print. However, knowing the full multimedia capabilities of optical discs can also provide an opportunity to create or apply other forms of media such as:

- Photography
- Slides
- Graphics
- Graphics Animation
- Audio

If the designer feels that any or all of the above options are required, the next step is to look at the size of such audio-visual media. For example:

- How much data must be stored?
- Are photographic images included—and how many?
- Are graphics to be created in digital or analog form? (for example, RGB graphics vs. Chryn or Paintbox graphics)
- Is the graphical animation to be supplied in cinematographical or digital (DYUV) form?
- How much audio is needed? Should audio files be separate from image or data files, or are they invariably linked to each other?

Then, the designer will analyze the expected size of the user "network" and estimate the number of "workstations" involved. She will also look at the volatility of the information about to be stored and attempt to predict the number of times this information must be updated. From this analysis, the profile of the optical medium required will emerge. If motion video is required, the choice is likely to be the laser videodisc. If data, graphics, and audio are the likely media in the program, CD-ROM is the preferred medium.

STEP 3: Application Development. With the usage profile, program objectives and media selection in place, the next step involves the actual application development. Here, we define the program elements in some greater detail:

- What is the primary retrieval engine for getting to the information? Will it be menu-driven or based on a full-text system using free terms to define a database search?
- To what extent will data, graphics, images and audio be used?
- What is the operating "environment" of the program? Sometimes, an environment other than "straightforward" PC DOS is required—as, for example, in the case of a word processing environment. (A good example is the new Bookshelf product from Microsoft.) Such environments, then, necessitate a true "multi-tasking" system for which the CD-ROM is a mere subset.
- Must access to the information be restricted? If so, is a unique user I.D. input sufficient, should "key" software be used in which the control (floppy) disc defines the range of access to the database, or should the data be encrypted to provide an additional layer of security?

These findings will help to select the specific software tools on the market today. There are some 50 different CD-ROM search programs on the market today and they all exhibit unique features and benefits.

STEP 4: System Design. The second important element in defining the applications format is to analyze the future "workstation." Usually, CD-ROM applications are developed for retrieval on an IBM PC or PC compatible, thus benefitting from the large installed base of PCs in the United States today. But several programs have been developed for systems like the DEC VAX or Rainbow system, the Apple Macintosh or even mainframe processors. Knowing the future "host environment" will be key to selecting the software retrieval system.

Likewise, the decision to use graphics or audio files will necessitate the provision of special hardware to display and/or "playback" multimedia information. Unlike the Macintosh or the Mac II, the IBM PC and its compatibles do not provide for digitized audio decoding, nor are its graphics capabilities sufficient to display true images. For graphics and their required hardware, one must:

- Choose between color and black & white.
- Define the resolution (expressed in picture elements or "pixels" on the display). A typical line graphic usually requires upwards of 640 × 400 pixels, but applications like CAD/CAM need 1024 × 800 or more.

- Define the "bit depth" of each pixel, which allows for a greater color and/or grey scale per picture.
- Likewise, define the frequency of samples for audio files. True "compact disc" or PCM sound runs at 44.1 thousand samples per second with a frequency range of 20,000 kHz. But this type of quality audio needs a large storage capacity with a maximum of 72 minutes for a full compact disc. Lower frequency ranges for audio result in lesser frequency—thus less "fidelity"—but allow the storage of much more audio.
- Like "bit depth," the quantization of audio expresses the range of information each sample can carry. In audio terms, this is expressed in signal-to-noise ratio. A high quantization will, for example, yield less background noise.

There are a range of color graphics and audio encoding/decoding adapters or "boards" available for the PC market today. In essence, their selection is a matter of cost—both in terms of the hardware purchase as well as the unique conditions under which the source material must be "produced." Remember that the issue of image resolution or color scale is of no consequence to the CD-ROM itself—satellite photography has successfully been recorded on CD-ROM—but that the cost and power of the retrieval workstation will determine how far you can go with visual information.

STEP 5: *Retrieval Software*. The results from the preceding steps will serve to select the software system which is used to access the future CD-ROM information based on program needs, system needs and user needs. There are, of course, other criteria to keep in mind when choosing what is known in the industry as a retrieval engine:

- How easily can the information or database be updated with new media sources?
- Can the software be "ported over" to other environments like Apple, DEC, SUN, etc.?
- What is the cost of using this software to create and prepare the database; and
- What is the cost of the "user license?" This item is often overlooked when planning a cost estimate for CD-ROM productions. In addition to the cost of applying the retrieval software to the database design (a process known as origination), most vendors will charge an additional fee for the retrieval diskette which must always be used to "unlock" the CD-ROM database. This is called a unit license and is charged for each individual diskette or workstation on which the CD-ROM is used. Typically, the cost of a user license is $100. This may not seem like much, but to acquire some 100 floppies can thus cost as much as $10,000! Compare this to the actual cost of applying software origination, which roughly will run about $2,000 per 10 megabytes of source data. (Naturally, substantial volume discounts will often apply.)

STEP 6: *Data Collection And Acquisition*. Once all requirements have been analyzed and a software tool (or tools) have been selected, we can proceed with the actual program "production." If there are pre-existing sources (usually data, graphics, or analog audio tapes), these can be reviewed, edited and formatted to the requirements of our CD-ROM database. But more often than not, we have to actively go out and "shoot" new material.

For text sources, this means the conversion to a machine-readable format. This can be done by using sophistical Optical Character Recognition (OCR) systems, which have an error rate of about 80 to 85 percent. Another method is to engage a specialty house to key in the material, often using skilled terminal operators. Such key facilities are likely to use services located abroad. Whether OCR or key-entry is the preferred format, the conversion cost will run about $1 to $2 per page (1,000-1,500 characters). If the material is typeset using a style font or fonts, the charge can run as high as $4—not only because style fonts (with their serif format and variable spacing between characters) are more difficult for an OCR to recognize, but also because more (and more dense) material is contained on a page.

Likewise, images are scanned to a digital format. There are many scanning systems on the market, running from $1,000 to as much as $9,000 or more for advanced color interpreters. Most of the low- to mid-range black & white scanners will record a page at 150 or 300 dots per inch. But again, it depends on your graphics adapter card and monitor whether this quality is what you ultimately get. Also, 300 dpi (dots per inch) images can run as high as 100KB per page, so that quite often, compression techniques must be used. The CCIT Group II or Group IV compression format is most often cited as a de facto standard. The reason is simple: It is used by fax machines worldwide and can thus rely on a vast scale of image applications.

Resolution, quality and storage requirements equally apply to audio files—where audio digitizing is a function of an encoder/adapter, often provided as a board set for an IBM XT or AT. For audio in range of frequencies and quantization factors, all the way up to full PCM audio (usually recorded on digital U-matic tape). With this process completed, all of our sources are "in the can."

STEP 7. Database Conversion And Inversion. Now, we can proceed to edit the materials—meaning format them for the specific program format we have in mind. As far as databases are considered, this is the time to create inverted tables of terms or words occurring throughout the database. This function, which is part of the software origination, is key to providing the future user free or full-text searchability of the database.

Finally, all sources are plotted and formatted in their proper length, form, and database address—ready for the concluding process of creating the program image.

STEP 8. The CD Disc Or Program Image. Up to this point, our source materials, now formatted in a coherent database, could be carried on virtually any medium—like an online database, for example, or a write-once (WORM) optical data disc. But the CD-ROM format has some unique physical aspects that must be adhered to: a blocking factor of 4 and a unique sector size of 2K (2048 bytes). Also, all files must be labelled according to the ANSI system of file systems (level 3).

Although these are rather simple operations that do not affect the contents of the sources we produced so far, it is critical to follow these CD specifications lest files or sectors be lost in the process.

Now, the program is ready to be mastered—and the result, soon, is a box of shiny compact disc ROMs! The production process is complete, and with the final testing of the floppy disc that will unlock the database, your product is ready for the most important step of all: use in the field.

The Benefits

Earlier, we said that CD-ROM could become an important alternative for interactive communications that did not require full motion video but relied heavily on digital sources. It could also benefit from multiple information access strategies and could be produced with existing PC and CD-ROM software tools in a form of desktop production.

One other key benefit is that CD-ROM is a physical standard worldwide—not just in terms of its naked readability (which, after all, Laservision implies as well), but that its driver utilities, operating software—even its logical directory and file structure—have all reached standardization.

By contrast, the interactive videodisc field must battle with a range of incompatible systems. *Videodisc Monitor* Editor Rockley Miller recently estimated that there are not less than 43, mostly incompatible "level 3" videodisc configurations on the market today—including some 73 graphics overlay devices which are all quite unique as well.

True, for most captive professional applications, such incompatibility is of little significance. However, the wide variety of different level 3 videodisc systems is the reason there is so little generic instructional programming on the marketplace today, seven years after the inception of the professional videodisc. What's more, the cost difference between a full-blown Sony VIEW System (a little under $10,000) or a multimedia CD-ROM station ($3,500, including a quality PC, a CD Audio/ROM player and a high-resolution graphics card) is significant. It is therefore highly likely that future generic instructional titles will prefer the CD-ROM rather than the videodisc format—simply because it makes a lot more business sense.

The bottom line is that CD-ROM as a *pars pro toto* for all other compact disc media should not make your publishing decision more difficult—it should expand your choices. This is not only because of the programming benefits as we have just seen, but also (and this may be news to some) because CD-ROM is the perfect springboard for virtually any future CD technology—including CD-I. That means if you and your design team have been plotting CD-I programming for some time but are waiting for ever-delayed player hardware and authoring systems, there is no reason why you cannot go and create your programs today on CD-ROM. You might as well gain valuable production experience with the CD medium and even maintain a good measure of upwards compatibility with CD-I in the future (whenever it appears on the market). The key to such an approach is a new, proposed file standard for multimedia programming.

Developed by Philips Du Pont Optical, this new standard called IXP (Information Exchange Protocol) is under scrutiny by software professionals around the world as the pre-eminent production tool for premaster tapes for ALL CD media, including CD-ROM, CD-V, and CD-I.

The IXP For Audiovisual Tapes

What would be the interest of mastering facility like Philips and Du Pont Optical to produce something of a premaster tape standard for CD-ROM? The answer is, quite simply, that producing a multi-media CD-ROM is a different affair altogether. To explain this, let's briefly review the unique technology of the compact disc.

Each CD, regardless of its application, is a CLV-format optical disc—something with which videodisc producers are very familiar. It means, in short, that unlike the CAV format in which each unique revolution represents one module of information equal in capacity to all other revolutions (whether near the inner or outer radius), all information is stored on one continuous track. Of course, that's more space-efficient, so you can listen to up to 75 minutes of music on one CD.

But because there is no structural distinction between modules or "frames" on the medium, the division becomes an absolute one, expressed in time: the time code (as with CLV videodiscs). As a result, designers of CD programs can use the time code to distinguish between segments, just like a producer can program different chapters on a CLV videodisc. Except, because the CD came forth from the music industry, they didn't call it "chapters" but "tracts," which is a DJ term for musical segments separated by a silent segment. Thus, as any CD listener will know, it is possible to search to a favorite moment in Wagner's Parsifal by entering the appropriate track number into the remote control. If this were a videodisc, we'd call it "level 1."

All CDs being digital, the technology provides for a layer of error correction code called "interleaved Reed-Salomon" to reduce the chance of a missed byte to 10^{-12}. However, this is not quite sufficient for a true data as used in a CD-ROM. For that purpose, Philips and Sony, the original licensers of the CD-ROM Yellow Book technology, created an additional safety net for digital information.

Now remember that a premaster tape for CD-ROM must be formatted in uniform blocks of 2048 (2K) bytes each—the individual "frames" of a CD-ROM. Each block, then, is enriched with an additional error detection and correction layer of 288 bytes. This processing is not usually done by the production facility (a software house, for example). It is commonly done just before the mastering at the mastering plant itself. Together with the error correction processing, we also add a sync pattern and header information, which expresses the physical location of sectors and files on the premaster tape into CD-ROM "framecode," although, as we have seen, this is an absolute timecode—stored not in the vertical interval but in a subchannel called "Q."

The point of all this is that all data-only CD-ROMs are "single-track": all sectors contain bit-accurate data, and thus the tape can be processed in one run. In the case of a multimedia CD-ROM, however, things are a bit more complex. If the author created some text or software files, additional error correction is necessary as usual (we call this format "Mode 1").

However, if a few audio files come along, you'd rather do without the protective code since regular EDAC will suffice, so use the extra "real estate" to store more audio time. This, then, is called "Mode 2" and provides the designer with sectors of not 2048, but 2352 bytes.

A full-fledged CD-ROM can contain a lot of such different files, including high-resolution images, graphics, audio, and text. To quite literally keep track of all these Mode 2/Mode2 switches and process error correction code appropriately would require a file protocol all of its own. To design such a protocol applies equally to multimedia CD-ROM as to CD-I, DVI, or even CD-V. they all share the same mode conversion requirements. They all need a very accurate system to keep track of individual file locations (particularly if those multimedia files are physically interleaved on the premaster tape to facilitate simultaneous retrieval—audio and graphics, for example). And because the correct implementation of this premaster processing is historically the responsibility of a mastering house, it was the initiative of Philips to develop the protocol.

So, in all truth, from the perspective of a facility, multimedia CD-ROM or CD-I or other media are all essentially similar. The bottom line is that if a file protocol were designed to exploit and formalize this similarity, the same benefits would apply to the designer and producer. A multimedia CD-ROM would become upwardly compatible with a CD-I premaster tape. And CD-I production can start today—using existing CD-ROM software tools, without waiting for CD-I to finally "happen." End of controversy.

A Common Language. Once the idea developed into a design for a file protocol (which in essence is nothing but a diverse set of "labels" to identify a group of files, describe their nature, and document their location on the disc), other ideas popped up. Why not provide a system for identifying different graphics resolutions, audio frequencies, data formats and software codes? Why not give the producer the tools to not only distinguish his files in terms of premastering, but in terms of design and production as well?

Which is shy the IXP protocol, as it took shape within Philips' ADVA Group in Baarn (Holland) and Hannover (West Germany), grew from a five-page encoding scheme to a 14-page file system. This system, which as a proposed standard is still being reviewed and amended by many software participants around the world, will likely become the driver behind authoring and origination software for all CDs. To give an idea of how IXP will perform in such an environment, let's review some labeling options that IXP will provide to design and production software.

IXP Production-Related Information. No matter what the shape of the "look and feel" of any such authoring or retrieval software program might be, an IXP protocol driver can identify each program element in the "flowchart" in terms of:

- its expected duration,
- its expected location, and
- its prescribed production format.

To give an example, when our designer plots a given real-time audio sequence at one point of his program, IXP will give him the terminology to (1) label its expected run-length by timecode; (2) determine the type of audio quality level or natural picture/graphics resolution; (3) specify the type of real-time interaction with any other such files; and (4) describe the production method(s) used.

The IXP File Labels. The following diagram shows the individual categories used in IXP's data field for multimedia sources. Like any other CD-ROM sector, this field is preambled by a Sync field, Mode byte, and ID. The following "user area" can contain any of the following:

IXP Data Field Information

1. The file name
2. the nature of the file:

   □ an audio segment
   □ a picture file
   □ a graphics file
   □ a data file (meaning "pure" data or bootable applications software

3. The "DISPLAY" of the file:

   □ Single layer of multiple layer
   □ Resolution or sampling factors
   □ Bit depth or frequency information

4. The post-production information:

   □ Sound or visual source
   □ Visual effects like wipes, window size, location and display periods
   □ Font type and size for text data

The time code used to describe the length and location of program files can be any absolute timescale: either SMPTE or EBU or CD-A time.

For remarks, production notes, producer/operator identification and addresses, ordering information or any data to be carried along the extra error protection layer and post-processing notes accompanied, a separate 32-byte data extension model is provided. The contents of this module are labeled using descriptor code in the preceding IXP data field.

IXP On the Pre-Master Tape. The result, then, is a separate IXP protocol file that is formatted as part of the IXP "driver" and stored on the premaster tape immediately *preceding* the start of the active program area.

This file looks, for all intents and purposes, just like the standard CD-ROM sector. It contains:

- An IXP Header field
- An IXP Data field
- An IXP Data-Extension field

In addition to the header and data field name information, an extension code contains production directives. These extensions take the form of 3-byte ASCII character sets with a wide range of production information. For example, if your CD-ROM graphic is an 8-bit deep RGB picture file on the first image plane of the display, IXP will give it the extension:

.R8(1)

There are a number of additional extension codes to identify the nature and production execution of material contained in the user file. For example, for bootable applications software, the extension [.SRC] will indicate a source code written in C; [.BAS] will obviously refer to a program in BASIC. In addition, numerous extension codes can be used to describe the font type for text, to flag a program as a real-time record and to add a range of other production-related remarks.

A Universal Protocol. In all, the IXP encoding scheme is a comprehensive attempt to identify all possible aspects of multimedia design, production, and premastering. What IXP might ultimately accomplish is that many of the standardization accomplishments of CD-I will benefit the world of CD-ROM multimedia production—at the same time, creating a program exchangeability between CD-I and CD-ROM premaster tapes. This would help the design and production community to get over the CD hurdle, evaluate each medium for its proper application benefits and start to exploit the unique features of these media.

As far as Philips and Du Pont Optical is concerned, we can only encourage as great an acceptance of the protocol as is possible. This body of work was not developed as a proprietary product or value-added service for our customers: it is the result of a conscientious effort on the company to resolve an apparent lack of communications standards in a very extensive production environment.

IXP was created by the Philips and Du Pont Optical Data Video Applications (ADVA) Group in Baarn (Holland) and Hannover (West Germany), the latter being the site of the largest optical manufacturing plant in the world today. It was further developed by the IXP Working Group that included American Interactive Media and The Record Group in Los Angeles, OptImage in Chicago, Philips' Home Interactive Systems Group in the Netherlands and Philips Du Pont Optical Professional Marketing in Wilmington, Delaware.

The chief architect of IXP was Mr. Bjoern Bluethgen, who is active today as Senior Product Manager for audio, video, and data applications of CD. It is no coincidence that Mr. Bluethgen was also a contributor to the documentations of the formal Digital Audio CD tape mastering and CD subcode/R-W specs as well as Green Book issues. These specifications, produced jointly by Philips and Sony, are the accepted standard for CD audio software and, as such, a universal foundation for all forms of compact disc production worldwide. It is our honest hope that the same will apply to the multi-media Information Exchange Protocol for CD production.

THE FIRST WAVE: CD-ROM ADOPTION IN OFFICES AND LIBRARIES
By William Paisley and Matilda Butler
Knowledge Access International, Mountain View, CA

The amount of information that could be distributed in the world increased by many orders of magnitude with the invention of movable type and the printing press. Then, however, the basic tools of publishing remained almost unchanged for four centuries after Gutenberg.

Publishing's grand second era began only 100 years ago with inventions made possible by 19th century chemistry, metallurgy and engineering: motor-driven cylindrical presses, hot-metal typesetting, the rotogravure process, continuous-sheet paper production and systems for transporting and distributing large quantities of the printed product.

Telecommunications emerged at the same time and within a few decades, the line between publishing and telecommunications began to blur. Text could be transmitted by wire and printed at the receiving station. A message could be sent to thousands of destinations simultaneously, which is tantamount to publishing. Picture transmission via telefacsimile followed, completing the parallel with print publishing.

The costs of these first forms of electronic publishing were much higher than print publishing. The full service of text and pictures had few markets other than newspapers. Electronic text itself became a necessity only in businesses requiring updates of fast-changing information, such as brokerages.

Until the 1960s, few additional developments altered the view that "electronic is quicker but printer is cheaper." Print also had a historical depth that was missing from electronic information. Information users in business, science, and the professions needed specific items of past information for planning, problem solving, and decision making. Transmitted electronic information had no memory for the past.

After its wartime invention, the first publishing applications of the computer were drudge work such as compilation and indexing. However, these were significant contributions to scientific and technical publishing, where, as Bush (1945) observed, "The summation of human experience is being expanded at a prodigious rate, and the means we use for threading through the consequent maze to the momentarily important item is the same as was used in the days of square-rigged ships."

Then came time-sharing systems with telecommunications links. The world of information changed as dramatically as it had in the 15th century. The computer could store past information with many access points provided by computer-generated indexes; users could retrieve the "momentarily important item."

Soon the term online replaced "time-sharing, telecommunicating computers" and database became a synonym of "computer-stored and computer-indexed information."

For the first time, a genuine alternative to print publishing existed for business, scientific, and professional information. The early converts to online database searching were researchers, both in science and in information-intensive fields such as law, journalism, and finance. Since they were already heavy users of print information, the speed and retrieval power of online systems justified the higher cost.

The number of databases available to online users grew from a handful to more than 3000. While the first databases were bibliographic, later databases contained numeric, directory, and full-text information. In some fields, much of the information needed for common tasks could be obtained from an online system. New computer-based tools, such as the *Science Citation Index*, went beyond equivalence with print. They fostered new types of research and created advantages for computer-literate researchers.

By the late 1970s, a more popular array of databases became available in the new videotext formats. Teletext, transmitted as part of a broadcast signal, provided user selection of a thousand or so screens. Videotext, transmitted via telephone or cable, provided access to a theoretically unlimited number of screens. Teletext and videotext required only keypads and decoders rather than computer terminals. They created a growing public market for news summaries, financial data, directories and schedules, as well as some entertainment and education.

When the first commercial microcomputers were introduced 10 years ago, it would have been a flight of fancy to predict a major role for them in electronic publishing. Now, however, with mass storage and fast processors, they are responsible for a new wave of interest and investment in electronic publishing.

What microcomputers represent in electronic publishing is offline power. In the early 1980s, this became evident in two ways. The first stand-alone databases were introduced on floppy discs by 1983. A good early example, which is still republished yearly, was *College Explorer*, the College Board's database of 2,700 colleges combined with a user-friendly search program. From the beginning, the stand-alone databases and their programs did not resemble online information. They took their design from microcomputer utilities like spreadsheets and word processors. They were colorful, easy to use, and very fast.

Another type of microcomputer program creates an offline "shell" around online searching. These "gateway" programs permit the online user to formulate a search within the microcomputer program before connecting with the online computer. Following the search, microcomputer programs permit the user to download or transfer records rapidly from the online computer into the memory of the microcomputer for later use. The microcomputer thus reduces costs before and after an online search.

These applications lent credibility to microcomputers as information tools, but they did not represent a major change in the cost/benefit equation of electronic publishing. What was missing was local mass storage capable of storing large databases in their entirety. Then the need to use online systems would contract toward the two extremes: information that changes too rapidly for disc-based updating and information that is consulted too seldom to justify local storage.

Twelve-inch laserdiscs for data storage were introduced around 1980. They are based on the same physical format as the earlier videodiscs, but they hold text and numbers rather than pictures. The extreme density of laser-written optical storage appeared to be the breakthrough that electronic publishers were waiting for. Conversions of large databases to optical storage began.

However, the 12-inch format was too much of a good thing. With a capacity of 2 billion characters and with expensive mastering, replication, and playback equipment, the 12-inch laserdisc has proved to be more of a solution for preserving and archiving collections of information than for distributing them.

At this juncture, the compact disc format was introduced. The 4.72-inch format had its roots in another medium, compact disc audio, which had already amortized its development costs. Except for unresolved issues of compatibility between the recording formats of CD-ROM, CD-I and DVI, the compact disc has entered electronic publishing as a mature technology. The compatibility issues might not be easily resolved because each of the recording formats has unique advantages, but present attention focuses on CD-ROM as a fully viable format that happened to reach the marketplace first.

To publishers, CD-ROM's half-billion character capacity represents the best and the worst of publishing opportunities: as many as 200,000 pages or 300 books per disc, indexed for the retrieval of every significant word. What is the demand for a library of information on one pocket-sized disc? Who will pay equivalent prices? Will the limits of CD-ROM pricing erode the narrow margin of profit in small, specialized publishing markets? Will CD-ROM products thrust publishers into the hardware business as well? How expensive will it be to provide technical support to users? Is there realistic protection for copyright in widely distributed computer-readable information?

Despite the small number of CD-ROM drives in offices and libraries, publishers are issuing a variety of CD-ROM products to address these questions. Perhaps at no time since the advent of publishing has a new technology raised so many challenging and stressful possibilities.

The growth that online systems has achieved in 20 years will probably be matched by the growth of the optical disc industry in less than 10 years. CD-ROM products are created from both online databases and print collections; the latter source is relatively inexhaustible. Because books and some entire databases are only the "chapters" of a CD-ROM product, many experimental combinations of information will be tested in the marketplace. As CD-ROM begins to climb the familiar S-shaped curve of adoption, the number of titles published each year will grow exponentially, compounded by growth in the number of discs pressed per title as the installed base of drives increases.

Figure 7-1 depicts the growth in publishing capacity that has resulted from the "four revolutions in publishing" described in this section. The pattern is one of successive S-curves separated by plateaus during which older technologies

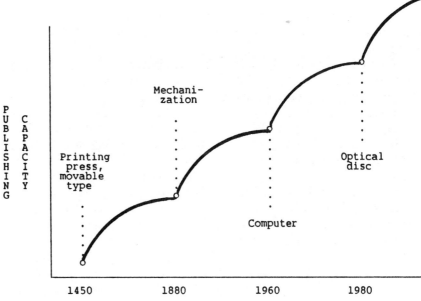

PUBLISHING CAPACITY

Printing press, movable type

Mechani-
zation

Computer

Optical
disc

1450   1880   1960   1980

Fig. 7-1. Four revolutions in publishing. Courtesy Knowledge Access International, Mountain View, CA.

operate at the limits of their capacity. The same pattern, in fact, characterizes the growth of capacity in fields as different from publishing as food production (from "the plough that broke the plains" to mechanized farming) and transportation (from the stagecoach to the airplane).

It is important to recognize in this pattern that the impact of new technologies is not limited to the sphere in which older technologies were successful. New agricultural technologies brought not only more food but also agribusiness. New transportation technologies brought not only faster travel but also a mobile society. No one involved with information should doubt that optical media will have impacts that are qualitatively as well as quantitatively different from those of the older technologies.

Phases of CD-ROM Development

A hundred or more CD-ROM applications have been announced as of the second quarter of 1987. These range from the Bible to census data, bibliographic files, directories, encyclopedias, government document collections, financial information, maintenance manuals, corporate archives, journal backfiles, and compilations of maps and other images. Only a few applications are "real" products with pricing and promotion that can establish them in the marketplace. The rest are prototypes for trial distribution primarily to offices and libraries. Some of the prototypes are technically deficient in comparison with their print or online counterparts. Others are technically adequate but unaffordably expensive to the end user. Still others will not be used to their full potential until users in business, science and the professions learn new procedures for manipulating information; they are "smart" products that required trained use similar to spreadsheets and decision-support programs. The remarkable variety of CD-ROM prototypes prompts us to ask, "If CD-ROM is the answer, what was the question?"

To understand the uncertainties of CD-ROM's early development (1984-1987), we can examine the common characteristics of this new technology and earlier technologies that emerged from the laboratory rather than the marketplace:

- The telephone in the 1870s. When the telephone was invented, most people lived and worked in small communities. They did not need electricity to talk with their neighbors. Early experiments with telephony in England included music broadcasting to wall-mounted receivers. In other countries, a few voice telephones per community were considered sufficient for the only application that could be foreseen: official communication. Only in the United States, where telephone systems could be added at low cost in the ongoing urban expansion, did telephony begin to play its many contemporary roles. One writer contends that the modern high-rise office building would be infeasible without the telephone, because the elevators would overflow with the business messengers that the telephone displaced. In the U.S. today, there are about 550 million daily local calls and an additional 50 million long-distance calls. What began as a solution in search of a problem is now a $60 billion annual business in the U.S. alone.
- The airplane in the 1900s. People were amazed that the airplane flew at all. How could they have imagined that 80 years later airplanes would carry more than 350 million passengers annually? The barnstorming novelty of county fairs is now a $20 billion annual business in the U.S. One-day intercontinental trips are the joy of vacationers and the bane of business travelers.
- Television in the 1930s. Seeing television for the first time at the 1939 World's Fair, a New York Times reporter wrote, "This will never be successful because no one will sit still to look at it." Television is now a $10 billion annual business in the U.S. that has transformed both cultural values and the political process.
- The microprocessor in the 1970s. Used originally in video games, microprocessors are now the "brains" in scores of devices from microcomputers to cars. Their contribution to the U.S. gross domestic product is evident in the Silicon Valley, Silicon Prairie or Silicon Forest that every state aspires to have. In countries of the Pacific Rim, microprocessors bring much-needed trade credits to fund the development of other industries.

Like the earlier technologies, CD-ROM leaves the laboratory as a solution in search of problems to solve. It will eventually play a large role in business and society. At first, its role will be to replace other information-dissemination technologies that it outperforms in cost or functionality. Later, it will perform new functions that in some cases will be unforeseen consequences of its unique characteristics. It is these functions, more than replacement functions, that will make CD-ROM as indispensable in our lives as the telephone, the airplane, and television.

Most of CD-ROM's brief history since 1984 falls in the first development phase: the demonstration of feasibility. Many of the existing CD-ROM prototypes are unremarkable except for the amount of information they contain. They are exactly parallel to the telephone in 1880, the airplane in 1910, television in 1940 and the microprocessor in 1975. Their purpose is to prove that the technology can live up to its claims at the technological level.

Another generation of CD-ROM products, already reaching the marketplace, represents the beginning of the second phase of development: as a potential replacement technology for large-scale print, microform, and online information products. Their adoption is proceeding as fast as the infrastructure for CD-ROM use comes together. Each installation requires a relatively powerful microcomputer, a CD-ROM drive and circuitry to connect the two. Where CD-ROM is introduced to replace some online uses, the cost of new equipment can be recovered from savings in online charges. However, CD-ROM as a replacement for printed information represents a new cost for offices and libraries that is recoverable only as the discs become less expensive than the printed information they replace. Presently, CD-ROM is more expensive than printed information, and it will remain so until economies of scale begin to operate in its favor.

Infrastructure for CD-ROM as a replacement technology is also being built where the information originates. Only a small fraction of non-online resources exist in computer-readable form. The costs of converting microform and print information to computer-readable form are in the range of $750 to $1,000 per million characters.

This innocuous sum grows to hundreds of thousands of dollars if one CD-ROM is entirely filled with newly converted information. Moreover, the need for mass conversion has arisen so recently that publishers have not had time to sort out the cost-effective methods for converting different types of information such as running text versus scientific equations and diagrams. Keyboard input is still cost-competitive with optical character recognition (OCR) because of OCR's reading errors that require hand editing, but the former is increasing in cost while the latter declines.

The second phase of CD-ROM development echoes the development of earlier technologies. After the feasibility of the telephone was demonstrated, its replacement functions could not be tested until wires were strung to connect large numbers of telephones. Aviation's second phase entailed the construction of airports and larger, safer aircraft. Television spent many years as a novelty waiting for broadcasting facilities to be built and inexpensive receivers to be produced.

CD-ROM products that have been introduced to replace online, microform or print information products perform ''as advertised''—they cost less to use than online, are more convenient to use than microform and retrieve information more precisely than print. Still, they are only retrieval systems designed to replace retrieval systems.

Retrieval is the central concept of the older technologies. Even online systems, with available power in the host computer, function only in retrieval mode. In the case of microforms and books, the question of what lies beyond retrieval is essentially meaningless, because these information "containers" are passive. They cannot do more for the user than surrender the information.

Except for cost, the host computer of an online information system could perform many functions beyond retrieval. The computer could aggregate, organize, analyze, summarize, tabulate, and extract information, as well as transform it from one presentation mode such as tabular to others such as text or graphics. In principle, the host computer could assist with many post-retrieval functions that users now perform manually with printouts. Costs of up to $3 per minute are a barrier to using the host computer in these ways. Therefore, online systems offer few functions beyond retrieval.

CD-ROM represents the historic separation of computer-readable mass storage from online charges. Although CD-ROM discs are not yet inexpensive, most are priced in the range of 10 to 20 hours of equivalent online time. In settings of moderate to high use, the cost of a disc is soon recovered from online savings. The only time-related concern in CD-ROM use is the minimum number of hours that amortizes the disc. Thus, the incentives for online versus CD-ROM use are opposite. The CD-ROM user is literally free to ask, "What more can this disc do for me?"

For the developers of CD-ROM applications, the question is only slightly different: "What do people want to do with CD-ROM information?" One answer lies as close as the utilities that are used on the same microcomputers that provide access to CD-ROM. Utilities are the tools of business, science and the professions for manipulating information. Each microcomputer user has from one to many favorite utilities such as word processors, personal database managers, spreadsheets, planners and schedulers, chart-makers, page layout programs, etc.

CD-ROM application developers have learned to watch the behavior of "power users" whose work gives them the motivation and experience to try out new functions on their own. Part of the 10-year-old folklore of microcomputing are the examples of "tricking" microcomputers into performing functions that they will not otherwise do. The user of a retrieval-only CD-ROM might want to extract some text and tabular material from the retrieved records, edit the text, and recompute the tables, then send the results through a formatter to a laser printer to produce the camera-ready original of a report. A power user would regard the deficiencies of the CD-ROM as a challenge and would later tell a story such as the following: "The CD-ROM would only let me print records, not save them, so I wrote a patch to redirect the information from the print buffer to the hard disc. Then I used my text editor to split the table out. The longest step was reformatting them for the spreadsheet and re-keying the row and column labels. After I could get them into the spreadsheet, it only took a minute to run my new formulas against the numbers. Then I brought the tables back over to the text editor, made the necessary revisions in the text, and sent the output to the page layout program. From the time I sat down to pull the information together, I had camera-ready printout in less than 2 hours."

These steps are a scandalous solution from the perspective of CD-ROM development. If file transfer, computation, text editing, and camera-ready printout were the user's goals, why weren't these functions an integral part of the CD-ROM program itself? Or, if a function is too unusual to be included, why doesn't the CD-ROM program transfer information that is properly formatted for input to another program?

A few products have taken the step beyond retrieval into CD-ROM's third phase of development. While their functions do not go beyond the common microcomputer utilities, the advantages of combining retrieval and information-manipulation utilities in the same program are impressively evident. One such product is Your Marketing Consultant (YMC), published by Market Statistics Inc. As a retrieval tool, it provides access to more than 3,800 counties and metropolitan areas in the U.S., displaying scores of variables and even map images of every area. When the user has chosen a set of counties or cities of interest based on any combination of search criteria, YMC shifts to utility mode. Would the user like to compute totals, averages or percentages for the chosen set? These are menu options for any variable in any set of records. Would the user like to generate a formula linking two or more variables? This can be done, and the output of one formula can even be used as input for another. Would the user like to enter data representing his or her own information about the counties or cities? The program accepts user input and provides full tabulation for the user variable, including formula combinations with the pre-existing variables. Would the user like to see variables or formula results ranked, first one way and then another? Any set of records can be ranked and re-ranked by all variables and formulas that pertain to those records.

If the user's application is too specialized for YMC's own library of functions, the program will transfer files to other utilities. Does the user want ASCII output for inclusion in a report or DIF output for entry to a spreadsheet? Both raw values and computed results can be transferred in these formats, complete with row and column labels.

Another example of a "smart" program provides a completely different set of utilities. The Harris Selectory of Electronics Industries, published by Harris Information Services, places its post-retrieval emphasis on useful forms of directory output such as mailing labels, telemarketing cards, and company profiles. Would the user like to print mailing labels from a chosen set of the more than 8,300 U.S. electronics companies in the database? After companies have been selected on 14 criteria such as region, products, or size, the user next works with a menu of choices for label format. Choices range from the *mechanical* (e.g., number of labels across the printout, number of spaces between labels, alphabetical or ZIP-ordered, company name first or executive's name first) to the *content-specific* (e.g., label codes derived from information in each record, such as SIC classification, order of preference for printing executives' names or titles if the first, second or third choices are not found in a given record). If name and address information is needed for computer-generated marketing letters, the Selectory creates a "comma-delimited" disc file as required by an external program like MailMerge. The external program will insert a name and address into each letter.

Different "smarts" for different applications: In a full-text database such as Consumer Drug Information on Disk, published by the American Hospital Pharmacists, the flexible extraction of relevant sections of records makes a smart program. The pharmacist who is filling a prescription for a pregnant woman with no health complications and the pharmacist who is filling the same prescription for an elderly man with high blood pressure will extract different sections from the same record and send the printout home with the patient. The program even has a "patient access mode" in which the sophisticated options available to the pharmacist leave the screen and are replaced by a simple menu choice of all the drugs in the database.

What these applications have in common is an analysis of the tasks for which people retrieve information in the first place. A retrieval-only system says to the user: "Here's the information you're looking for. Feel free to copy it down and use it as you wish." Smarter products now being released in the third phase of CD-ROM development treat retrieval as the mid-point in a session. After retrieval, the programs shift to utility mode and provide the tools for using the information.

Technology Seeks Its Own Level

The developers of a technology are guided by images of what it may become. CD-ROM development thus far has been dominated by an image of reference use. Even the unique capabilities of CD-ROM in a microcomputer environment have been characterized as post-retrieval functions. However, a new image of what CD-ROM might become is capturing the interest of developers.

Kuhn (1970) argues that major advances in science are not evolutionary but revolutionary; they involve an unexpected change in perspective. The change does not abandon the previously valid model of research, but it establishes an alternative model that will often yield better results. The timing and inspiration for each change are somewhat mysterious. Butterfield (1957) suggests a process in which scientists "handle the same bundle of data as before but place them in a new system of relations with each other putting on a different kind of thinking cap . . . picking up the opposite end of the stick."

This process aptly describes the ongoing change in CD-ROM development. Instead of taking the database as a given and providing tools for using it in different tasks, why not take each task as a given and create a knowledge base of well-focused information from different databases? The former image shows us a database with a shell of tools around it. The new image shows us a smart program that contains whatever information it needs to facilitate a well-defined task even if the information is drawn from many databases and contains a variety of full-text, numeric, directory, image, and bibliographic formats.

A shock of recognition occurs. We are reinventing the concept of the "expert system," that consists of a knowledge base and a set of rules for manipulating the knowledge. But now the knowledge base and the "inference engine" are contained on a CD-ROM disc rather than a mainframe or minicomputer. Fully serviceable expert systems can sit on the desks of physicians, nurses, engineers, lawyers, managers, accountants, architects, researchers, students, and in fact, anyone who uses information for problem solving or decision making.

It is said that the future, writ small, always exists in the present. CD-ROM expert systems are no exception. Products under development contain carefully chosen "key resources" for particular professional specialties, containing the variety of information formats described above. These are not yet expert systems by any stretch of the imagination. Their rules are based on association ("show the relationships of X"). However, they are shifting the focus from given databases to given tasks.

One example, yet unnamed, is being developed with funding from the U.S. National Center for Nursing Research. This CD-ROM will contain a reference shelf of research-based knowledge for nurses in six professional roles: nursing administrators, nurse practitioners, clinical nurse specialists, staff nurses, nursing educators and nursing researchers. The different resources will be drawn into a unified structure through "hypertext" indexing (a now-feasible procedure that was envisioned by Bush, 1945). Hypertext is a computer-generated network of relationships in the knowledge base that lead the user from any starting point, such as a paragraph that responds to the user's first query, to all related text, tables, figures, citations, etc. In a journey through the knowledge base, the user may leave the original query terms behind. In other words, hypertext's map of second-order relationships ("relationships of relationships") leads the user to information that the original query terms would not have found.

A technology seeks and finds its own level in relation to older technologies with overlapping capabilities. However, it does not then function only in its unique range. A technology represents investment in design, production, acquisition and the skills of use. To be cost-effective, a technology will be required to perform less powerful as well as more powerful functions. For example, a car will often be driven along the same route as a less expensive bus, and when traffic is heavy, the car might cross the city more slowly than a bicycle. But the car is an "adopted technology" that its owner will use in as many ways as possible in order to have it available for the types of uses that other transportation technologies cannot provide.

CD-ROM will be an adopted technology in offices and libraries at first, followed by schools and other institutional settings and, finally, homes. It will be required to perform the less powerful reference functions as well as the more powerful problem solving and decision support functions. Even if it is used primarily as a reference tool, the image of what it can do at its own level will be an important factor in its adoption.

Rethinking Information

New communications media select and reshape the information that they will convey. Without the hyperbole, this is McLuhan's theory of the progression of communication media (1964). Early films were indeed only stage plays performed in front of a camera, but it was not long before films inspired scripts and production techniques that would not have worked on the stage. As mentioned previously, the mainframe computer of two decades ago inspired a new information product, the Science Citation Index, which could not have been produced otherwise at an affordable cost.

Conversely, the relationship between an older medium and its message becomes static over time. Scientific journal articles have not changed fundamentally since the 17th century despite their well-documented shortcomings. They are the message of their medium, and apparently, they will remain so.

It is understandable that all of us, information producers as well as information users, think of information in terms of packages created by this interaction between medium and message. We think of information as we customarily see it in the form of reports, articles, books, online databases, etc. We think of the generally homogeneous content of each package, whether textual, numeric or graphic. But the information will be different when it has been selected and reshaped by the new medium of CD-ROM.

CD-ROM requires a fresh look at the properties of information. New distinctions are needed along information dimensions that are now defined only in terms of print and online publishing. The immediate need for these distinctions is to guide conversions of print and online information to CD-ROM. Over time, they may change CD-ROM technology itself, overcoming any limitations it may have in relation to desirable forms of information for CD-ROM publication.

CD-ROM's greatest present limitation is the cost of updating and re-issuing discs to stay abreast of new information. The more rapidly a disc must be updated, the more it costs the information user. Furthermore, even with the most ambitious updating schedule, CD-ROM cannot keep pace with online systems in reporting certain types of information.

The concept of timeliness is not as simple as the number of new items in a database per day or the percentage of a database that turns over per month. Many databases are updated daily with changes that a user can do without for a month or longer.

Imagine that three databases were updated yesterday. One contains new projections of employment indicators for the end of 1987. Many users of the indicators risk little by using last month's set until the update arrives "in due time."

The second contains changes in mortgage rates. The user risks the possibility that decisions made today in ignorance of these changes will prove to be more costly than the updated information would have been.

The third contains new information on poisons and antidotes. If this information relates to any poisoning case that occurs today, then a life is at risk. The cost of information that may or may not be needed is never an irrelevant consideration, but toxicological updates are close to being priceless.

In these examples, timeliness is constant, while risk, which can range from a missed opportunity to life versus death, varies. Risk is just one of the complex motives underlying the need for information. Other examples show how timeliness and need are related:

- Rapidly Changing Information, Urgent Need—Life and death are not the only urgent matters. On an exchange, buy and sell decisions are urgent. Exchange prices are also rapidly changing information.
- Rapidly Changing Information, Non-urgent Need—News wires carry information that changes almost as fast as exchange prices. However, only in the newsroom do the latest bulletins matter more than the gist of a whole day's story. Even there, the only urgent use of bulletins occurs just before press time.
- Slowly Changing Information, Urgent Need—A toxicological database changes slowly in comparison with market information, but the need to consult it is even more urgent. Another family of databases contains information for dealing with controllable environmental disasters such as forest fires and chemical spills. For example, the U.S. Forest Service's Firebase system to guide forest fire fighting contains information accumulated over many years on the behavior of fires according to several variables.
- Slowly Changing Information, Non-urgent Need—Information resulting from research, scholarship or artistic creativity fills the libraries with volumes that retain all or some of their value from year to year. Usually, such information does not have to be consulted urgently, and decisions based on it are seldom as risky as the examples given above. Figure 7-2 summarizes this discussion and provides additional examples.

In its present form, CD-ROM is not an appropriate medium for all types of information shown in Fig. 7-2. It certainly cannot be used for information that changes rapidly and is needed on an urgent basis. Conversely, it may be the future medium of choice for information that changes slowly or is not urgently needed. Early CD-ROM products include examples of encyclopedic informa-

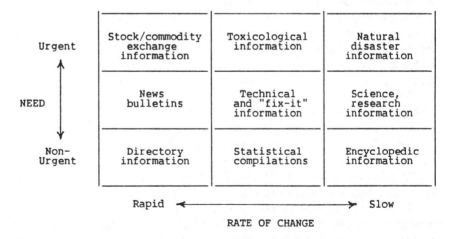

Fig. 7-2. Types of information by urgency of need and rate of change. Courtesy Knowledge Access International, Mountain View, CA.

117

tion, science and research information, statistical compilations, technical information, and directory information.

Apart from the extreme case of rapidly changing and urgently needed information, other examples of information that combine these characteristics to some degree (such as toxicological information and news bulletins) suggest adapting the information to avoid the limitations of CD-ROM while capitalizing on its strengths. Recent updates of such information cannot be ignored, but the back-files are very rich and would benefit from CD-ROM's retrieval power as well as post-retrieval manipulation of the retrieved information. There are research uses of the information for which the backfiles are nearly self-sufficient. However, a publisher of toxicological information on CD-ROM would probably arrange for online or "hotline" updates to anticipate liability issues.

These examples all take CD-ROM in its present form as a given, just as hand-crank starters were a given on early automobiles. Can CD-ROM be equipped with a built-in "starter" for updated information? Procedures have already been developed to distribute floppy disc updates during the periods between new editions of the CD-ROM. Two installments of monthly floppy discs would supplement a quarterly CD-ROM; three installments of weekly floppy disks would supplement a monthly CD-ROM, etc.

However, floppy disc updates cannot keep up with yesterday's changes. Two telecommunication-based updating strategies have been proposed, and prototypes of the first are beginning to appear.

In the first strategy, the CD-ROM system is a "gateway" to one or more online systems. After using the CD-ROM information up to its cut-off date, the user is assisted in logging on to the online system(s) for the latest information. This is an excellent interim solution that minimizes online charges, but information obtained online may not be accessible to post-retrieval utilities in the CD-ROM program, since "smart" features expect to find the data preprocessed and tagged in certain ways.

The second strategy is more seamless and may be less expensive for the user, but it requires more equipment at the CD-ROM workstation. Satellite links are now routinely used to transmit data to microcomputers. Narrow-band, small-antenna systems (such as the one pioneered by Equatorial Communications) cost about $2500, which falls in the middle of the price range for some microcomputer peripherals like laser printers.

Under the control of a program in the microcomputer, the satellite transmission is received and stored on the hard disc. This can happen moment by moment during the day, but a single nighttime transmission of the full day's updates might be the preferred strategy in terms of convenience and cost. To the user, the CD-ROM and the hard disc drive function as one unit. Old and new information can be searched simultaneously.

Telecommunication updating of CD-ROM will undoubtedly be an integral feature of the technology in a few years. It overcomes CD-ROM's updating problem without remastering discs with only a few changes from edition to edition. In a new conceptualization of information, whatever is not present in local memory is probably available through a telecommunication link in an identical

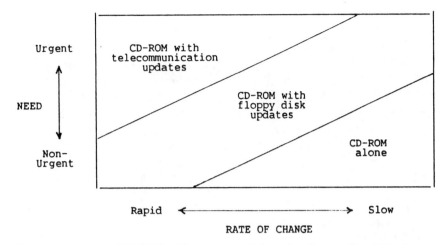

Fig. 7-3. Suitability of CD-ROM for different types of information. Courtesy Knowledge Access International, Mountain View, CA.

format. Users can make economic decisions to buy fast or slow updating based on the importance of updates to them. For some research purposes, each edition of the CD-ROM would be used without telecommunication updates. Other users would subscribe to an online or satellite updating service. Satellite updating, invisible to the user, will be valued in settings like libraries where less experienced users are being assisted.

Figure 7-3 summarizes this discussion of the suitability of CD-ROM, alone or in combination with updated procedures, as a publication medium for different types of information.

We will conceptualize information in many new ways because of CD-ROM. In particular, though, we will move beyond the dichotomy of static-but-available information in books and journals versus dynamic-but-transitory information in online systems. Information will become a more fluid concept in our minds.

In the optical memory of our microcomputer, we have a "lake" of information. In library settings it may be an ocean, at home only a pond. A river of information flows constantly into the lake. We can see it enter the lake, but after that we cannot tell it apart from the information that was already in the lake. All of the information is equally fluid and available to us.

Metaphors are part of the image of what a technology may become. After starting on dirt roads, the automobile moved across continents on "rivers of concrete." Traveling on a river is quite different from traveling on a dirt road; one expects to travel long distances comfortably in a boat-like vehicle, which is exactly what the automobile became. Similarly, CD-ROM will develop in one way if it is viewed as a box of static information that is used for a while and then discarded; it will develop differently if it is viewed as a lake of fluid information into which new information constantly flows.

Building Capacity

The CD-ROM disc gleams in its crystal case. It is the totem of electronic publishing. People pick it up to squint at the spiral track, which they have been told is 3 miles long. They look for 500 million characters etched on 15 square inches of recording surface.

The library's CD-ROM reference corner shows signs of too much use and too little maintenance. Many discs are out of their cases and scattered on the tables. An update shipment sits on the cart waiting to be shelved. The library began cataloging when updates became more numerous than the originals. Finally, sequential shelf numbers were added. The newest CD-ROM on the shelf bears the number "9,147." However, there are not 9,147 discs in the room; older discs are in general circulation, and some discs have been lost and not yet replaced (the problem of lost discs is mitigated by a "no fault" replacement policy that most publishers have accepted as a condition of selling CD-ROMs to libraries). The catalog indicates that proportionate numbers of CD-ROM titles occur in five categories:

- science, technology and medicine
- business
- education
- general reference, literature and art
- best sellers and fads

This is now; that is the future. The gleaming disc will soon be dusty and covered with fingerprints. The publicity surrounding CD-ROM will wane. Stories of wise decisions or ingenious solutions or timely interventions based on information will not mention that the information came from CD-ROM. Users will wish they had more time to keep up with the latest CD-ROMs; there will be sales of condensed CD-ROMs for busy executives. Companies will donate outdated CD-ROMs to schools and universities for tax advantages. Publishers will complain that their CD-ROM divisions are losing money. In short, CD-ROM will become a mundane technology like the telephone, the automobile, the airplane, and television.

By various estimates, by the end of 1987 there will be 20,000—or is it 90,000—CD-ROM drives in use. In the future their numbers will grow rapidly as production capacity and demand reinforce each other.

Attention has focused on the drives as the weak link in the chain of CD-ROM adoption in offices and libraries. However, the drives will soon be plentiful; there already exists a drive that costs less than even one CD-ROM title in some categories. More critical issues in building capacity for CD-ROM demand our attention.

Production

How will publishers fund the costly conversion process that is just beginning? Will new technologies such as optical character recognition or a specialized service industry bring economies of scale to the conversion of print information to computer-readable form?

120

- At present, every CD-ROM product has its own procedures for manipulating information. A user who needs to use several CD-ROM products will spend more time learning how to use them than in working with the information. How many years will it take for CD-ROM products to converge on procedures that require as little relearning from product to product as, for example, the controls of different automobiles?
- To some extent, CD-ROM manufacturers are cooperating to standardize disc recording formats, but only a very patient user can make discs from different manufacturers work interchangeably. Will a true standard solve this problem?
- Will manufacturers agree on updating procedures using telecommunication links so that workstations can be equipped to receive updates for more than one database?
- CD-ROM development and production is much more capital-intensive than the brilliant software written by small teams of programmers in small companies that launched the microcomputer revolution. Will small companies be able to compete in this well-capitalized industry? What market niches will they find where creativity balances capital or attracts capital?

Pricing and Use Costs

- If CD-ROM titles in 1988 and 1990 cost an average of $300 (less than now), how will offices and libraries budget for their initial collections of 50 to 100 titles?
- How will libraries budget for CD-ROM workstations? What are the unbudgeted costs of establishing and operating a CD-ROM reference area? How can demand and technological change be projected in order to install adequate equipment without piecemeal acquisition and replacement?
- Many businesses will pay for CD-ROM with savings from reduced online use, but libraries have generally recovered online costs from patrons or have not offered online searches at all. Should libraries levy CD-ROM fees on patrons? Can this be done without penalizing the use of "smart" CD-ROMs that are designed to be used by the hour in performing tasks?
- What is the role of government agencies in sponsoring CD-ROM products in areas such as health care, where they have information dissemination responsibilities?

User Training and Support

- Many workers and library users who are not computer literate will have a need to use high-level CD-ROM products that combine the functions of several microcomputer utilities. Who will train them? Who will provide problem-solving support?
- The reference librarian's traditional role as information finder began to change with the advent of online systems. CD-ROM will place still more information-finding power in user's hands. Users will need less help in finding inform-

ation and more help in processing it. Is this a new role for the reference librarian? What new skills does it require?

- Information is said to be the great equalizer, but the experience of recent communication experiments tells us otherwise. New communication media and information products, even when they are easy to use, are adopted first by the information "haves" rather than the "have nots." The benefits of CD-ROM will not extend to most people unless awareness, trail, learning and use are stimulated by schools, libraries, business training programs and government information programs.

Future Development

- Will the market pay back the large investment in research that will be required to develop CD-ROM expert systems?
- What changes in compiling, editing, and processing CD-ROMs will drop their prices into the range of trade books—for example, a scholar's edition of Shakespeare for $29.95?

Each of these issues will be resolved in turn. The question is not whether, but when. CD-ROM presents a complex and costly revolution in publishing that has been international in scope from the outset. The talent and energy that invented CD-ROM must now be tapped to solve the even more complex and costly problems of building capacity for its wide distribution and adoption.

THE EVOLUTION OF ELECTRONIC PUBLISHING TOWARD AN INTELLIGENT DISTRIBUTION MEDIUM
by Steven C. Corum, Director
Strategic Business Development
AMTEC Information Services, an EDS Company

Since the advent of Johann Gutenberg's printing press in 1440, the sole goal of the publishing process has been to place information at the disposal of the reader. Regardless of content or technique, this information has been provided over the last four hundred years in the form of words on paper collected into books. These books have reflected our civilization's technological development and, as a result, an ever-increasing number are devoted to highly complex, technical reference information.

Technical references are, by their nature, read in a unique manner. Whereas a book of fiction or history is written and intended to be read serially, i.e., front to back, a technical reference is constructed to allow the reader to access specific items of information independent of preceding or succeeding pages. For example, a reader looking in an encyclopedia for information on photolithography doesn't really care that the pertinent article is preceded by an article on photography or succeeded by an article on photolysis. These other articles may be of peripheral interest, but they actually only provide physical delimiters for the article of primary interest.

How does a reader go about finding the desired information? In the example above, we'll assume that the reader is dealing with a single-volume encyclopedia and that the articles are in alphabetical sequence by title. First, the reader opens the book in a semi-random manner, knowing both intuitively and be experience that the articles beginning with the letter P lie somewhere in the middle of the book. The reader looks at the titles on the pages to which he has opened to determine where he is positioned relative to the desired article. Depending on this perceived relative location, the reader then proceeds to flip through pages, individually or in chunks, forward or backward, until the desired article is finally found.

Alternatively, our reader might have elected to use an index or table of contents to find the desired article. This still involves the same basic process of flipping through pages and making relative location decisions to find the reference to the article. Once found, this reference provides a page number which the reader then searches for in the same manner as before. Only the target of the search has changed from the title of the article to the number of the page on which the article is located. The methodology of the search has not changed.

The example we have explored is extremely simplistic in nature. In today's professional and technical environments, the necessary information is often contained in multiple locations in a reference matter and may or may not be explicitly referenced by seemingly unrelated material. It has been the publishers' challenge to embody the printed information with sufficient ancillary information, also printed, to enable the reader to locate all the pertinent information wherever it may have been placed by the writers. With reference works of several thousand pages not being uncommon, this is no mean task, as it involves cross-referencing many thousands of terms in a manner meaningful to the reader.

The typical approach to implementing this cross-reference has been the creation of an index of significant terms and their location(s) on physical pages within a document. This approach requires a plethora of human value judgments as to what constitutes a significant term. Even with the more modern and sophisticated word processing applications, the writer must "tell" the word processor what is and is not significant. A more brute force approach is to index every occurrence of every word in a document and then remove all insignificant references. Of course, there are many variations within and between these extremes, but it still amounts to the same end result. A human must make the final decision as to what is to be included in the index in order to protect the reader from a meaningless overwhelm of useless information.

Therein lies the rub. The publisher constantly walks a very thin line between providing all the information required to reference the desired material and obfuscating those references with too much information. The bottom line for the publisher, from a business perspective, is that readers only use those reference materials that make themselves easy for the reader to use. And, typically, we don't buy what we won't use. Therefore, it is in the publisher's best financial interest to provide reference materials that the readers will want to use because they don't require a great deal of effort on the reader's part.

At the same time, the publisher must also be aware of the time and effort, with their related costs, involved in creating easy-to-use reference materials.

Even though these costs are reasonably expected to be recouped through the sales of the final product, i.e., the book or document, there is a point at which the costs drive the price prohibitively high for an acceptable return on investment. Although this point varies from document to document, there is always a trade-off between useability and costs.

Why must this be so? In the past quarter-century, the development and availability of electronic data processing systems with their associated capabilities has greatly benefitted the publishing industry. The latest and greatest database techniques allow vastly improved storage and management of the raw data that go into reference materials. Creation and manipulation of index references and cross-references have been automated and streamlined to a large extent. Yet the question of useability still exists and is a major consideration in the publication of reference materials. Is there some basic, underlying concept that continues to cause conundrums for publishers of reference materials? In a word, Yes!

Since its inception in the early 1970s, the electronic publishing industry has been geared toward increasing the efficiency and productivity of the publication process through the use of ever more powerful data processing systems. More sophistication means more functionality which, in turn, leads to more flexibility in creating the final product. However, all this technology and its concomitant potential to handle larger and larger quantities of information is still oriented toward the same final product as Gutenberg produced centuries ago—words on paper collected into books.

Initiates of the electronic publishing industry discuss such arcane terms as photoconductive image transfer, ion deposition, magnetography, and electroerosion. To a person unfamiliar with the technical vernacular, these terms conjure up visions of scientists in white lab coats watching with baited breath as sub-atomic particles react in mysterious, dimly understood ways to create a spectacular effect. In actuality, these terms all refer to various methods of creating little black dots on a piece of paper to form letters. The end result is words on paper collected into books which the reader must search through to find the desired information.

The technology available to the publisher today is truly remarkable, and the intent here is not to denigrate or belittle the awesome strides made in the last 25 years. Yet technology is only as useful as its application allows, and up to now all this technology has been applied to aid the publisher and not the reader. In the last few years, however, publishers have made the decision to provide information to the reader in a more usable form which actually assists the reader in the search process. Part of this decision was based on (yes, you quessed it) the availability of a new technology called CD-ROM.

Before we examine CD-ROM technology and its application by publishers, we need to lay out a scenario to put CD-ROM publications in some type of perspective. Let's select the case of a reader, technically skilled, required to perform a highly critical, fairly technical, and complex task based on information consisting of instructions and procedures found in a technical reference document. In this scenario, a technician must remove a critical component from a complex system, perform safety checks and maintenance, and reinstall the component. Our technician relies on two primary sources of information in order to perform this task—a maintenance manual and an illustrated parts catalog. Both of these references are massive and contain thousands of pages of extremely detailed instructions, procedures, descriptions, cautions, warnings, and lists of materials required, along with detailed engineering drawings showing component relationships and other pertinent information. The inherently critical nature of performing this maintenance task demands that our technician have complete and total access to all necessary information so that the component, once reinstalled, can be returned to duty and will safely perform its intended function until its next maintenance cycle.

Now that we've set the stage, let's walk our technician through the maintenance process. First, because each system configuration has its own unique set of documents, the technician goes to a wall filled with bulky binders and finds the section pertaining to the configuration to be serviced. Next, using memory or a printed index, the technician searches for the specific maintenance binder containing the instructions for the task to be performed. Once the binder is located, a search is made of the hundreds of pages in the binder for the specific set of procedures required. These procedures are then removed from the binder, copied, and the originals returned to the binder. After this time-consuming process is complete, our technician takes the copied pages and uses the lists of special tools, consumable materials, and parts to assemble all material required for the maintenance. If one or more of the parts are, in fact, an assembly, then our technician repeats the above process to find and search through the related parts catalog to find all the parts associated with that assembly.

Only after all of this searching and researching has been fully and thoroughly finished can our technician even begin to think about actually performing the maintenance. Is this scenario unfair or untypical? Unfortunately, it is not. Most major service facilities would recognize and sympathize with our technician. Is this situation caused by the writers of the manuals? The engineers and technical writers who actually wrote these manuals are responsible for thoroughness and accuracy in providing complete information to the service personnel, and the amount of information required cannot be reduced or condensed to any great extent. Is this situation caused by the publisher of the manuals? Every binder is rife with tables of contents, indexes, cross-references and every other mechanism possible to assist the technician, including massive, separate volumes of location information. What is the real cause of this situation?

Paper. For all its versatility and abundance, paper is a "dumb" medium for transmitting information. Paper doesn't know what's printed on it, it can't tell the reader if the desired information is on the page being looked at, and paper just sits there waiting to be manipulated by the reader. Paper just isn't an adequate medium for conveying complex information quickly and effectively.

What are the alternatives? Many publishers of complex, high-volume reference materials have attempted to reduce the sheer bulk of their products by using microfilm "fiche." This allows many printed pages to be contained in a relatively small space, but fiche are no more intelligent than the paper they are depicting. Worse, instead of the familiar action of flipping pages, now the reader must scroll two-dimensionally through a matrix of images to find the required information. Fiche still require the reader to perform all the searching.

The latest alternative to paper and fiche is CD-ROM. Originally developed as an optically-based medium for the storage of high-fidelity, digitally-encoded sound such as stereo music albums, CD has evolved into a high-density storage medium for electronic data. Publishers have embraced CD-ROM technology and the functionality it provides to supplant the printed page as the primary source of complex technical information. With the ability to store 200,000 pages worth of information and graphics on a single CD platter less than 5 inches in diameter, and the ability of the CD application system to perform extremely complex searches of that information, the reader now has virtually instant access to whatever information may be desired. That information is also now available for further processing in any number of ways by the application system.

Let's replay our technician's scenario, but this time we'll provide the maintenance manual and parts catalog on CD-ROM. First, our technician opens a small box next to the CD-ROM player and pulls out the disc for the system configuration to be serviced. This disc is inserted into the player and the technician calls up the maintenance manual. Search parameters are requested by the application system and entered by the technician. Assuming the parameters entered are sufficiently specific, the next thing the technician sees is the information required. If not, a list of possible matches is presented and the technician narrows the search or selects one of the matches. In either event, our technician has the information in very short order.

Once this information is available, the technician uses the application system interface, either keyboard or perhaps a mouse, to select the material necessary for the maintenance task. If an assembly is included in the list of parts, the technician can branch to the parts catalog, and the application system will automatically display a complex breakdown of the indicated assembly. Now the technician tells the application to order all necessary tools and components, and the inventory management system receives all appropriate orders transparently to the technician. Assured that everything is available and waiting, the technician prints out the full procedure description to take to the actual work area to begin the component service (yes, it was printed on paper).

As we see in our revised scenario, CD-ROM removes the bulk of the searching burden from the reader and does the search itself. The reader only has to know what information is required and not where it is located or how to find it. This is an obvious and tremendous advantage in the use of highly complex reference works. Even so, paper is cheap and technology usually isn't. Realistically, we must pay a price for functionality and ease of use. Once more, there is a trade-off in cost versus performance. Now, however, there are distinct, quantifiable cost justifications that both the publisher and reader may consider in the decision to go with CD-ROM.

From the publisher's perspective, the technological investments made to produce paper products are not really wasted. All the processing power required to print the paper is still required to generate the CDs. Only the final output phase changes with some ancillary processing to format the data for CD and instill the necessary "intelligence" to make that data searchable by the application system. Instead of their investments being wasted, publishers can now realize further returns on those same investments by expanding the scope of their offerings into the CD-ROM arena. Naturally, this makes the publishers happy. Fortunately, the resultant flexibility and power of the CD applications also make the reader happy. This "win-win" situation is a driving force behind the rapidly growing CD-ROM industry.

It has been our experience at AMTEC that our existing customer base for paper products is extremely interested in our OPTI-Search Publishing System for CD-ROM applications. AMTEC's clients include major players in the automotive and aerospace industries where the need for quick, effective access to highly complex, technical information is a constant imperative. Our familiarity with publishing this type of information comes from long experience that was painstakingly acquired through the cooperative efforts of our staff and clients.

The decision to pursue and produce a CD-ROM product was not made in a day, a week, or even a month. We took a long, hard look at the marketplace and its long-term potential. We talked to many vendors and explored a myriad of alternatives. We participated in prototype developments and drove our in-house resources to determine the feasibility of creating our own offering. After many months of doing our homework, AMTEC decided that it was in our best interests and that of our clients to pursue CD-ROM in a major effort. We are very happy to report that our efforts were made wisely and that we have succeeded.

We still print paper, but there's a very viable alternative—in CD-ROM.

CD-ROM AS AN INTERNATIONAL MEDIUM
by John Lowry, President
Reteaco Inc.

The subject of CD-ROM as an international medium is one that has great relevance for me for two reasons. First, I am a Canadian. Second, I have spent thirty years working internationally in the field of television.

Canada is a country with two official languages—English and French. It is also what one Canadian historian has termed a "vertical mosaic" of many ethnic cultures and languages—in contrast with our United States neighbor—dubbed a "melting pot" by the same historian. As a result of an immigration policy that was intended to help Canada's population grow to match its geography, we have attracted people from all over the world—including, for example, the largest Italian population outside of Italy. As a result, effective communications in Canada necessarily means consideration of many languages and cultures.

I've been involved in television from the early days of the medium. To me, television is both an example of our global village and evidence of how incompatible technologies in different countries can create a high-tech nightmare for communicators. One obvious example of this incompatibility is today's use of the NTSC, PAL, and SECAM broadcast standards in various parts of the world.

Technological differences of this kind seem to come from two roots—the diverse solutions to technical problems developed in labs around the world and the combination of politically driven cultural isolation and protection of home industries. In either case, effective communication and global understanding is certainly impaired.

Reteaco was founded four years ago, which I suppose means that we've been involved in the CD-ROM medium from more or less its beginning. We were among the first to develop a powerful indexing system specifically for CD-ROM and have since developed more than sixty CD-ROM databases.

It is clear that CD-ROM is a communications medium that will not be troubled by the basic standards difficulties that television and other industries have had to face. In fact, very few so-called "high tech" products have started their life being born out of international research and cooperation.

Adoption of the Philips/Sony physical specifications for CD-ROM has guaranteed that development work done in one country can be applied in another. This is an important foundation for CD-ROM's international usefulness. But by itself, this standard is not enough. What will continue to make CD-ROM a truly successful international industry is more than this consistent optical technology. CD-ROM must be combined with powerful software to ensure that the needs it addresses are global in nature.

In every industrialized country and in every sector from private enterprise to education to government, people today are faced with the paradox of an overabundance of data and too little usable information. CD-ROM, combined with the right search and retrieval software, addresses this by giving you all the information you might need plus the ability to find what is specifically relevant to you at any point in time. And because this need for relevant information is the same worldwide, so are the basic features that will make CD-ROM systems succeed or fail in the market, regardless of whether you are in Europe, Japan, Africa, North America, etc.

The principal criteria for CD-ROM success are:

- Ease of use—systems must be intuitively obvious to the non-technical user if CD-ROM is to fulfill its promise of becoming a primary new medium of communication. The CD-ROM industry depends upon broad distribution, without training to people who are technical, non-technical, executives, researcher, students, office and plant workers, and so on.
- Speed—CD-ROM search and retrieval systems must, I believe, be more than just faster than the next best alternative. They should ideally retrieve and display the needed information so quickly that the search time is transparent to the user. Moreover, we must consider total search time—not just CD-ROM access time. This means considering how long it takes to load a disc, choose a database, formulate a query and access the records. The process must be fast enough and productive enough to encourage a few variations on a search or "what-ifs" to broaden our understanding of the chosen subject.
- Integration of text and images—CD-ROM systems, to meet the requirements of many applications, must allow for the integration of text and numeric data with images. And these images must be displayed in a high definition manner

with high enough frame rates to eliminate the fatigue still associated with reading from a computer screen. The competition for CD-ROM is still paper— with the crisp, clear, non-flickering images and type fonts we all take for granted.

- Price— And let's not forget that CD-ROM today is a business, a marketplace, not just a technology. CD-ROM systems must offer competitive price/performance advantages over alternative media—both to information providers and their end users. For those of us working in the database service, search and retrieval software or mastering and replication areas, it means establishing prices that recognize psychological price barriers and limits on departmental signing authority. And for information providers or publishers, it means setting prices for discs that will encourage wide penetration of CD-ROM databases rather than high price ''skimming'' strategies.

So far, I've said that information distribution and management needs are the same the world over, but there is also an additional set of needs related specifically to international information distribution and access. They actually arise from the need to do business internationally—and they too can be answered by CD-ROM-based solutions.

CD-ROM-based databases can make an important contribution through translation dictionaries that are more complete and more easily accessible than ever before. One such example is the Termium III CD-ROM that Reteaco created for the Secretary of State within the Canadian government. It contains the official translations from English to French and French to English used by government departments, legislative groups, agencies, and private industry, both within and outside Canada. It contains 500,000 records and 1,139,000 search terms. In this case, the Secretary of State had been providing Termium III online for years. Due to increased demand for the database, the department was faced with a multi-million dollar computer expansion. Instead, they have chosen CD-ROM.

CD-ROM systems can easily be configured for multilingual user environments—enabling users to switch from one language to another with a few keystrokes.

The Canadian Centre for Occupational Health and Safety is a tripartite body representing government, labor and industry. One of their mandates is the distribution throughout Canada of information regarding hazardous materials in the workplace. In the past, this has been handled by mailing large volumes of Materials Safety Data Sheets printed in both French and English.

We are currently producing 20,000 such data sheets—each containing several pages of information. This is combined with ten other safety-related databases and a major bibliographic listing of chemicals—on a set of two CD-ROM's with quarterly updates. In our retrieval software, all headings, functions, on-screen prompts, help windows and field identifiers can be changed at will by the user from one language to another. This means that even where some data does not exist in the preferred language of the user, the CD-ROM environment provides an interface that enables the user to search in his or her own language.

In the CCOHS example, it is the software rather than all the data that is fully bilingual. However, with its access capacity, a single CD-ROM can accommodate multiple language versions of even quite large databases. For users who are fluent in more than one language, it is even possible to compare and perhaps gain new insights into subtleties of meaning by reviewing information in more than one language. One of Reteaco's customers, the Canadian Department of Justice, is doing just this with English and French versions of Canadian law.

CD-ROM also enables organizations to distribute multilanguage text and numeric databases integrated within a single image database. For example, a multinational automotive manufacturer could deliver CD-ROM auto parts catalogues to its branches and dealerships around the world. A single image database showing illustrations of specific product parts and sub-assemblies could be linked with individual text databases in the local languages of the countries in which its dealers operate—all on one CD-ROM.

What is significant here is that the storage requirements for full-screen, high-definition images is high. Yet I believe that clear, flicker-free images are a necessity if CD-ROM is to be accepted in the workplace.

Even with data compression such as the two-dimensional CCITT Group 4 standard, the image portion of a text/image database typically represents five times that of the text. Reteaco recently completed an auto-parts database for one of the American "Big Three" automakers. It links compressed images, with a resolution 1280×1024 picture elements, to the corresponding identifying text, including part number, part or subassembly name, car model and year, price, etc.

Adding a second, third, or more languages to this database would contribute relatively little to its size. Such an approach would reduce costs to the information provider with no corresponding reduction in the usefulness of the data at the end-user level. Our analysis indicates that large parts catalogues can be created and distributed to a wide range of users on CD-ROM for less than the shipping cost of paper catalogues.

The concept of a personal database is given a new dimension when users can select their language of choice with ease and flexibility. Similarly, the marketing advantages for publishers offering these kinds of options within their information products is significant when selling to mixed language environments.

Although the need to provide multilingual solutions in the international marketplace is perhaps the most obvious one that CD-ROM can provide, there are several other specifically international needs, that the technology can also address. They include:

• The need to keep track of and quickly access relevant information on many marketplaces and sovereign nations—CD-ROM is a natural way to distribute large policies or operations manuals, regulations, or statistical data. When a user is trying to keep track of such information for many marketplaces and the laws of different countries, CD-ROM becomes an even more valuable resource. We are now working on a database for Statistics Canada containing

130

information on the Canadian economy derived in part from census data. I am sure similar undertakings will be developed for most other industrialized nations in the near future. They are a wealth of easily usable information for the international marketer.

- The need to bridge the boundaries of national telephone and telegraph systems—Up to now, online has been used on an international basis where there is a need to distribute information with random access search capability. But this practice introduces its own set of difficulties related to the linking of the PTT's—the public telephone/telegraph system of one country with that of another. CD-ROM can now offer a lower-cost, and frequently less problematic, solution.

Moreover, in some developing countries, where communications systems are not reliable, CD-ROM might be the only practical solution to ensure data integrity and timely delivery because the system is truly stand-alone at the user level. This is an interesting thought when we remember that early expectations of CD-ROM were that it would only be useful for static databases. In fact, 3M Corporation in the United States recently announced a one-day turnaround option on mastering and replication. Three-day turns are already the norm. Some data service organizations, including our own, can now provide one- to two-week update cycles including sophisticated indexing.

I believe CD-ROM will succeed because of universal needs. I have further suggested major areas where CD-ROM can, and indeed is, contributing to international communications. CD-ROM, with the right indices and search software, has the storage capacity for handling multiple languages on a single disc. It can be a new tool for international business people dealing with many sets of regulations, procedures or other detailed data on a global marketplace. And finally, CD-ROM can reduce dependence on sometimes incompatible or unreliable international telephone and telegraph systems.

These general areas suggest, but by no means exhaustively cover, the full range of international applications for CD-ROM. But I hope they do convey how exciting an opportunity CD-ROM is for global information distribution.

With apologies to those of you who are tired of Gutenberg comparisons, CD-ROM today will, I believe, contribute as much to the international flow of ideas as the printing press did in the fifteenth century. Researchers, business people, scientists, educators—we will all benefit.

As a closing note I would like to mention one small database project that Reteaco was involved in earlier this year. Our company worked with Philips and Du Pont Optical, and U.S.-based publisher, CW Communications, to develop a special disc for distribution at the second annual Microsoft conference on CD-ROM. Articles were contributed by CW Communications' various divisions throughout the United States, and database services were provided by Reteaco in our Toronto headquarters.

The processed tapes, ready for mastering, were forwarded to Eindhoven, and finished discs were received in Seattle a few days later. These discs are now in the hands of conference attendees from Japan, Europe, South America, the United States and Canada. And most importantly, they can be used by any of these people because a single standard exists for CD-ROM.

CD-ROM is already international. It is already providing solutions. And given the direction of the industry, it promises a great deal more.

AN EDUCATOR'S POINT OF VIEW
by Elissa J. Tivona, M.A., Instructional Designer and
Production Manager
Arapahoe Community College, Littleton, Colorado

Like a limitless ocean filled with exotic fish, some which delight and entertain and some which nourish and sustain us, technological marvels swim by on a daily basis. For some people, CD-I may be one more elusive and beautiful tropical fish flitting in and out of view in this sea of possibilities. But for others who spend days immersed in these waters, CD-I has come into much sharper focus. CD-I stands for compact disc interactive, and it promises a three-way merger of digital audio capability (which compact-disc audio currently provides) with optical data storage and video images. Such an accomplishment begins to unlock the imagination: illustrated volumes of encyclopedias on a disc the size of a 45 RPM record; unparalleled "how-to" packages including narration, visuals, and databases of information; enhanced music delivery combining flawless audio with imagery . . . the possibilities go on and on.

Yet even as Philips, in conjunction with Sony, leaders in CD-I development, complete a comprehensive Green Book of specifications that defines technically what a CD-I disc will be, the marketplace is posing the more difficult question: "Why? Why do we need yet another form of media delivery?" The manufacturers, competing for the public's attention in what amounts to a high-tech battle of the bands, can and will give us this new wave of delivery systems. But the market will determine if what the system can do actually measures up to what it does do. What CD-I does, in reality, falls into the realm of the software or courseware developed to operate on the system. These applications will be critical to the success or failure of CD-I. And as educators and consumers of "smart" delivery systems, we may be holding an unexpected trump card at this point in time. What niche do we need filled by a new breed of systems? What will we invite into our classrooms and homes to sit side by side with the television and CD audio player? And why?

Many would pay dearly for a look into a crystal ball to predict the answers to these questions. I won't presume to answer for everyone, but I'd like to offer some predictions of my own. When trolling for a spot in the consumer's private pond, there are some variables that must be taken into account:

- Price - We will want to know if CD-I will be affordable.
- Compatibility - We will want the courseware/software to play on any brand of CD-I player, regardless of manufacturer.
- Performance - We will want CD-I to perform comparable to, if not better than, related and known technologies, i.e., CD audio.

Okay, where are we now with respect to these issues? American Interactive Media (a division of Polygram Corporation) is a new company that came into existence expressly to develop interactive video software, has begun to address these immediate concerns. Guided by the standards set forth in the Philips Green Book, AIM contends that CD-I is to be a universal standard. Software will be interchangeable from system to system. The "base" case standard is also intended to result in an affordable player—accessible, at least eventually, to the consumer of, say, a high quality stereo system for the home. In addition, the standards guarantee the capability for broadcast-quality picture portions of CD-I, with some specified limitations in other areas.

Having taken into account these three initial milestones, CD-I, has at least arrived at the user's door. What gets it inside? What will ensure a place for CD-I in the users' environment? There are two possible answers, with one based on the CD audio model and the other based on the television model. In the first model, CD audio capitalizes on the adage, "Build a better mouse trap and the world will beat a path to your door." When mice are running rampant, unquestionably the need exists to get rid of them. A reasonably intelligent person will use the best, most efficient means to do so. So it is with CD audio. The consumer has definitely demonstrated a strong desire (if not actually a need) for musical entertainment in the home through the purchase of records and tapes. CD audio declared itself as a better delivery method and proved its claim. Relative to both the LP and the audio tape, the CD offers a more noise-free listening experience on a less fragile medium. Add to that the affordable price and compatibility and you have a sure-fire recipe for success.

The second model is, by far, the more challenging. Volumes have been written as to why television, as an informational delivery system, has become so entrenched. It is far beyond the scope of this piece to enumerate the reasons. But in my opinion, there is one critical factor that has guaranteed television an unshakeable niche: it has evolved into a technological "member" of the family. We invite it into our homes, give it a central role in our daily lives and have ongoing dialogues with respect to its presence. Is the programming good or bad for us? Should we or shouldn't we watch? Do we listen to television more than to other members of our households? How does its "personality" impact on us as individuals or as a society? Television is relative, and we wrestle with our relationship to this relative on a continuing basis. If this metaphor has any basis, then clearly it would require an exceptional emerging technology to unseat this relationship.

I am intrigued at the possibility CD-I holds in this regard. I am intrigued by the challenge of making CD-I the technological companion of the 21st century. If we examine the potentials inherent in CD-I, we are on the brink of this changeover. We can ask CD-I to provide, in addition to the friendly presence of easy entertainment, a wealth of information resources comparable to having libraries in our own homes. We are looking at a transition from simple, preprogrammed entertainment to "edu-tainment." Programming will become not only a source for information but a window to information on levels that current television programming cannot possibly provide. The user will be able to ask this personal tele-tutor not only to be at home or in the class, but also to assist in exploring the larger world in greater depth and detail. CD-I is like graduating from the childhood relationship of cousins to a deeper, more meaningful relationship with, for example, a wise and worldly grandparent. Can CD-I live up to such lofty expectations? Can it accomplish this friendly "takeover" from the passive medium of television? Will it, in fact, be embraced in the home and classroom as video has? If designers of vision can conscientiously work toward creating this new niche, I predict it will become the newest resident in our homes as well as in other learning environments. Yet developers must not delay or skimp with the production of applications. After all, how long would we have lived with a box that simply issued forth flickering light? We were captivated by the programming on television, as will undoubtedly be the case for CD-I. I'm ready now for the Smithsonian at my fingertips. That's not too much to ask, is it?

According to Larry Lowe, Applications Design Engineer for American Interactive Media, "If you are a visionary, CD-I is a stunning new evolutionary event along the path from the cave to the stars. It is a quantum synergy of various technologies, all standardized and consumer-application driven. It might prove to be the most profound advance in communication technology in the history of the planet. Just one of the applications of CD-I would be to teach the universal language Esperanto to everyone on the planet. It is this view of CD-I that will lead to the kind of applications that will turn its promise into a self-fulfilling prophecy. On the other hand, if you are a healthy skeptic, CD-I is vaporware. Merely a couple of speeches and a handful of specifications."

Furthermore, as the engineers at Philips, Sony, and AIM ponder the possibilities, competitors at RCA and GE are hard at work on another entry into the field called DVI. In the DVI scenario, end users add a sophisticated chip set to their IBM PC, which makes existing CD-ROM technology capable of playing back full motion video. Previous to this breakthrough, CD-ROM players were most notable as computer peripherals capable of providing users with access to vast amounts of optically stored data. But digital, full motion video presented hardware designers and engineers with another magnitude of challenge altogether. In order to produce 30 frames of video per second—the rate at which visual information is refreshed to create the perception of motion—18 million bytes of data per second is required. GE/RCA have actually demonstrated that compressed digital information stored on CD-ROMs can be decompressed through the DVI board in the IBM PC controllers. This process now allows a single CD-ROM to become a storage medium for over an hour of motion video, albeit with picture quality far below the broadcast quality standards specified by CD-I. And to add to the chagrin of CD-I developers, prototype hardware and software was successfully demonstrated publicly at the March 1987 Microsoft CD-ROM Conference.

So the race is on, with GE/RCA and Philips/Sony battling it out to see who can get to the marketplace first with their delivery systems. But while manufacturers wrestle with the merger of sciences that will undoubtedly bring the hardware to use within a perceived window of opportunity, the issues remain unchanged. What educational or entertainment value will the media end products have? What software is currently under development that will make either of these systems meaningful?

These questions emerge in my mind from the basis of personal experience. I raise them both from my point of view as an educator and as an instruction media producer. Hindsight often turns out to be 20/20. Therefore, when I'm examining, somewhat ruefully, my experience as a media developer, I am forced to approach these newest "kids" on the technological block, CD-I and DVI, with more cautious optimism. I know I share the frustrations of a significant handful of instructional video producers who caught the interactive video (IAV) fever in the late seventies and early eighties. At that time, I became mesmerized by the marriage of the microprocessor to video. The optical laserdisc, with its potential for storing visual databases, and the interface boards that allowed for computers to "talk" to these videodisc players (or to videotape players, for that matter) became personal obsessions. I became a one-person sales force in many instances where my intended audiences—personnel trainers and classroom instructors—hadn't the slightest idea what I was talking about. Interactive video is still discussed today in professional conferences and meetings throughout the country as a revolutionary new technology even though the technical achievement of random access to video information is yesterday's news. Sadly, actual interactive applications—transportable among hardware systems, accessible to technology-shy individuals, and affordable—are simply not in place in very many practical settings. Most IAV applications are highly customized for specific needs, such as point-of-purchase displays for specific products or are highly sophisticated training devices, such as a welding simulator. These applications, although suggestive of the powerful potential of IAV, are simply not available to the average person, either in the home or in the typical learning environment. Generic, consumer-ready, or even classroom-ready applications have not kept pace with the inherent talents of the machinery. Therefore, the fledgling industry, calling itself interactive video, languishes. Those of us with skills as developers remain impassioned believers, but often with little in our hands to make a point. By contrast, in Japan, videodisc players did find a niche in the consumer market, and consequently, educational videodiscs on everything from tropical fish to the Louvre Museum in Paris are readily available at the local video vendor.

Still, if I poke fun at myself for my wild enthusiasm as a media specialist with an irrepressible flare for the technological, I must then take myself more seriously as an educator. I don that hat with a sincerity which cannot be denied. As technology advances, methods of learning—up until now inconceivable—become real possibilities. Simulations for physicians in training of real emergency situations such as gunshot wounds; exhibits of ancient artifacts from biblical times offering me the opportunity to study the minutest detail with the touch of a finger on the video screen; trips through Mayan ruins where I can "snap" a photograph and get a hard-copy printout of the actual image—these are among actual applications either currently up and running or under development. Applications like these, as well as countless others, are well within the realm of the possible.

The ultimate question I am posing here is will these applications also be within the realm of the practical? Will these astonishing opportunities for expanding our knowledge and awareness of the universe dissolve like castles of sand in the waves of economic reality—hardware and software just too far out of reach for education? I would be greatly saddened by that outcome, which is why I cheer on yet another generation of educational technology, although this time with slightly more reserve. I know that I feel a real rush of excitement when I ponder the educational opportunities that CD-I, DVI, and IAV promise; tomorrow, perhaps, our children will not just ponder these promises. Rather, it is my hope that they can be active participants in this imminent revolution in learning.

CD-ROM MARKET ANALYSIS
by LINK Resources Corporation and InfoTech

CD-ROM is a fundamental electronic medium that will continue to evolve and unfold its potential for the remainder of this century. Like the videodisc, it enters its initial commercial stages situated at the confluence of three industries: information processing, information publishing and entertainment. But while the videodisc represented a similar convergence, CD-ROM's uniqueness as a publishing medium stems from its already-recognized technology development costs, high degree of standardization, and committed backing by major manufacturers—all bequeathed by the consumer market success of the compact audio disc.

The *information processing industry* will exploit CD-ROMs' 600-megabyte capacity (equivalent to 1000 floppy discs, 250,000 printed pages, one dictionary with several thousand full-color pictures supported by pronounced words) to integrate database reference sources squarely into the kinds of communications and problem-solving tasks already performed on personal computers. In a largely parallel development, the industry will also attempt to bring about a rebirth for small computers through new applications on CD-ROM and CD-I.

- A period of several years will be required to work out the investments, applications, partnerships and distribution arrangements necessary to fully exploit the CD-ROM medium in large retail and value-added reseller markets.
- Some early applications will be successfully integrated on a fairly broad scale (e.g., knowledge worker productivity aids, product information, directories, and internally published documentation).
- As a distribution medium for software-only products, CD-ROM has short-term potential for public domain software in retail settings and for use with sophisticated systems in specialized markets. As CD-ROM becomes established as a computer peripheral, the distinction between data and software (applications) will disappear, replaced by integrated database application environments.
- Key to widespread acceptance will be the combination of personal computers equipped with built-in, half-height, low-cost CD-ROM drives and "trigger" applications able to address horizontal markets.

- CD-ROM drive manufacturing is not considered viable by U.S. computer hardware companies. Most will seek to capitalize through various joint ventures with drive and interface manufacturers to take advantage of their strengths in integration, distribution, marketing, and support.
- In their initial CD-ROM strategies, large computer manufacturers will tend to follow the example of Digital Equipment Corporation—which is to say that they will focus CD-ROM marketing efforts on their existing customers and on the support of applications involving internal information distribution.

The *information publishing industry* has recognized CD-ROM's potential as a low-cost delivery system (relative to online) for existing electronic information products and as a medium high in utility and convenience for information not now delivered electronically.

- The information industry did not sponsor any of the development of optical media. Yet it is the information industry that has the greatest opportunity to capitalize on optical publishing, for not many customers will buy a CD-ROM system or peripheral except for the content, which has a compelling use of attractiveness.
- Early emphasis on migration of existing online databases to the stand-alone CD-ROM medium will produce difficult pricing dilemmas for database providers; and the result will be high prices for CD-ROM database products and slow development outside the existing high-volume markets for static information (i.e., libraries and information centers, and specialized professionals).
- This industry, which captures, selects, edits, packages, and delivers information products, largely regards CD-ROM as a long-term catalyst to growth, facilitating new products, new packages, new markets, new revenues.
- Hundreds of information-based organizations have made serious commitments to examine the options or to actually enter optical publishing.
- Information company objectives include increasing market share and breaking into new markets or levels of markets; from an operations standpoint, CD-ROM is evaluated for its potential to lower production and distribution costs in the long term, improve marketing effectiveness and increase control.
- The production costs of transferring existing machine-readable databases to CD-ROM are much less than transferring hard copy; yet many products currently on paper or microforms are among the strongest candidates for CD-ROM products because the cost/benefit of automating such storage is believed to be justified.
- Information providers must establish new marketing strategies that take into account the role of CD-ROM in a multimedia product mix.
- CD-ROM will be a vehicle for expansion of the information industry, but its impact will take a few years to be felt.

The *entertainment/consumer electronics industry* is riding the wave of compact audio disc's huge success and formulating a new attack on the home computer market, this time with computers disguised as music/entertainment appliances. With the introduction of CD-I, the entertainment industry will have a more appropriate technology to exploit in its efforts to expand its product line by offering a more versatile home entertainment/educational product than CD audio.

- CD-I is a set of specification . . . . . Backed by Philips and Sony (the partners in the development of the compact audio disc and CD-ROM standards) with other Japanese manufacturers on board, CD-I expands upon CD-ROM in two important ways:

  ☐ By defining how data for video, graphics and sound are encoded on the disc, it standardizes a multimedia format.
  ☐ By specifying a microprocessor family (Motorola 68000) and operating system (CD-RTOS), based on OS 9, made by Microware of Des Moines, Iowa, it enables real-time applications such as entertainment and education/training, and ensures that CD-I disc carrying audio, video, text, binary data, and applications programs will work on all CD-I drives from all manufacturers.

- CD-I is intended to piggy-back on the success of CD audio by providing a CD player which can also function as a "viewer" for interactive programming. Although target retail price at introduction in 1987 is $1000, eventually it is expected to be priced at approximately $200 above the price of compact audio disc-only players.
- In terms of CD-I's impact on the overall CD-ROM market:

  ☐ The prospect of a consumer electronic publishing medium with the same level of standardization that has enabled the compact audio disc system to achieve such rapid success can only facilitate the growth of an infrastructure supportive to the development of optical media publishing in general.
  ☐ Most current CD-ROM applications involving either text-only online database migrating to locally-stored media or text-oriented internal data, and relatively low-resolution images will not be directly affected by the prospect of CD-I.
  ☐ Many relatively mass-market oriented professional and institutional publishers who have been eyeing CD-ROM as an entry into electronic publishing will now opt to wait for CD-I and its greater multimedia facilities and assurance of standardization.
  ☐ Educational and library buyers, for whom a single system to handle all optical storage needs is highly desirable and standardization crucial, will think twice before making commitments to CD-ROM.

CD-ROM Market Overview

- Between 1985 and the end of the decade, sales of CD-ROM hardware and

138

information products will constitute a $2.3 billion market.
- Nearly one million CD-ROM drives and CD-I players will be sold during this period, for a total hardware market of $645 million.
- By 1990, the CD-ROM hardware and information products will generate $1.3 billion in annual sales.
- Unit sales of CD-ROM drives and CD-I players in 1990 will exceed $.5 million.
- The sales of content will grow inexorably in proportion to hardware, constituting about 79 percent of 1990's total CD-ROM systems market.
- The number of discs manufactured will similarly outpace drives sold; by 1990, close to 20 million CD-ROM discs will be stamped for the U.S. market.
- The market outlook has changed considerably with the unveiling of plans by electronic giants Philips, Sony, and others to manufacture and market a system called CD-I.
- Table 7-1 summarizes drives, discs, and total system revenues for the CD-ROM market as a whole through 1990.
- Tables 7-2 and 7-3 present expected development of the four major market segments (professional productivity, library, education, and consumer) in terms of drives shipped and total system revenues, respectively.

Table 7-1. CD-ROM Market Summary, 1985-1990. Courtesy LINK Resources Corporation.

	Drives Sold (1)	Drives Installed	Dics Manufactured (2)	Value of Drives Sold (3)	Total Value of Systems (4)
1985	80	80	200	$120,000	$288,000
1986	6,178	6,258	18,392	$9,051,400	$15,338,000
1987	36,627	42,885	204,940	$40,929,700	$80,702,600
1988	115,907	158,792	1,107,064	$105,046,300	$249,103,200
1989	289,172	447,964	4,210,834	$204,780,400	$653,823,400
1990	534,713	982,677	12,319,270	$285,096,500	$1,283,093,400
1985- 1990 Total	982,677	982,677	17,860,700	$645,024,300	$2,282,348,600

1. Includes CD-ROM and CD-I, to end users.
2. Sold to end users.
3. End user prices, including cards and cabling, estimated.
4. Includes CD-ROM hardware and content (software and data) purchases and subscriptions.

The Professional Market

- CD-ROM will find its largest market through the early 1990s in professional applications—though the consumer and education categories will gradually increase their share of the CD data market.

Table 7-2. CD-ROM Drive Shipments*, 1985-1990, by Major Market Segment. Courtesy LINK Resources Corporation.

	1985 Units	%	1986 Units	%	1987 Units	%	1988 Units	%	1989 Units	%	1990 Units	%
Professional Productivity	40	50	4,800	78	28,000	76	85,400	74	182,800	64	275,200	51
Libraries	40	50	678	11	2,427	7	4,007	3	6,372	2	9,513	2
Consumers	-	-	700	11	3,700	10	14,500	13	50,000	17	130,000	24
Education	-	-	-	-	2,500	7	12,000	10	50,000	17	120,000	23
Total	80	100	6,178	100	36,627	100	115,907	100	289,172	100	534,713	100

*To end users.

Table 7-3. Value of CD-ROM Systems Sold*, 1985-1990, by Major Market Segment. Courtesy LINK Resources Corporation.

	1985 $000	%	1986 $000	%	1987 $000	%	1988 $000	%	1989 $000	%	1990 $000	%
Professional Productivity	180	63	12,095	79	61,660	76	186,665	75	448,720	69	811,265	63
Libraries	108	37	2,123	14	9,797	12	22,713	9	45,748	7	82,373	6
Consumers	-	-	1,120	7	4,645	6	15,100	6	45,605	7	110,440	9
Education	-	-	-	-	4,600	6	24,625	10	113,740	17	279,015	22
Total	288	100	15,338	100	80,702	100	249,103	100	653,823	10	1,283,093	100

*To end users.

- Internal databases for distribution within a single company or organization are least dependent upon standardization. These typically closed-loop applications will account for the majority of shipments in the professional productivity category, especially in the early years.
- However, other professional categories such as business reference, medical/scientific, engineering/construction/design, and especially law, will account for 90 percent of the total value of CD-ROM systems sold into the professional market in 1990 because of the high value of information discs.

The Library Market

- Although their interest in and knowledge of CD-ROM is high, most library managements are cautious about committing precious acquisitions and equipment funds to a new medium.

- Sixty-five percent of 510 libraries we surveyed (and over 70 percent of a special library expert sample) expected that it would take three or more years for CD-ROM to become a standard information format in their own institutions.
- Still, installations at the remaining 30 to 35 percent will provide many people both in and out of the corporate/professional world their initial encounter with CD-ROM systems—in the form of electronic card catalogs, indexes to journals and periodicals and other database services.
- The types of information most desired by libraries on optical media are, in descending order: indexing/abstracting database, periodicals, substitutes for microforms of all content types, older portions of online databases, bibliographies and other reference works, and government and technical reports.
- Librarians expect to see CD-ROM products return graphics to the text of journals; provide software allowing multiple levels of access by novice and experienced users, and hybrid online/optical disc products.

CDs in Education

- Before CD-ROM and/or CD-I deliver on their instructional and software management potential, familiar hurdles such as constrained school budgets, difficulties in digesting and utilizing existing equipment and a lack of good educational software must be cleared.
- But costs and other problems of software acquisition and management of software libraries are key problems that CD-ROM could address in the K-12 environment, aided by a re-emergence of interest in centralized mini- or supermicro-based systems to which optical drives could be networked.
- In post-secondary education, state-of-the-art technology is much more important to the major vendors such as DEC, IBM, Apple, and Hewlett-Packard, as well as new contenders like Sun Microsystems or Next, Inc. For all of them, CD-ROM will play a role in the development of advanced products for this demanding community.

The Consumer Market

- Grolier's Electronic Encyclopedia has served Grolier's long-term and the CD-ROM industry's short-term interests by creating some leading-edge consumer awareness.
- The announcement by Philips and Sony of CD-I has, for now, altered the prospects for CD-ROM in consumer applications.
- For the potential players in a consumer CD-ROM industry (publishers, movie studios, software companies like Microsoft), CD-I has the potential to establish a large foothold in the mass market. But because both home computing and CD-I require consumers to change habits and acquire a new mode of playing/learning/working/shopping, we have adopted a conservative stance in forecasting the consumer market for CD-I in its first few years.
- To be assured of success in the wide marketplace, CD-I must offer a completely new kind of experience. It must be an experience that bears returning to frequently. It must compete successfully with existing uses of time, whether

entertainment-, education- or work-related. And the CD-I industry must begin now to (re)create what both compact disc audio players and videocassette recorders were born with: a pre-existing storehouse of content (in the latter cases, records and movies) ready to be transferred to a new medium.

Appendix A

Standard ECMA-119

Volume and File Structure
of CD ROM
for Information Interchange

ECMA
EUROPEAN COMPUTER MANUFACTURERS ASSOCIATION

December 1986

BRIEF HISTORY

In the past years, compact discs originally developed for recording music have also been used for recording data, as they allow recording of large amounts of information in a reliable and economic manner. As a read-only medium, they are particularly suitable for use in applications such as auditing and legal documents. It appeared very quickly that there is an urgent need for a stable standard for the structure of such compact discs and of the files recorded thereon.

In October 1985, a number of industrial and software companies in the USA invited experts to participate in the elaboration of a working paper for such a project. The result of this work, in which also expert members of ECMA/TC15 as well as from Japan participated, was a report dated May 1986 and known as the "High Sierra Group" proposal.

This proposal was submitted in Europe to ECMA for their consideration. ECMA TC15, in collaboration with experts from user organizations, invested a considerable amount of work into this proposal in order to clarify and complete its technical contents and to re-edit it in a form suitable for an international standard. Particular attention was given to conformance aspects by applying the same editing principles as for the other standards for labelling, such as ECMA-13 (ISO 1001) and ECMA-107 (ISO 9293). As a result the present standard was produced.

This ECMA Standard has been submitted by ECMA to ISO for further processing as an international standard under the ISO fast-track procedure with a view to issuing an ISO standard possibly as soon as 1988.

Adopted as an ECMA Standard by the General Assembly of Dec. 11, 1986.

TABLE OF CONTENTS

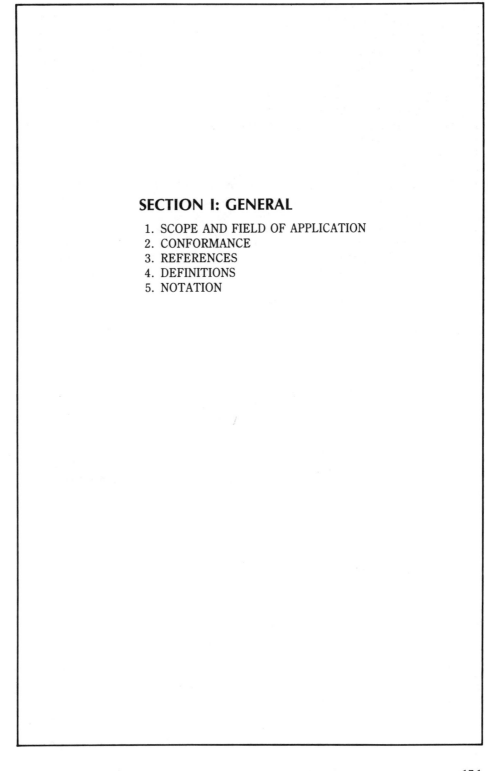

SECTION I: GENERAL

1. SCOPE AND FIELD OF APPLICATION
2. CONFORMANCE
3. REFERENCES
4. DEFINITIONS
5. NOTATION

1. *SCOPE AND FIELD OF APPLICATION*

   This Standard specifies the volume and file structure of compact read only optical discs (CDROM) for the interchange of information between users of information processing systems.

   This Standard specifies:
   - the attributes of the volume and the descriptors recorded on it;
   - the relationship among volumes of a volume set;
   - the placement of files;
   - the attributes of the files;
   - record structures intended for use in the input or output data streams of an application program when such data streams are required to be organized as sets of records;
   - three nested levels of interchange;
   - requirements for the processes which are provided within information processing systems, to enable information to be interchanged between different systems, utilizing recorded CDROM as the medium of interchange; for this purpose it specifies the functions to be provided within systems which are intended to originate or receive CDROM which conform to this Standard.

2. *CONFORMANCE*
   2.1 *Conformance of a CDROM*
   A CDROM conforms to this Standard when all information recorded on it conforms to the specifications of Section II of this Standard. A statement of conformance shall identify the lowest level of interchange to which the contents of the CDROM conform.

   A prerequisite to such conformance is conformance of the CDROM to a standard for recording (see 4.15).
   2.2 *Conformance of an Information Processing System*
   An information processing system conforms to this Standard if it meets the requirements specified in Section III of this Standard either for an originating system, or for a receiving system, or for both types of system. A statement of conformance shall identify which level of these requirements can be met by the system.

3. *REFERENCES*

ECMA-6	:	7-Bit Coded Character Set
ECMA-35	:	Code Extension Techniques
ECMA-43	:	8-Bit Code - Structure and Rules
ISO 1539	:	Programming languages - FORTRAN
ISO 2375	:	Data processing - Procedure for registration of escape sequences

International Register of Coded Character Sets to Be Used With Escape Sequences
Standards for recording : This Standard assumes the existence of a standard for recording (see 4.15).

4.   *DEFINITIONS*
         For the purposes of this Standard, the following definitions apply:

4.1   *Application Program*
         A program that processes the contents of a file, and may also process
         selected attribute data relating to the file or to the volume(s) on which the
         file is recorded.

         NOTE 1

         An application program is a specific class of user, as defined in this Standard.

4.2   *Byte*
         A string of eight binary digits operated upon as a unit.

4.3   *Data Field of a Sector*
         A fixed-length field containing the data of a sector.

4.4   *Data Preparer*
         A person or other entity which controls the preparation of the data to be
         recorded on a volume group.

         NOTE 2

         A data preparer is a specific class of user as defined in this Standard.

4.5   *Descriptor*
         A structure containing descriptive information about a volume or a file.

4.6   *Extent*
         A set of logical blocks, the logical block numbers of which form a continuous
         ascending sequence.

4.7   *File*
         A named collection of information.

4.8   *File Section*
         That part of a file that is recorded in any one extent.

4.9   *Implementation*
         A set of processes which enable an information processing system to behave
         as an originating system, or as a receiving system, or as both types of
         system.

4.10   *Logical Block*
         A group of 2^{n+9} bytes treated as a logical unit, where n equals 0 or a
         positive integer.

4.11   *Originating System*
         An information processing system which can create a set of files on a vol-
         ume set for the purpose of data interchange with another system.

4.12   *Record*
         A sequence of bytes treated as a unit of information.

4.13   *Receiving System*
         An information processing system which can read a set of files from a vol-
         ume set which has been created by another system for the purpose of data
         interchange.

4.14   *Sector*
        The smallest addressable part of the recorded area on a CDROM that can
        be accessed independently of other addressable parts of the recorded area.

4.15   *Standard for Recording*
        A standard that specifies the recording method and the addressing method
        for the information recorded on a CDROM.
        The specifications of the standard for recording that are relevant for this
        Standard are:
        - a unique Physical Address for each recorded sector;
        - the location of the Data Field within each sector;
        - the length of the Data Field within each sector;
        NOTE 3
        The standard for recording used in conjuction with this Standard is subject to agreement be-
        tween the originator and the recipient of the volumes.

4.16   *User*
        A person or other entity (for example, an application program) that causes
        the invocation of the services provided by an implementation.

4.17   *Volume*
        A dismountable CDROM.

4.18   *Volume Set*
        A collection of one or more volumes, on which a set of files is recorded.

5.   *NOTATION*
        The following notation is used in this Standard.

5.1   *Decimal and Hexadecimal Notations*
        Numbers in decimal notation are represented by decimal digits, viz. 0 to 9.
        Numbers in hexadecimal notation are represented by hexadecimal digits,
        viz. 0 to 9 and A to F, shown in parentheses.

5.2   *Other Notation*
        BP   Byte position within a descriptor, starting with 1
        RBP   Byte position within a descriptor field, starting with 1
        ZERO   A single bit with the value 0
        ONE   A single bit with the value 1
        Digit(s) Any digit from DIGIT ZERO to DIGIT NINE

SECTION II: REQUIREMENTS FOR THE MEDIUM

1. VOLUME STRUCTURE
2. DIRECTORY STRUCTURE
3. FILE STRUCTURE
4. RECORD STRUCTURE
5. RECORDING OF DESCRIPTOR FIELDS
6. VOLUME DESCRIPTORS
7. FILE AND DIRECTORY DESCRIPTORS
8. LEVELS OF INTERCHANGE

6. VOLUME STRUCTURE
6.1 Arrangement of Data on a CDROM
6.1.1 Physical Addresses

Each sector shall be identified by a unique Physical Address as specified in the relevant standard for recording.

6.1.2 Logical Sector

The sectors of a volume shall be organized into Logical Sectors. Each Logical Sector shall consist of a number of bytes equal to 2048 or 2^n, whichever is larger, where n is the largest integer such that 2^n is less than, or equal to, the number of bytes in the Data Field of any sector recorded on the volume. The number of bytes in a Logical Sector shall be referred to as the Logical Sector Size. Each Logical Sector shall begin in a different sector from any other Logical Sector, and shall begin with the first byte of the Data Field of the sector in which it begins. If the number of bytes of the Data Field of each sector recorded on the volume is less than 2048, a Logical Sector shall comprise more than one sector, and the set of the Physical Addresses of its constituent sectors shall form a consecutive ascending sequence. The data of a Logical Sector shall be recorded in the Data Fields of its constituent sectors.

Each Logical Sector shall be identified by a unique Logical Sector Number. Logical Sector Numbers shall be integers assigned in an ascending sequence, in order of ascending Physical Addresses of the constituent sectors, starting with 0 for the Logical Sector containing the sector having the lowest Physical Address which may contain recorded information. The numbering shall continue through successive Logical Sectors, each of which begins with the sector with the next higher Physical Address than that of the last sector constituting the previous Logical Sector.

6.1.3 Volume Space

The information on a volume shall be recorded in the set of all Logical Sectors on the volume. This set shall be referred to as the Volume Space of the volume.

The bytes in the Volume Space shall be numbered consecutively. The numbering shall start with 1, which shall be assigned to the first byte of the first Logical Sector of the Volume Space. The numbering shall continue through successive bytes of the first Logical Sector, and then through successive bytes of each successive Logical Sector, of the Volume Space.

6.2 Arrangement of the Volume Space
6.2.1

The Volume Space shall be divided into a System Area and a Data Area. The System Area shall occupy the Logical Sectors with Logical Sector Numbers 0 to 15. The System Area shall be reserved for system use. Its content is not specified by this Standard.

The Data Area shall occupy the remaining Logical Sectors of the Volume Space.

6.2.2 Logical Block

The Volume Space shall be organized into Logical Blocks. Each Logical Block shall consist of 2^{n+9} bytes, where n equals 0 or a positive integer. The number of bytes in a Logical Block shall be referred to as the Logical Block Size which shall not be greater than the Logical Sector Size. The data of a Logical Block shall be recorded in the Data Fields of its constituent Logical Sectors.

Each Logical Block shall be identified by a unique Logical Block Number. Logical Block Numbers shall be integers assigned in ascending order starting with 0. Logical Block Number 0 shall be assigned to the Logical Block which begins with the first byte of the Volume Space. Each successive Logical Block Number shall be assigned to the Logical Block which begins with the byte in the Volume Space immediately following the last byte of the preceding Logical Block.

6.3   Arrangement of the Data Area

File Sections shall be recorded in the Data Area. More than one File Section of a file may be recorded on the same volume.

The following types of descriptors shall be recorded in the Data Area to describe the use of the Data Area:
- Volume Descriptors
- File Descriptors
- Directory Descriptors
- Path Tables

The Volume Descriptors shall be recorded in consecutively numbered Logical Sectors starting with the Logical Sector having Logical Sector Number 16. The Logical Sectors in the Data Area shall be available for the assignment of Volume Partitions and the recording of File Sections, File Descriptors, Directory Descriptors and Path Tables.

Each File Section shall be recorded in an Extent, and shall be identified by a descriptor in a directory. An Extended Attribute Record can be associated with the File Section. If present, it shall be recorded in the same Extent and identified by the same descriptor. Each directory shall be recorded as a file in a single Extent, and shall be identified by a Directory Descriptor either in another directory or in a Volume Descriptor. Each directory shall also be identified by a record in a Path Table. Each Path Table shall be identified in a Volume Descriptor.

Space within the Data Area may be assigned to one or more Volume Partitions. Each Volume Partition shall be recorded in an Extent and shall be identified by a Volume Descriptor.

6.4   Arrangement of Extents

6.4.1   Extent

An Extent shall be set of Logical Blocks, the Logical Block Numbers of which form a continuous ascending sequence.

6.4.2   Mode of Recording a File Section

A File Section, and its associated Extended Attribute Record if any, shall be recorded in an Extent either in interleaved mode or in non-interleaved mode.

6.4.3   Interleaved Mode

6.4.3.1   File Unit

A File Unit shall comprise a set of Logical Blocks that are within an Extent and the Logical Block Numbers of which form a continuous ascending sequence.

When a File Section is recorded in interleaved mode, one or more File Units, each consisting of the same number of Logical Blocks, shall be assigned to the File Section within the same Extent. The number of Logical Blocks in the File Unit shall be the assigned File Unit Size for the File Section.

The first Logical Block of each File Unit shall have a Logical Block Number which is the lowest Logical Block Number in the Logical Sector that contains that Logical Block.

The sequence of the File Units in an Extent shall correspond to the sequence of the Logical Block Numbers of the first Logical Block of each File Unit.

NOTE 4

The Logical Blocks comprising a File Unit assigned to a File Section may:

- also each be assigned to a different File Section, and/or

- comprise part of one or more Volume Partitions.

6.4.3.2   Interleave Gap

The set of Logical Blocks the Logical Block Numbers of which lie between the last Logical Block Number of a File Unit and the first Logical Block Number of the next File Unit, if any, in the sequence, shall be an Interleave Gap. All Interleave Gaps between the File Units assigned to a File Section shall comprise the same number of Logical Blocks. This number shall be the assigned Interleave Gap Size for the File Section.

NOTE 5

The Logical Blocks comprising an Interleave Gap between the File Units assigned to a File Section may:

- also each be assigned to a different File Section, and/or

- comprise part of one or more Volume Partitions.

6.4.3.3   Relation of File Section to File Unit

When a File Section is recorded in interleaved mode, the File Section, and its associated Extended Attribute Record, if any, shall be recorded over the sequence of File Units assigned to the File Section.

6.4.3.4   Recording of an Extended Attribute Record

If an Extended Attribute Record is recorded it shall be recorded in the first File Unit of the sequence. The recording shall begin at the first byte of the first Logical Block of the File Unit. It shall continue through successive bytes of that Logical Block, and then through successive bytes of successive Logical Blocks, if any, of the File Unit, until all of the Extended Attribute Record is recorded.

The assigned Extended Attribute Record length shall be equal to the assigned File Unit Size.

6.4.3.5   Recording of a File Section

The successive parts, if any, of the File Section Shall be recorded in successive File Units, starting from the second File Unit in the sequence if an Extended Attribute Record is recorded, and starting from the first File Unit in the sequence if no Extended Attribute Record is recorded.

6.4.3.6   Data Space

The set of File Units in which the successive parts of the File Section are recorded shall be the Data Space of the File Section.

The bytes in the Data Space shall be numbered consecutiviely. The numbering shall start from 1 which shall be assigned to the first byte of the first Logical Block of the first File Unit, if any, of the Data Space. The numbering shall continue through successive bytes of that Logical Block, then through successive bytes of each successive Logical Block, if any, of the first File Unit, and then through successive bytes of the Logical Block(s) of each successive File Unit, if any, assigned to the File Seciton.

The numbering shall end with a number equal to the product of the number of bytes in a Logical Block, the number of Logical Blocks in the File Unit, and the number of File Units assigned to the File Section; or shall equal zero if there are no bytes in the Data Space.

6.4.4   Non-Interleaved Mode

When a File Section is recorded in non-interleaved mode the File Section, and its associated Extended Attribute Record, if any, sxhall be recorded over the sequence of Logical Blocks in an Extent.

6.4.4.1   Recording of an Extended Attribute Record

If an Extended Attribute Record is recorded, it shall be recorded over one or more Logical Blocks, the Logical Block Numbers of which form a continuous ascending sequence. The recording shall begin at the first byte of the first Logical Block of the Extent. It shall continue through successive bytes of that Logical Block, and then through successive bytes of successive Logical Blocks, if any, of the Extent, until all of the Extended Attribute Record is recorded.

The number of Logical Blocks over which the Extended Attribute Record is recorded shall be the assigned Extended Attribute Record length for the File Section.

NOTE 6

The Logical Blocks comprising an Extended Attribute Record assigned to a File Section may:

- also each be assigned to a different File Section, and/or
- comprise part of one or more Volume Partitions.

6.4.4.2   Recording of a File Section

The File Section shall be recorded over zero or more Logical Blocks, the Logical Block Numbers of which form a continuous ascending sequence. If no Extended Attribute Record is recorded, the sequence shall start with the first Logical Block of the Extent. If an Extended Attribute Record is recorded, the sequence shall start with the first Logical Block, if any, immediately following the last Logical Block over which the Extended Attribute Record is recorded.

6.4.4.3   Data Space

The set of Logical Blocks over which the File Section is recorded shall be the Data Space of the File Section.

The bytes in the Data Space shall be numbered consecutively. The numbering shall start from 1 which shall be assigned to the first byte of the first Logical Block, if any, of the Data Space. The numbering shall continue through successive bytes of that Logical Block, and then through successive bytes of each successive Logical Block, if any, of the Data Space.

The numbering shall end with a number equal to the product of the number of bytes in a Logical Block, and the number of Logical Blocks in the Data Space; or shall equal zero if there are no Logical Blocks in the Data Space.

6.4.5   Data Length of a File Section

The data length of a File Section shall be the number of consecutive bytes in the Data Space, starting from the first byte, if any, that are intended for interchange. If this number is less than the number of bytes in the Data Space, then any remaining bytes in the Data Space shall be ignored in interchange.

6.4.6   Relation of Extended Attribute Record to File Section

An Extended Attribute Record may be associated with a File Section. If present, the Extended Attribute Record shall identify certain attributes of the file of which the File Section forms a part.

A subset of those attributes shall apply to all File Sections of a file that contains records according to 6.10. If any of those attributes are assigned to the file, an Extended Attribute Record shall be recorded in association with each of the File Sections of the file.

The other attributes identified in an Extended Attribute Record shall apply to that File Section and all preceding File Sections of the file (see 6.5.1). If no Extended Attribute Record is recorded in association with the last File Section of a file, then these attributes are not specified for the file.

6.4.7   Recording of a Volume Partition

If a Volume Partition is recorded, it shall be recorded over one or more Logical Blocks, the Logical Block Numbers of which form a continuous ascending sequence. The recording shall begin at the first byte of the first Logical Block of the Extent. It shall continue through successive bytes of that Logical Block, and then through successive bytes of successive Logical Blocks, if any, of the Extent, until all of the Volume Partition is recorded. The first Logical Block of each Volume Partition shall have a Logical Block Number which is the lowest Logical Block Number in the Logical Sector that contains that Logical Block.

The number of Logical Blocks over which the Volume Partition is recorded shall be the assigned Volume Partition Size for the Volume Partition.

6.5   File Structure

6.5.1   Relation to File Sections

Each file shall consist of one or more File Sections. Each File Section of a file shall be identified by a record in the same directory. The sequence of the File Sections of a file shall be identified by the order of the corresponding records in the directory.

A File Section may be part of more than one file and may occur more than once in the same file. A File Section may be identified by more than one record in the same or a different directory.

Each File Section of a file may be recorded on a different volume.

6.5.2   File Space

The set of Data Spaces over which a file is recorded shall be the File Space of the file.

The bytes in the File Space shall be numbered consecutively. The numbering shall start from 1 which shall be assigned to the first byte of the first Data Space, if any. The numbering shall continue through successive bytes of that Data Space, and then through successive bytes of each successive Data Space, if any, of the file.

The numbering shall end with a number equal to the sum of the number of bytes in all Data Spaces of the file.

6.5.3   Contents of a File

The information in a file shall be interpreted according to the relevant standards for the coded representation of information.

NOTE 7

The identification of these standards is the subject of an agreement between the originator and the recipient of the file.

6.5.4   Associated File

An Associated File has a relationship not specified by this Standard to another file that has been assigned the same File Identifier (see 7.5) as that of the Associated File in the same directory.

6.6   Volume Set

A Volume Set shall be the set of volumes on which a set of files is recorded. A Volume Set shall consist of one or more volumes having a common Volume Set Identifier (see 8.4.19 and 8.5.13). All volumes in a Volume Set shall be numbered consecutively starting from 1.

A Volume Group within a Volume Set shall consist of one or more consecutively numbered volumes the contents of which are established at the same time. The sequence number of the volume that has the highest sequence number within the Volume Group shall be the assigned Volume Set Size.

Each volume of a Volume Set shall contain a description of all the directories and files that are recorded on those volumes the sequence number of which is less than, or equal to, the assigned Volume Set Size of the volume.

NOTE 8

Such description recorded on a volume shall supersede the description recorded on any volume of the Volume Set having a lower assigned Volume Set Size.

The Logical Block Size shall be the same for all volumes of a Volume Set.

6.7   Volume Descriptors

A Volume Descriptor shall be one of the following types:
- Primary Volume Descriptor
- Supplementary Volume Descriptor
- Volume Partition Descriptor
- Boot Record
- Volume Descriptor Set Terminator

6.7.1   Volume Descriptor Set

A Volume Descriptor Set shall be a sequence of volume descriptors recorded in consecutively numbered Logical Sectors starting with the Logical Sector with Logical Sector Number 16. Each successive Volume Descriptor shall be recorded in the Logical Sector with the next higher Logical Sector Number than that of the Logical Sector in which the previous Volume Descriptor is recorded. The sequence shall consist of two or more volume descriptors consecutively recorded as follows.

6.7.1.1	The sequence shall contain one Primary Volume Descriptor (see 8.4) recorded at least once.
	The Primary Volume Descriptor shall describe the Volume Space, and identify the attributes of the volume, the locations of a Root Directory and of a group of Path Tables, and the number of volumes in the Volume Set.
6.7.1.2	The sequence may contain zero or more Supplementary Volume Descriptors (see 8.5) each recorded at least once.
	A Supplementary Volume Descriptor shall describe the Volume Space, and identify the attributes of the volume, the locations of a Root Directory and of a group of Path Tables, and the number of volumes in the Volume Set. It shall also identify the coded graphic character set used within selected fields of this descriptor, and of the records in associated File Descriptors, Directory Descriptors and Path Tables.
6.7.1.3	The sequence may contain zero or more Volume Partition Descriptors (see 8.6).
	A Volume Partition Descriptor shall identify a Volume Partition within the Volume Space, its position and size, and its attributes.
6.7.1.4	The sequence may contain zero or more Boot Records (see 8.2).
	A Boot Record shall contain information which may be used to achieve a specific state in a receiving system or an application program.
6.7.1.5	The sequence shall be terminated by the recording of one or more Volume Descriptor Set Terminators (see 8.3).

6.8 Directory Structure

6.8.1 Directory

A directory shall be recorded as a file containing a set of records each of which identifies a File Section or another directory. A directory shall not be recorded as an Associated File, shall not be recorded in interleaved mode and shall consist of only one File Section.

The identification of a file shall be different from the identification of any other file, unless the file is an Associated File (see 6.5.3), or of any directory identified in the same directory. The identification of a directory shall be different from the identification of any file or of any other directory identified in the same directory.

The first Logical Block of the Extent in which a directory is recorded shall have a Logical Block Number which is the lowest Logical Block Number in the Logical Sector that contains that Logical Block.

6.8.1.1 Directory Record

A Directory Record shall contain:
- information to locate a File Section,
- information to locate any Extended Attribute Record associated with the File Section,
- the identification of the file,
- certain attributes of the file,
- certain attributes of the File Section.

The first or only Directory Record recorded in a Logical Sector shall begin at the first byte of the first Data Field of that Logical Sector. Each subsequent Directory Record recorded in that Logical Sector shall begin at the byte immediately following the last byte of the preceding Directory Record in that Logical Sector. Each Directory Record shall end in the Logical Sector in which it begins. Unused positions after the last Directory Record in a Logical Sector shall be set to (00).

6.8.1.2   Order of Directory Records

The records in a Directory shall be ordered according to 9.3.

The order of the directory records for a file in a directory shall specify the order of the File Sections in the File Space of the file.

6.8.1.3   Directory Length

The length of a directory shall be the sum of:
- the lengths of all Directory Records in the directory;
- the number of unused positions after the last Directory Record in all Logical Sectors in which the directory is recorded.

6.8.2   Directory Hierarchy

A Directory Hierarchy shall be a set of directories related to each other as follows.

The Root of the hierarchy, called the Root Directory, shall be a directory identified either in a Primary Volume Descriptor or in a Supplementary Volume Descriptor.

Each directory, other than the Root Directory, shall be identified by a record in another directory.

A directory identifying another directory shall be called the Parent Directory of the identified directory. Each directory shall contain a record which identifies its Parent Directory. Different directories may have the same Parent Directory.

A hierarchical relationship shall exist between the Root Directory and all other directories:

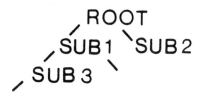

The hierarchy shall consist of a number of levels (i.e. for n levels: level 1, level 2, . . ., level n). The Root Directory shall be the one and only directory at level 1 of the hierarchy.

If a Directory is at level m of the hierarchy, its Parent Directory shall be at level (m–1). The Parent Directory of the Root Directory shall be the Root Directory.

6.8.2.1   Depth of Directory Hierarchy

The number of levels in the hierarchy shall not exceed eight. In addition, for each file recorded, the sum of the following shall not exceed 255:
- the length of the File Identifier (see 7.5.2),

- the length of the Directory Identifiers (see 7.6) of all relevant directories,
- the number of relevant directories.

6.8.2.2   Identification of Directories

For a Root Directory:
- the first Directory Record of the Root Directory shall describe the Root Directory and shall have a Directory Identifier consisting of a single (00) byte;
- the second Directory Record of the Root Directory shall describe the Root Directory itself and shall have a Directory Identifier consisting of a single (01) byte;
- a Directory Record describing the Root Directory shall be contained in the Root Directory field of the volume descriptor that identifies the directory hierarchy.

For each directory other than the Root Directory:
- the first Directory Record of the directory shall describe that directory and shall have a Directory Identifier consisting of a single (00) byte;
- the second Directory Record of the directory shall describe the Parent Directory for that directory and shall have a Directory identifier consisting of a single (01) byte;
- a Directory Record in its Parent Directory shall describe the directory.

6.8.3   Relation of Directory Hierarchies

One or more Directory Hierarchies shall be recorded on a volume.

A Directory Hierarchy shall be identified in the Primary Volume Descriptor.

Each additional Directory Hierarchy shall be identified in a Supplementary Volume Descriptor.

The directories within each hierarchy shall identify zero or more of the files that are recorded in those volumes, the sequence numbers of which are less than, or equal to, the assigned Volume Set Size of the volume.

A directory shall not be a part of more than one Directory Hierarchy.

6.9   Path Table

A Path Table recorded on a volume of a Volume Set shall contain a set of records describing a directory hierarchy for those volumes of the Volume Set the sequence numbers of which are less than, or equal to, the assigned Volume Set Size of the volume.

For each directory in the directory hierarchy other than the Root Directory, the Path Table shall contain a record which identifies the directory, its Parent Directory and its location. The records in a Path Table shall be numbered starting from 1. The first record in the Path Table shall identify the Root Directory and its location.

The directory number of a directory shall be the ordinal number of the Path Table Record that identifies the directory.

6.9.1   Order of Path Table Records

The records in a Path Table shall be ordered by the following criteria in descending order of significance:

- in ascending order according to level in the directory hierarchy;
- in ascending order according to the directory number of the Parent Directory of the directory identified by the record;
- in ascending order according to the relative value of the Directory Identifier field in the record, where the Directory Identifiers shall be valued as follows:
  - If the two Directory identifiers do not contain the same number of byte positions, the shorter Directory Identifier shall be treated as if it were padded on the right with all padding bytes set to (20), and as if both Directory Identifiers contained the identical number of byte positions.
  - After any padding necessary to treat the Directory Identifiers as if they were of equal length, the characters in the corresponding byte positions, starting with the first position, of the Directory Identifiers are compared until a byte position is found that does not contain the same character in both Directory Identifiers. The greater Directory Identifier is the one that contains the character with the higher code position value in the coded graphic character set used to interpret the Directory Identifier of the Path Table Record.

6.9.2   Path Table Group

A Path Table shall be either a Type L Path Table or a Type M Path Table. In a Type L Path Table, a numerical value shall be recorded according to 7.2.1 if represented as a 16-bit number and according to 7.3.1 if represented as a 32-bit number.

In a Type M Path Table, a numerical value shall be recorded according to 7.2.2 if represented as a 16-bit number and according to 7.3.2 if represented as a 32-bit number.

A Path Table Group shall comprise one or two identical Type L Path Tables and one or two identical Type M Path Tables.

6.9.3   Recorded Occurrences of the Path Table

One or more Path Table Groups shall be recorded on a volume. The Primary Volume Descriptor shall identify the size and locations of the constituent Path Tables of a Path Table Group. These Path Tables shall identify the directories in the Directory Hierarchy which is identified by the Primary Volume Descriptor.

Corresponding to each additional Directory Hierarchy recorded on a volume an additional Path Table Group shall be recorded on the volume. For each such Path Table Group the corresponding Supplementary Volume Descriptor shall identify the size and locations of its constituent Path Tables. These Path Tables shall identify the directories in the corresponding Directory Hierarchy.

6.9.4   Consistency of Path Tables between Volumes of a Volume Group

6.9.4.1   The contents of a Type L Path Table identified in a Primary Volume Descriptor shall be identical with the contents of any other Type L Path Table identified in a Primary Volume Descriptor on a volume of the same Volume Group.

The contents of a Type M Path Table identified in a Primary Volume

Descriptor shall be identical with the contents of any other Type M Path Table identified in a Primary Volume Descriptor on a volume of the same Volume Group.

6.9.4.2 The contents of a Type L Path Table identified in a Supplementary Volume Descriptor shall be identical with the contents of any other Type L Path Table identified in a Supplementary Volume Descriptor, having the same volume set identification and identifying the same coded graphic character set for use within selected descriptor fields (see 7.4), on a volume of the same Volume Group.

The contents of a Type M Path Table identified in a Supplementary Volume Descriptor shall be identical with the contents of any other Type M Path Table identified in a Supplementary Volume Descriptor, having the same volume set identification and identifying the same coded graphic character set for use within selected descriptor fields (see 7.4), on a volume of the same Volume Group.

6.10 Record Structure

The information in a file may be organized as a set of records according to this clause of this Standard.

6.10.1 Characteristics

A record shall be a sequence of bytes treated as a unit of information. The length of a record shall be the number of bytes in the record.

A record shall be either a fixed-length record, or a variable-length record. All records in a file shall be either fixed-length records or variable-length records.

6.10.2 Measured Data Units (MDU)

A Measured Data Unit shall contain either a fixed-length record or a variable-length record. An MDU shall comprise an even number of bytes.

6.10.2. Relationship to File Space

Each MDU shall be recorded in successive bytes of the File Space. The first or only MDU shall begin at the first byte of the File Space. Each successive MDU shall begin at the byte in the File Space immediately following the last byte of the preceding MDU.

6.10.3 Fixed-Length Records

A fixed-length record shall be a record contained in a file that is assigned to contain records that all must have same length.

A fixed-length record shall be contained in an MDU. The MDU shall consist of the fixed-length record, immediately followed by a (00) byte if necessary to give the MDU an even length.

The minimum assigned length of a fixed-length record shall be 1.

6.10.4 Variable-Length Records

A variable-length record shall be a record contained in a file that is assigned to contain records that may have different lengths. The value recorded in the Record Format field of an Extended Attribute Record for a file containing variable-length records shall contain the same value as that recorded in the Record Format field of any other Extended Attribute Record of that same file.

A variable-length record shall be contained in an MDU. The MDU shall consist of a Record Control Word (RCW) immediately followed by the variable-length record, immediately followed by a (00) byte if necessary to give the MDU an even length.

The RCW shall specify as a 16-bit number the length of the record. The RCW shall be recorded according to:
- 7.2.1, if the value in the Record Format field of the Extended Attribute Record describing the Extent is 2, or
- 7.2.2, if the value in the Record Format field of the Extended Attribute Record describing the Extent is 3.

A maximum record length shall be assigned for a file. The length of any record in the file shall not exceed this value. The assigned maximum record length shall be in the range 1 to 32767.

The minimum length of a variable-length record shall be 0.

7. RECORDING OF DISCRIPTOR FIELDS

7.1 8-Bit Numerical Values

A numerical value represented in binary notation by an 8-bit number shall be recorded in a field of a descriptor in one of the following two formats. The applicable format is specified in the description of the descriptor fields.

7.1.1 8-Bit Unsigned Numerical Values

An unsigned numerical value shall be represented in binary notation by an 8-bit number recorded in a one-byte field.

7.1.2 8-Bit Signed Numerical Values

A signed numerical value shall be represented in binary notation by an 8-bit two's complement number recorded in a one-byte field.

7.2 16-Bit Numerical Value

A numerical value represented in binary notation by a 16-bit number shall be recorded in a field of a descriptor in one of the following three formats. The applicable format is specified in the description of the descriptor fields.

7.2.1 Least Significant Byte First

A numerical value represented by the hexadecimal representation (wx yz) shall be recorded in a two-byte field as (yz wx).

NOTE 9

For example, the decimal number 4660 has (12 34) as its hexadecimal representation and shall be recorded as (34 12).

7.2.2 Most Significant Byte First

A numerical value represented by the hexadecimal representation (wx yz) shall be recorded in a two-byte field as (wx yz).

NOTE 10

For example, the decimal number 4660 has (12 34) as its hexadecimal representation and shall be recorded as (12 34).

7.2.3 Both Byte Orders

A numerical value represented by the hexadecimal representation (wx yz) shall be recorded in a four-byte field as (yz wx wx yz).

NOTE 11

For example, the decimal number 4660 has (12 34) as its hexadecimal representation and shall be recorded as (34 12 12 34).

7.3 32-Bit Numerical Values

A numerical value represented in binary notation by a 32-bit number shall be recorded in a field of a descriptor in one of the following three formats. The applicable format is specified in the description of the descriptor fields.

7.3.1 Least Significant Byte First

A numerical value represented by the hexadecimal representation (st uv wx yz) shall be recorded in a four-byte field as (yz wx uv st).

NOTE 12

For example, the decimal number 305419896 has (12 34 56 78) as its hexadecimal representation and shall be recorded as (78 56 34 12).

7.3.2   Most Significant Byte First

A numerical value represented by the hexadecimal representation (st uv wx yz) shall be recorded in a four-byte field as (st uv wx yz).

NOTE 13

For example, the decimal number 305419896 has (12 34 56 78) as its hexadecimal representation and shall be recorded as (12 34 56 78).

7.3.3   Both Byte Orders

A numerical value represented by the hexadecimal representation (st uv wx yz) shall be recorded in an eight-byte field as (yz wx uv st st uv wx yz).

NOTE 14

For example, the decimal number 305419896 has (12 34 56 78) as its hexadecimal representation and shall be recorded as (78 56 34 12 12 34 56 78).

7.4   Character Sets and Coding

7.4.1   d-Characters and a-Characters

The characters in the descriptors shall be coded according to ECMA-6 (see Appendix A), except as specified in 7.4.4.

The 37 characters in the following positions of the International Reference Version are referred to as d-characters:

3/0	to	3/9
4/1	to	5/10
5/15		

The 57 characters in the following positions of the International Reference Version are referred to as a-characters:

2/0	to	2/2
2/5	to	2/15
3/0	to	3/15
4/1	to	4/15
5/0	to	5/10
5/15		

The applicable set of characters is specified in the description of the descriptor fields.

7.4.2   c-Characters

The characters of the coded graphic characters sets identified by the escape sequences in a Supplementary Volume Descriptor are referred to as c-characters.

7.4.2.1   a1-Characters

A subset of the c-characters will be referred to as a1-characters. This subset shall be subject of agreement between the originator and the recipient of the volume.

7.4.2.2   d1-Characters

A subset of the a1-characters will be referred to as d1-characters. This subset shall be the subject of agreement between the originator and the recipient of the volume.

7.4.3   Separators

The characters separating the components of a File Identifier shall be:

SEPARATOR 1   represented by the bit combination (2E)

SEPARATOR 2   represented by the bit combination (3B)

7.4.4   Use of Characters in Descriptor Fields

The characters in the fields of the following descriptors shall be a-characters or d-characters as specified in 9.

- Directory records within a Directory Hierarchy that is identified in a Primary Volume Descriptor,
- Path Table records within a Path Table Group identified in a Primary Volume Descriptor,
- Extended Attribute records identified in a directory of a Directory Hierarchy that is identified in a Primary Volume Descriptor.

The characters in the fields in the following descriptors shall be al or d1-characters as specified in 9.

- Directory records within a Directory Hierarchy that is identified in a Supplementary Volume Descriptor,
- Path Table records within a Path Table Group identified in a Supplementary Volume Descriptor,
- Extended Attribute records identified in a directory of a Directory Hierarchy that is identified in a Supplementary Volume Descriptor.

7.4.5   Justification of Characters

In each fixed-length field the content of which is specified by this Standard to be characters, the characters shall be left-justified and any remaining positions on the right shall be set to (20).

7.5   File Identifier

7.5.1   File Identifier Format

A File Identifier shall consist of the following sequence:

- File Name: A sequence of zero or more d-characters or d1-characters;
- zero or one SEPARATOR 1;
- File Name Extension: A sequence of zero or more d-characters or d1-characters;
- zero or one SEPARATOR 2;
- File Version Number: Digits representing a number from 1 to 32767.

This sequence shall meet the following requirements:

- If no characters are specified for the File Name then the File Name Extension shall consist of at least one character.
- If no charaters are specified for the File Name Extension then the File Name shall consist of at least one character.
- If the File Version Number is not specified then it shall be assumed to be 1.
- If the File Name Extension is specified then the SEPARATOR 1 shall be present.
- If the File Version Number is specified then the SEPARATOR 2 shall be present.
- The sum of the following shall not exceed 31:

- if there is a File Name, the length of the File Name,
- if there is a File Name Extension, the length of the File Name Extension,
- if there is a SEPARATOR 1, + 1.

NOTE 15

If the File Name Extension is not specified, the SEPARATOR 1 may be present. If the File Version Number is not specified, the SEPARATOR 2 may be present.

7.5.2   File Identifier Length
The length of the File Identifier shall be the sum of the following:
- if there is a File Name, the length of the File Name,
- if there is a File Name Extension, the length of the File Name Extension,
- if there is a File Version Number, the number of digits in the File Version Number,
- the number of SEPARATORs.

7.6   Directory Identifier
7.6.1   Directory Identifier Format
A Directory Identifier shall consist of a sequence of one or mode d-characters or d1-characters (see 7.4.4), except as specified in 7.6.2.

7.6.2   Reserved Directory Identifiers
- The Directory Identifier of a Directory Record describing the Root Directory shall consist of a single (00) byte.
- The Directory Identifier of the Directory Record of each directory shall consist of a single (00) byte.
- The Directory Identifier of the second Directory Record of each directory shall consist of a single (01) byte.

7.6.3   Directory Identifier Length
The length of a Directory Identifier shall not exceed 31.

8.   VOLUME DESCRIPTORS
The Volume Descriptors shall identify the volume, the partitions recorded on the volume, the volume creator(s), certain attributes of the volume, the location of other recorded descriptors and the version of the standard which applies to the volume descriptor.

8.1   Format of a Volume Descriptor

BP	Field Name	Content
1	Volume Descriptor Type	numerical value
2-6	Standard Identifier	CD001
7	Volume Descriptor Version	numerical value
8-2048	(Depends on Volume Descriptor Type)	(Depends on Volume Descriptor Type)

8.1.1   Volume Descriptor Type (BP 1)
This field shall specify as an 8-bit number the Volume Descriptor Type.

Number 0   shall mean that the Volume Descriptor is a Boot Record.

Number 1   shall mean that the Volume Descriptor is a Primary Volume Descriptor.

Number 2   shall mean that the Volume Descriptor is a Supplementary Volume Descriptor.

Number 3   shall mean that the Volume Descriptor is a Volume Partition Descriptor.

Numbers 4-254   are reserved for future standardization.

Number 255   shall mean that the Volume Descriptor is a Volume Descriptor Set Terminator.

This field shall be recorded according to 7.1.1.

8.1.2   Standard Identifier (BP 2-6)

This field shall specify an identification of this Standard.

The characters in this field shall be CD001.

8.1.3   Volume Descriptor Version (BP 7)

This field shall specify as an 8-bit number the version of the specification for the Volume Descriptor.

The content and the interpretation of this field shall depend on the content of the Volume Descriptor Type field.

This field shall be recorded according to 7.1.1.

8.1.4   Depends on Volume Descriptor Type (BP 8-2048)

The content and the interpretation of this field shall depend on the Volume Descriptor Type field.

8.2   Boot Record

The Boot Record shall identify a system which can recognize and act upon the content of the field reserved for boot system use in the Boot Record, and shall contain information which is used to achieve a specific state for a system or for an application.

BP	Field Name	Content
1	Volume Descriptor Type	numerical value
2-6	Standard Identifier	CD001
7	Volume Descriptor Version	numerical value
8-39	Boot System Identifier	a-characters
40-71	Boot Identifier	a-characters
72-2048	Boot System Use	not specified

8.2.1   Volume Descriptor Type (BP 1)

This field shall specify an 8-bit number indicating that the Volume Descriptor is a Boot Record.

The number in this field shall be 0.

This field shall be recorded according to 7.1.1.

8.2.2   Standard Identifier (BP 2-6)

This field shall specify an identification of this Standard.

The characters in this field shall be CD001.

8.2.3   Volume Descriptor Version (BP 7)

This field shall specify as an 8-bit number the version of the specification for the Boot Record structure.

1 shall indicate the structure of the present Standard.

This field shall be recorded according to 7.1.1.

8.2.4 Boot System Identifier (BP 8-39)

This field shall specify an identification of a system which can recognize and act upon the content of the Boot Identifier and Boot System Use fields in the Boot Record.

The characters in this field shall be a-characters.

8.2.5 Boot Identifier (BP 40-71)

This field shall specify an identification of the boot system specified in the Boot System Use field of the Boot Record.

The characters in this field shall be a-characters.

8.2.6 Boot System Use (BP 72-2048)

This field shall be reserved for boot system use. Its content is not specified by this Standard and shall be ignored in interchange.

8.3 Volume Descriptor Set Terminator

The recorded set of Volume Descriptors shall be terminated by a sequence of one or more Volume Descriptor Set Terminators.

BP	Field Name	Content
1	Volume Descriptor Type	numerical value
2-6	Standard Identifier	CD001
7	Volume Descriptor Version	numerical value
8-2048	(Reserved for future standardization)	(00) bytes

8.3.1 Volume Descriptor Type (BP 1)

This field shall specify an 8-bit number indicating that the Volume Descriptor is a Volume Descriptor Set Terminator.

The number in this field shall be 255.

This field shall be recorded according to 7.1.1.

8.3.2 Standard Identifier (BP 2-6)

This field shall specify an identification of this Standard.

The characters in this field shall be CD001.

8.3.3 Volume Descriptor Version (BP 7)

This field shall specify as an 8-bit number the version of the specification for the Volume Descriptor Set Terminator.

1 shall indicate the structure of the present Standard.

This field shall be recorded according to 7.1.1.

8.3.4 Reserved for Future Standardization (BP 8-2048)

This field shall be set to (00).

8.4 Primary Volume Descriptor

The Primary Volume Descriptor shall identify the volume, the system specifying the content of the Logical Sectors with Logical Sector Numbers 0 to 15, the size of the Volume Space, the version of the standard which applies to the Volume Descriptor, the version of the specification which applies to the directory records and the Path Table records and certain attributes of the volume.

BP	Field Name	Content
1	Volume Descriptor Type	numerical value
2-6	Standard Identifier	CD001
7	Volume Descriptor Version	numerical value
8	Unused Field	(00) byte
9-40	System Identifier	a-characters
41-72	Volume Identifier	d-characters
73-80	Unused Field	(00) bytes
81-88	Volume Space Size	numerical value
89-120	Unused Field	(00) bytes
121-124	Volume Set Size	numerical value
125-128	Volume Sequence Number	numerical value
129-132	Logical Block Size	numerical value
133-140	Path Table Size	numerical value
141-144	Location of Occurrence of Type L Path Table	numerical value
145-148	Location of Optional Occurrence of Type L Path Table	numerical value
149-152	Location of Occurrence of Type M Path Table	numerical value
153-156	Location of Optional Occurrence of Type M Path Table	numerical value
157-190	Directory Record for Root Directory	34 bytes
191-318	Volume Set Identiifer	d-characters
319-446	Publisher Identifier	a-characters
447-574	Data Preparer Identifier	a-characters
575-702	Application Identifier	a-characters
703-739	Copyright File Identiifer	d-characters, SEPARATOR 1, SEPARATOR 2
740-776	Abstract File Identifier	d-characters, SEPARATOR 1, SEPARATOR 2
777-813	Bibliographic File Identifier	d-characters, SEPARATOR 1, SEPARATOR 2
814-830	Volume Creation Date and Time	Digit(s), numerical value
831-847	Volume Modification Date and Time	Digit(s), numerical value
848-864	Volume Expiration Date and Time	Digit(s), numerical value
865-881	Volume Effective Date and Time	Digit(s), numerical value
882	File Structure Version	numerical value
883	(Reserved for future standardization)	(00) byte
884-1395	Application Use	not specified
1396-2048	(Reserved for future standardization)	(00) bytes

8.4.1   Volume Descriptor Type (BP 1)
This field shall specify an 8-bit number indicating that the volume

descriptor is a Primary Volume Descriptor.

The number in this field shall be 1.

This field shall be recorded according to 7.1.1.

8.4.2   Standard Identifier (BP 2-6)

This field shall specify an identification of this Standard.

The characters in this field shall be CD001.

8.4.3   Volume Descriptor Version (BP 7)

This field shall specify as an 8-bit number an identification of the version of the specification for the Primary Volume Descriptor.

1 shall indicate the structure of the present Standard.

This field shall be recorded according to 7.1.1.

8.4.4   Unused Field (BP 8)

This field shall be set to (00).

8.4.5   System Identifier (BP 9-40)

This field shall specify an identification of a system which can recognize and act upon the content of the Logical Sectors with Logical Sector Numbers 0 to 15 of the volume.

The characters in this field shall be a-characters.

8.4.6   Volume Identifier (BP 41-72)

This field shall specify an identification of the volume.

The characters in this field shall be d-characters.

8.4.7   Unused Field (BP 73-80)

This field shall be set to (00).

8.4.8   Volume Space Size (BP 81-88)

This field shall specify as a 32-bit number the number of Logical Blocks in which the Volume Space of the volume is recorded.

This field shall be recorded according to 7.3.3.

8.4.9   Unused Field (BP 89-120)

This field shall be set to (00).

8.4.10   Volume Set Size (BP 121-124)

This field shall specify as a 16-bit number the assigned Volume Set Size of the volume.

This field shall be recorded according to 7.2.3.

8.4.11   Volume Sequence Number (BP 125-128)

This field shall specify as a 16-bit number the ordinal number of the volume in the Volume Set of which the volume is a member.

This field shall be recorded according to 7.2.3.

8.4.12   Logical Block Size (BP 129-132)

This field shall specify as a 16-bit number the size, in bytes, of a Logical Block.

This field shall be recorded according to 7.2.3.

8.4.13   Path Table Size (BP 133-140)

This field shall specify as a 32-bit number the length in bytes of a recorded occurrence of the Path Table identified by this Volume Descriptor.

This field shall be recorded according to 7.3.3.

8.4.14   Location of Occurrence of Type L Path Table (BP 141-144)

This field shall specify as a 32-bit number the Logical Block Number of the first Logical Block allocated to the Extent which contains an occurrence of the Path Table. Multiple-byte numerical values in a record of this occurrence of the Path Table shall be recorded with the least significant byte first.

This field shall be recorded according to 7.3.1.

8.4.15   Location of Optional Occurrence of Type L Path Table (BP 145-148)

This field shall specify as a 32-bit number the Logical Block Number of the first Logical Block allocated to the Extent which contains an optional occurrence of the Path Table. If the value is 0, it shall mean that the Extent shall not be expected to have been recorded. Multiple-byte numerical values in a record of this occurrence of the Path Table shall be recorded with the least significant byte first.

This field shall be recorded according to 7.3.1.

8.4.16   Location of Occurrence of Type M Path Table (BP 149-152)

This field shall specify as a 32-bit number the Logical Block Number of the first Logical Block allocated to the Extent which contains an occurrence of the Path Table. Multiple-byte numerical values in a record of this occurrence of the Path Table shall be recorded with the most significant byte first.

This field shall be recorded according to 7.3.2.

8.4.17   Location of Optional Occurrence of Type M Path Table (BP 153-156)

This field shall specify as a 32-bit number the Logical Block Number of the first Logical Block allocated to the Extent which contains an optional occurrence of the Path Table. If the value is 0, it shall mean that the Extent shall not be expected to have been recorded. Multiple-byte numerical values in a record of this occurrence of the Path Table shall be recorded with the most significant byte first.

This field shall be recorded according to 7.3.2.

8.4.18   Directory Record for Root Directory (BP 157-190)

This field shall contain an occurrence of the Directory Record for the Root directory.

This field shall be recorded according to 9.1.

8.4.19   Volume Set Identifier (BP 191-318)

This field shall specify an identification of the Volume Set of which the volume is a member.

The characters in this field shall be d-characters.

8.4.20   Publisher Identifier (BP 319-446)

This field shall specify an identification of the user who specified what shall be recorded on the Volume Group of which the volume is a member. If the first byte is set to (5F), the remaining bytes of this field shall specify an identifier for a file containing the identification of the user. This file shall be described in the Root Directory. The File Name shall not contain more than eight d-characters and the File Name Extension shall not contain more than three d-characters.

If all bytes of this field are set to (20), it shall mean that no such user is identified.

The characters in this field shall be a-characters.

8.4.21   Data Preparer Identifier (BP 447-574)

This field shall specify an identification of the person or other entity which controls the preparation of the data to be recorded on the Volume Group of which the volume is a member.

If the first byte is set to (5F), the remaining bytes of this field shall specify an identifier for a file containing the identification of the data preparer. This file shall be described in the Root Directory. The File Name shall not contain more than eight d-characters and the File Name Extension shall not contain more than three d-characters.

If all bytes of this field are set to (20), it shall mean that no such data preparer is identified.

The characters in this field shall be a-characters.

8.4.22 Application Identifier (BP 575-702)

This field shall specify an identification of the specification of how the data are recorded on the Volume Group of which the volume is a member.

If the first byte is set to (5F), the remaining bytes of this field shall specify an identifier for a file containing the identification of the application. This file shall be described in the Root Directory. The File Name shall not contain more than eight d-characters and the File Name Extension shall not contain more than three d-characters.

If all bytes of this field are set to (20), it shall mean that no such application is identified.

The characters in this field shall be a-characters.

8.4.23 Copyright File Identifier (BP 703-739)

This field shall specify an identification for a file described by the Root Directory and containing a copyright statement for the Volume Set. If all bytes of this field are set to (20), it shall mean that no such file is identified.

The File Name of a Copyright File Identifier shall not contain more than 8 d-characters. The File Name Extension of a Copyright File Identifier shall not contain more than 3 d-characters.

The characters in this field shall be d-characters, SEPARATOR 1 and SEPARATOR 2.

This field shall be recorded as specified in 7.5.

8.4.24 Abstract File Identifier (BP 740-776)

This field shall specify an identification for a file described by the Root Directory and containing an abstract statement for the Volume Set. If all bytes of this field are set to (20), it shall mean that no such file is identified.

The File Name of an Abstract File Identifier shall not contain more than 8 d-characters. The File Name Extension of an Abstract File Identifier shall not contain more than 3 d-characters.

The characters in this field shall be d-characters, SEPARATOR 1 and SEPARATOR 2.

The field shall be recorded as specified in 7.5.

8.4.25 Bibliographic File Identifier (BP 777-813)

This field shall specify an identification for a file described by the Root Directory and containing bibliographic records interpreted according to standards that are the subject of an agreement between the originator and the recipient of the volume. If all bytes of this field are set to (20), it shall mean that no such file is identified.

The File Name of a Bibliographic File Identifier shall not contain more than eight d-characters. The File Name Extension of a Bibliographic File Identifier shall not contain more than three d-characters.

	The characters in this field shall be d-characters, SEPARATOR 1 and SEPARATOR 2. The field shall be recorded as specified in 7.5.
8.4.26	Volume Creation Date and Time (BP 814-830) This field shall specify the date and the time of the day at which the information in the volume was created. It shall be recorded according to 8.4.26.1.
8.4.26.1	Date and Time Format The date and time shall be represented by a 17-byte field recorded as follows.

RBP	Interpretation	Content
1-4	Year from 1 to 9999	Digits
5-6	Month of the year from 1 to 12	Digits
7-8	Day of the month from 1 to 31	Digits
9-10	Hour of the day from 0 to 23	Digits
11-12	Minute of the hour from 0 to 59	Digits
13-14	Second of the minute from 0 to 59	Digits
15-16	Hundredths of a second	Digits
17	Offset from Greenwich Mean Time in number of 30 minute intervals from -24 (West) to +24 (East) recorded according to 7.1.2	numerical value

	If all characters in RBP 1-16 of this field are the digit ZERO and the number in RBP 17 is zero, it shall mean that the date and time are not specified.
8.4.27	Volume Modification Date and Time (BP 831-847) This field shall specify the date and the time of the day at which the information in the volume was last modified. This field shall be recorded according to 8.4.26.1.
8.4.28	Volume Expiration Date and Time (BP 848-864) This field shall specify the date and the time of the day at which the information in the volume may be regarded as obsolete. If the date and time are not specified then the information shall not be regarded as obsolete. This field shall be recorded according to 8.4.26.1
8.4.29	Volume Effective Date and Time (BP 865-881) This field shall specify the date and the time of the day at which the information in the volume may be used. If the date and time are not specified then the information may be used at once. This field shall be recorded according to 8.4.26.1
8.4.30	File Structure Version (BP 882) This field shall specify as an 8-bit number the version of the specification for the records of a directory and of a Path Table. 1 shall indicate the structure of the present Standard. This field shall be recorded according to 7.1.1.

	8.4.31	Reserved for future standardization (BP 883)

8.4.31   Reserved for future standardization (BP 883)
          This field shall be set to (00).

8.4.32   Application Use (BP 884-1395)
          This field shall be reserved for application use. Its content is not specified by this Standard.

8.4.33   Reserved for future standardization (BP 1396-2048)
          This field shall be set to (00).

8.5   Supplementary Volume Descriptor
          The Supplementary Volume Descriptor shall identify the volume, the system specifying the content of the Logical Sectors with Logical Sector Numbers 0 to 15, the size of the Volume Space, the version of the standard which applies to the Volume Descriptor, the version of the specification which applies to the directory records and the Path Table records, certain attributes of the volume and the coded graphic character set used to interpret descriptor fields that contain characters.

BP	Field Name	Content
1	Volume Descriptor Type	numerical value
2-6	Standard Identifier	CD001
7	Volume Descriptor Version	numerical value
8	Volume Flags	8 bits
9-40	System Identifier	a1-characters
41-72	Volume Identifier	d1-characters
73-80	Unused Field	(00) bytes
81-88	Volume Space Size	numerical value
89-120	Escape Sequences	32 bytes
121-124	Volume Set Size	numerical value
125-128	Volume Sequence Number	numerical value
129-132	Logical Block Size	numerical value
133-140	Path Table Size	numerical value
141-144	Location of Occurrence of Type L Path Table	numerical value
145-148	Location of Optional Occurrence of Type L Path Table	numerical value
149-152	Location of Occurrence of Type M Path Table	numerical value
153-156	Location of Optional Occurrence of Type M Path Table	numerical value
157-190	Directory Record for Root Directory	34 bytes
191-318	Volume Set Identifier	d1-characters
319-446	Publisher Identifier	a1-characters
447-574	Data Preparer Identifier	a1-characters
575-702	Application Identifier	a1-characters
703-739	Copyright File Identifier	d1-characters, SEPARATOR 1, SEPARATOR 2
740-776	Abstract File Identifier	d1-characters, SEPARATOR 1, SEPARATOR 2
777-813	Bibliographic File Identifier	d1-characters, SEPARATOR 1, SEPARATOR 2

814-830	Volume Creation Date and Time	Digit(s), numerical value
831-847	Volume Modification Date and Time	Digit(s), numerical value
848-864	Volume Expiration Date and Time	Digit(s), numerical value
865-881	Volume Effective Date and Time	Digit(s), numerical value
882	File Structure Version	numerical value
883	(Reserved for future standardization)	(00) byte
884-1395	Application Use	not specified
1396-2048	(Reserved for future standardization)	(00) bytes

Within a Volume Descriptor Set the contents of the fields of this descriptor shall be identical with the contents of the corresponding fields in a Primary Volume Descriptor except for the following fields.

8.5.1   Volume Descriptor Type (BP 1)

This field shall specify an 8-bit number indicating that the Volume Descriptor is a Supplementary Volume Descriptor.

The number in this field shall be 2.

This field shall be recorded according to 7.1.1.

8.5.2   Volume Descriptor Version (BP 7)

This field shall specify as an 8-bit number an identification of the version of the specification for the Supplementary Volume Descriptor.

1 shall indicate the structure of the present Standard.

This field shall be recorded according to 7.1.1.

8.5.3   Volume Flags (BP 8)

The bits of this field shall be numbered from 0 to 7 starting with the least significant bit.

This field shall specify certain characteristics of the volume as follows.

Bit 0   if set to ZERO, shall mean that the Escape Sequences field specifies only escape sequences registered according to ISO 2375;

if set to ONE, shall mean that the Escape Sequences field specifies at least one escape sequence not registered according to ISO 2375.

Bits 1-7   These bits are reserved for future standardization and shall all be set to ZERO.

8.5.4   System Identifier (BP 9-40)

This field shall specify an identification of a system which can recognize and act upon the content of the Logical Sectors with Logical Sector Numbers 0 to 15 of the volume.

The characters in this field shall be a1-characters.

8.5.5   Volume Identifier (BP 41-72)

This field shall specify an identification of the volume.

The characters in this field shall be d1-characters.

8.5.6   Escape Sequences (BP 89-120)

This field shall specify one or more escape sequences according to ECMA-35 that designate the G0 graphic character set and, optionally, the G1 graphic character set to be used in an 8-bit environment according to ECMA-35 to interpret descriptor fields related to the Directory Hierarchy identified by this Volume Descriptor (see 7.4.4). If the G1 set is designated, it is implicitly invoked into columns 10 to 15 of the code table.

These escape sequences shall conform to ECMA-35, except that the ESCAPE character shall be omitted from each designating escape sequence when recorded in this field. The first or only escape sequence shall begin at the first byte of the field. Each successive escape sequence shall begin at the byte in the field immediately following the last byte of the preceding escape sequence. Any unused positions following the last sequence shall be set to (00).

If Bit 0 of the Volume Flags field is set to ZERO, it shall mean that this field specifies only escape sequences registered according to ISO 2375. If all the bytes of this field are set to (00), it shall mean that the set of a1-characters is identical with the set of a-characters and that the set of d1-characters is identical with the set of d-characters. In this case both sets are coded according to ECMA-6.

8.5.7	Path Table Size (BP 133-140)

This field shall specify as a 32-bit number the length in bytes of a recorded occurrence of the Path Table identified by this Volume Descriptor.

This field shall be recorded according to 7.3.3.

8.5.8	Location of Occurrence of Type L Path Table (BP 141-144)

This field shall specify as a 32-bit number the Logical Block Number of the first Logical Block allocated to the Extent which contains an occurrence of the Path Table. Multiple-byte numerical values in a record of this occurrence of the Path Table shall be recorded with the least significant byte first.

This field shall be recorded according to 7.3.1.

8.5.9	Location of Optional Occurrence of Type L Path Table (BP 145-148)

This field shall specify as a 32-bit number the Logical Block Number of the first Logical Block allocated to the Extent which contains an optional occurrence of the Path Table. If the value is 0, it shall mean that the Extent shall not be expected to have been recorded. Multiple-byte numerical values in a record of this occurrence of the Path Table shall be recorded with the least significant byte first.

This field shall be recorded according to 7.3.1.

8.5.10	Location of Occurrence of Type M Path Table (BP 149-152)

This field shall specify as a 32-bit number the Logical Block Number of the first Logical Block allocated to the Extent which contains an occurrence of the Path Table. Multiple-byte numerical values in a record of this occurrence of the Path Table shall be recorded with the most significant byte first.

This field shall be recorded according to 7.3.2.

8.5.11	Location of Optional Occurrence of Type M Path Table (BP 153-156)

This field shall specify as a 32-bit number the Logical Block Number of the first Logical Block allocated to the Extent which contains an occurrence of the Path Table. If the value is 0, it shall mean that the Extent shall not be expected to have been recorded. Multiple-byte numerical values in a record of this occurrence of the Path Table shall be recorded with the most significant byte first.

This field shall be recorded according to 7.3.2.

8.5.12   Directory Record for Root Directory (BP 157-190)

This field shall contain an occurrence of the Directory Record for the Root Directory.

This field shall be recorded according to 9.1.

8.5.13   Volume Set Identifier (BP 191-318)

This field shall specify an identification of the Volume Set of which the volume is a member.

The characters in this field shall be d1-characters.

8.5.14   Publisher Identifier (BP 319-446)

This field shall specify an identification of the user who specified what shall be recorded on the Volume Group of which the volume is a member.

If the first byte is set to (5F), the remaining bytes of this field shall specify an identifier for a file containing the identification of the user. This file shall be described in the Root Directory.

If all bytes of this field are set to (20), it shall mean that no such user is identified.

The characters in this field shall be a1-characters.

8.5.15.   Data Preparer Identifier (BP 447-574)

This field shall specify an identification of the person or other entity which controls the preparation of the data to be recorded on the Volume Group of which the volume is a member.

If the first byte is set to (5F), the remaining bytes of this field shall specify an identifier for a file containing the identification of the data preparer. This file shall be described in the Root Directory.

If all bytes of this field are set to (20), it shall mean that no such data preparer is identified.

The characters in this field shall be a1-characters.

8.5.16   Application Identifier (BP 574-702)

This field shall specify an identification of the specification of how the data are recorded on the Volume Group of which the volume is a member.

If the first byte is set to (5F), the remaining bytes of this field shall specify an identifier for a file containing the identification of the application. This file shall be described in the Root Directory.

If all bytes of this field are set to (20), it shall mean that no such application is identified.

The characters in this field shall be a1-characters.

8.5.17   Copyright File Identifier (BP 703-739)

This field shall specify an identification for a file described by the Root Directory and contain a copyright statement for the Volume Set. If all bytes of this field are set to (20), it shall mean that no such file is identified. The characters in this field shall be d1-characters, SEPARATOR 1 and and SEPARATOR 2.

The field shall be recorded as specified in 7.5.

8.5.18   Abstract File Identifier (BP 740-776)

This field shall specify an identification for a file described by the Root Directory and contain an abstract statement for the Volume Set. If all bytes of this field are set to (20), it shall mean that no such file is identified. The characters in this field shall be d1-characters, SEPARATOR 1 and SEPARATOR 2.

The field shall be recorded as specified in 7.5.

8.5.19   Bibliographic File Identifier (BP 777-813)

This field shall specify an identification for a file described by the Root Directory and contain bibliographic records interpreted according to standards that are the subject of an agreement between the originator and the recipient of the volume. If all bytes of this field are set to (20), it shall mean that no such file is identified.

The characters in this field shall be d1-characters, SEPARATOR 1 and SEPARATOR 2.

The field shall be recorded as specified in 7.5.

8.5.20   Application Use (BP 884-1395)

This field shall be reserved for application use. Its content is not specified by this Standard.

8.6   Volume Partition Descriptor

The Volume Partition Descriptor shall identify a volume partition within the Volume Space, the system specifying the content of fields reserved for system use in the Volume Descriptor, the position and size of the volume partition, and the version of the standard which applies to the Volume Descriptor. The contents of the volume partition are not specified by this Standard.

BP	Field Name	Content
1	Volume Descriptor Type	numerical value
2-6	Standard Identifier	CD001
7	Volume Descriptor Version	numerical value
8	Unused Field	(00) byte
9-40	System Identifier	a-characters
41-72	Volume Partition Identifier	d-characters
73-80	Volume Partition Location	numerical value
81-88	Volume Partition Size	numerical value
89-2048	System Use	not specified

8.6.1   Volume Descriptor Type (BP 1)

This field shall specify an 8-bit number indicating that the Volume Descriptor is a Volume Partition Descriptor.

The number in this field shall be 3.

This field shall be recorded according to 7.1.1.

8.6.2   Standard Identifier (BP 2-6)

This field shall specify an identification of this Standard.

The characters in this field shall be CD001.

8.6.3   Volume Descriptor Version (BP 7)

This field shall specify as an 8-bit number an identification of the version of the specification for the Volume Partition Descriptor.

1 shall indicate the structure of the present Standard.
This field shall be recorded according to 7.1.1.

8.6.4   Unused Field (BP 8)
This field shall be set to (00).

8.6.5   System Identifier (BP 9-40)
This field shall specify an identification of a system which can recognize and act upon the content of the System Use field in the Volume Descriptor.
The characters in this field shall be a-characters.

8.6.6   Volume Partition Identifier (BP 41-72)
This field shall specify an identification of the Volume Partition.
The characters in this field shall be d-characters.

8.6.7   Volume Partition Location (BP 73-80)
This field shall specify as a 32-bit number the Logical Block Number of the first Logical Block allocated to the Volume Partition.
This field shall be recorded according to 7.3.3.

8.6.8   Volume Partition Size (BP 81-88)
This field shall specify as a 32-bit number the number of Logical Blocks in which the Volume Partition is recorded.
This Field shall be recorded according to 7.3.3.

8.6.9   System Use (BP 89-2048)
This field shall be reserved for system use. Its content is not specified by this Standard.

9.   FILE AND DIRECTORY DESCRIPTORS
9.1   Format of a Directory Record

BP	Field Name	Content
1	Length of Directory Record (LEN__DR)	numerical value
2	Extended Attribute Record Length	numerical value
3-10	Location of Extent	numerical value
11-18	Data Length	numerical value
19-25	Recording Date and Time	numerical value
26	File Flags	8 bits
27	File Unit Size	numerical value
28	Interleave Gap Size	numerical value
29-32	Volume Sequence Number	numerical value
33	Length of File Identifier (LEN__FI)	numerical value
34-(33 + LEN__FI)	File Identifier	d-characters, d1-characters, SEPARATOR 1, SEPARATOR 2, (00), (01)
(34 + LEN__FI)	Padding Field	(00) byte
(LEN__DR-LEN SU + 1) -(LEN__DR)	System Use	LEN__SU bytes

NOTE 16

LEN__SU denotes the length of the System Use field.

9.1.1   Length of Directory Record (LEN DR) (BP 1)

This field shall specify as an 8-bit number the length in bytes of the Directory Record.

This field shall be recorded according to 7.1.1.

9.1.2   Extended Attribute Record Length (BP 2)

This field shall contain an 8-bit number. This number shall specify the assigned Extended Attribute Record Length if an Extended Attribute Record is recorded. Otherwise this number shall be zero.

This field shall be recorded according to 7.1.1.

9.1.3   Location of Extent (BP 3-10)

This field shall specify as a 32-bit number the Logical Block Number of the first Logical Block allocated to the Extent.

This field shall be recorded according to 7.3.3.

9.1.4   Data Length (BP 11-18)

This field shall specify as a 32-bit number the data length of the File Section.

This field shall be recorded according to 7.3.3.

NOTE 17

This number does not include the length of any Extended Attribute Record.

9.1.5   Recording Date and Time (BP 19-25)

This field shall indicate the date and the time of the day at which the information in the Extent described by the Directory Record was recorded.

The date and time shall be represented by seven 8-bit numbers each of which shall be recorded according to 7.1.1 as follows.

RBP	Interpretation	Content
1	Number of years since 1900	numerical value
2	Month of the year from 1 to 12	numerical value
3	Day of the month from 1 to 31	numerical value
4	Hour of the day from 0 to 23	numerical value
5	Minute of the hour from 0 to 59	numerical value
6	Second of the minute from 0 to 59	numerical value
7	Offset to Greenwich Mean Time in number of 30 minute intervals from -24 (West) to +24 (East) recorded according to 7.1.2.	numerical value

If all seven numbers are zero, it shall mean that the date and time are not specified.

9.1.6   File Flags (BP 26)

The bits of this field shall be numbered from 0 to 7 starting with the least significant bit.

If this Directory Record identifies a directory then bit positions 2, 3 and 7 shall be set to ZERO.

If no Extended Attribute Record is associated with the File Section identified by this Directory Record then bit positions 3 and 4 shall be set to ZERO.

This field shall specify certain characteristics of the file as follows.

Bit Postion	Bit Name	
0	Existence	if set to ZERO, shall mean that the existence of the file shall be made known to the user upon an inquiry by the user; if set to ONE, shall mean that the existence of the file need not be made known to the user.
1	Directory	if set to ZERO, shall mean that the Directory Record does not identify a directory; if set to ONE, shall mean that the Directory Record identifies a directory.
2	Associated File	if set to ZERO, shall mean that the file is not an Associated File; if set to ONE, shall mean that the file is an Associated File.
3	Record	if set to ZERO, shall mean that the structure of the information in the file is not specified by the Record Format field of any associated Extended Attribute Record (see 9.5.8); if set to ONE, shall mean that the structure of the information in the file has a record format specified by a number other than zero in the Record Format Field of the Extended Attribute Record (see 9.5.8).

4	Protection	if set to ZERO, shall mean that:
		- an Owner Identification and a Group Identification are not specified for the file (see 9.5.1 and 9.5.2),
		- any user may read or execute the file (see 9.5.3).
		if set to ONE, shall mean that:
		- an Owner Identification and a Group Identification are specified for the file (see 9.5.1 and 9.5.2),
		- at least one of the even-numbered bits or bit 0 in the Permissions field of the associated Extended Attribute Record is set to ONE (see 9.5.3).

5-6	Reserved	these bits are reserved for future standardization and shall be set to ZERO.
7	Multi-Extent	if set to ZERO, shall mean that this is the final Directory Record for the file; if set to ONE, shall mean that this is not the final Directory Record for the file.

9.1.7 File Unit Size (BP 27)

This field shall contain an 8-bit number. This number shall specify the File Unit Size for the File Section if the File Section is recorded in interleaved mode. Otherwise this number shall be zero.

This field shall be recorded according to 7.1.1.

9.1.8   Interleave Gap Size (BP 28)

This field shall contain an 8-bit number. This number shall specify the Interleave Gap Size for the File Section if the File Section is recorded in interleaved mode. Otherwise this number shall be zero.

This field shall be recorded according to 7.1.1.

9.1.9   Volume Sequence Number (BP 29-32)

This field shall specify as a 16-bit number the ordinal number of the volume in the Volume Set or which the Extent described by this Directory Record is recorded.

This field shall be recorded according to 7.2.3.

9.1.10   Length of File Identifier (LEN_FI) (BP 33)

This field shall specify as an 8-bit number the length in bytes of the File Identifier field of the Directory Record.

This field shall be recorded according to 7.1.1

9.1.11   File Identifier (BP 34-(33 + LEN_FI))

The interpretation of this field depends as follows
on the setting of the Directory bit of the File Flags field.

If set to ZERO, shall mean	:	The field shall specify an identification for the file. The characters in this field shall be d-characters or d1-characters, SEPARATOR 1, SEPARATOR 2. The field shall be recorded as specified in 7.5.
If set to ONE, shall mean	:	The field shall specify an identification for the directory. The characters in this field shall be d-characters or d1-characters or only a (00) byte, or only a (01) byte. The field shall be recorded as specified in 7.6.

9.1.12   Padding Field (BP 34 + LEN_FI))

This field shall be present in the Directory Record only if the number in the Length of the File Identifier field is an even number.

If present, this field shall be set to (00).

9.1.13   System Use (BP LEN_DR-LEN_SU + 1)-LEN_DR)

This field shall be optional. If present, this field shall be reserved for system use. Its content is not specified by this Standard. If necessary to cause the Directory Record to comprise an even number of bytes, a (00) byte shall be added to terminate this field.

9.2   Consistency of File Attributes between Directory Records of a File

The following fields of each Directory Record for the same file shall contain the same values:

- Existence bit of the File Flags field
- Directory bit of the File Flags field

- Associated File bit of the File Flags field
- Record bit of the File Flags field
- Reserved bits of the File Flags field
- Length of File Identifier field
- File Identifier field
- Padding field

9.3   Order of Directory Records

The records of a Directory shall be ordered according to the relative value of the File Identifier Field by the following criteria in descending order of significance:

- in ascending order according to the relative value of File Name, where File Names shall be valued as follows:
  - If two File Names have the same content in all byte positions, then these two File Names are said to be equal in value.
  - If two File Names do not contain the same number of byte positions, the shorter File Name shall be treated as if it were padded on the right with all padding bytes set to (20) and as if both File Names contained the identical number of byte positions.

    After any padding necessary to treat the File Names as if they were of equal length, the characters in the corresponding byte positions, starting with first position, of the File Names are compared until a byte position is found that does not contain the same character in both File Names. The greater File Name is the one that contains the character with the higher code position value in the coded graphic character set used to interpret the File Identifier field of the Directory Record.

- in ascending order according to the relative value of File Name Extension, where File Name Extensions shall be valued as follows:
  - If two File Name Extensions have the same content in all byte positions, then these two File Name Extensions are said to be equal in value.
  - If two File Name Extensions do not contain the same number of byte positions, the shorter File Name Extension shall be treated as if it were padded on the right with all padding bytes set to (20) and as if both File Name Extensions contained the identical number of byte positions.

    After any padding necessary to treat the File Name Extensions as if they were of equal length, the characters in the corresponding byte positions, starting with the first position, of the File Name Extensions are compared until a byte position is found that does not contain the same character in both File Name Extensions. The greater File Name Extension is the one that contains the character with the higher code position value in the coded graphic character set used to interpret the File Identifier field of the Directory Record.

- in descending order according to the relative value of File Version Number, where File Version Numbers shall be valued as follows:
  - If two File Version Numbers have the same content in all byte positions, then these two File Version Numbers are said to be equal in value.

- If two File Version Numbers do not contain the same number of byte positions, the shorter File Version Number shall be treated as if it were padded on the left with all padding bytes set to (30) and as if both File Version Numbers contained the identical number of byte positions.

  After any padding necessary to treat the File Version Numbers as if they were of equal length, the characters in the corresponding byte positions, starting with the first position, of the File Version Numbers are compared until a byte position is found that does not contain the same character in both File Version Numbers. The greater File Version Number is the one that contains the character with the higher code position value in the coded graphic character set used to interpret the File Identifier field of the Directory Record.
  - in descending order according to the value of the Associated File bit of the File Flags field.
  - The order of the File Sections of the File Space.

9.4   Format of a Path Table Record

BP	Field Name	Content
1	Length of Directory Identifier (LEN__DI)	numerical value
2	Extened Attribute Record Length	numerical value
3-6	Locaton of Extent	numerical value
7-8	Parent Directory Number	numerical value
9-(8+LEN__DI)	Directory Identifier	d-characters, d1-characters, (00) byte
(9+LEN__DI)	Padding field	(00) byte

9.4.1   Length of Directory Identifier (LEN__DI) (BP 1)
           This field shall specify as an 8-bit number the length in bytes of the Directory Identifier field of the Path Table Record.
           This field shall be recorded according to 7.1.1.

9.4.2   Extended Attribute Record Length (BP 2)
           This field shall contain an 8-bit number. This number shall specify the assigned Extended Attribute Record Length if an Extended Attribute Record is recorded. Otherwise this number shall be zero.
           This field shall be recorded according to 7.1.1.

9.4.3   Location of Extent (BP 3-6)
           This field shall specify as a 32-bit number the Logical Block Number of the first Logical Block allocated to the Extent in which the directory is recorded.
           This field shall be recorded according to 7.3.

9.4.4   Parent Directory Number (BP 7-8)
           This field shall specify as a 16-bit number the record number in the Path Table for the parent directory of the directory.
           This field shall be recorded according to 7.2.

	9.4.5	Directory Identifier (BP 9-(8 + LEN__DI))

9.4.5 — Directory Identifier (BP 9-(8 + LEN__DI))
This field shall specify an identification for a directory.
The characters in this field shall be d-characters or d1-characters or only a (00) byte.
This field shall be recorded as specified in 7.6.

9.4.6 — Padding field (BP (9 + LEN__DI))
This field shall be present in the Path Table Record only if the number in the Length of Directory Identifier field is an odd number.
If present, this field shall be set to (00).

9.5 — Format of an Extended Attribute Record
If present, an Extended Attribute Record shall be recorded over at least one Logical Block. It shall have the following contents.

BP	Field Name	Content
1-4	Owner Identification	numerical value
5-8	Group Identification	numerical value
9-10	Permissions	16 bits
11-27	File Creation Date and Time	Digit(s), numerical value
28-44	File Modification Date and Time	Digit(s), numerical value
45-61	File Expiration Date and Time	Digit(s), numerical value
62-78	File Effective Date and Time	Digit(s), numerical value
79	Record Format	8 bits
80	Record Attributes	8 bits
81-84	Record Length	numerical value
85-116	System Identifier	a-characters, a1-characters
117-180	System Use	not specified
181	Extended Attribute Record Version	numerical value
182	Length of Escape Sequences (LEN__ESC)	numerical value
183-246	(Reserved for future standardization)	(00) bytes
247-250	Length of Application Use (LEN__AU)	numerical value
251-(250 + LEN__AU)	Application Use	LEN__AU bytes
(251 + LEN__AU)- (250 + LEN__ESC + LEN__AU)	Escape Sequences	LEN__ESC bytes

9.5.1 — Owner Identification (BP 1-4)
This field shall specify as a 16-bit number an identification of the file owner who is a member of the group identified by the Group Identification field of the Extended Attribute Record.
If the number in this field is 0, this shall indicate that there is no owner identification specified for the file. In this case, the Group Identification field shall contain zero.

	This field shall be recorded according to 7.2.3.
9.5.2	Group Identification (BP 5-8)

This field shall specify as a 16-bit number an identification of the group of which the file owner is a member.

The values for this number from 1 to a number subject to agreement between the data preparer and receiving system shall identify the group as belonging to the class of user referred to as System.

If the number in this field is 0, this shall indicate that there is no group identification specified for the file. In this case, the Owner Identification field shall contain zero.

This field shall be recorded according to 7.2.3.

9.5.3	Permissions (BP 9-10)

The bits of this 16-bit field shall be numbered from 0 to 15 starting with the least significant bit of the byte recorded in byte position 10.

Bits 0 to 3 may be ignored in interchange.

If requested by the owner, bits 4 to 7 may be ignored in interchange.

This field shall specify access permissions for certain classes of users as follows.

Bit 0	if set to ZERO, shall mean that an owner who is a member of a group of the System class of user may read the file; if set to ONE, shall mean that an owner who is a member of a group of the System class of user may not read the file.
Bit 1	shall be set to ONE.
Bit 2	if set to ZERO, shall mean that an owner who is a member of a group of the System class of user may execute the file; if set to ONE, shall mean that an owner who is a member of a group of the System class of user may not execute the file.
Bit 3	shall be set to ONE.
Bit 4	if set to ZERO, shall mean that the owner may read the file; if set to ONE, shall mean that the owner may not read the file.
Bit 5	shall be set to ONE.
Bit 6	if set to ZERO, shall mean that the owner may execute the file; if set to ONE, shall mean that the owner may not execute the file.
Bit 7	shall be set to ONE.
Bit 8	if set to ZERO, shall mean that any user who is a member of the group specified by the Group Identification field may read the file; if set to ONE, shall mean that of the users who are members of the group specified by the Group Identification field, only the owner may read the file.
Bit 9	shall be set to ONE.
Bit 10	if set to ZERO shall mean that any user who is a member of the group specified by the Group Identification field may execute the file; if set to ONE, shall mean that of the users who are members

of the group specified by the Group Identification field, only the owner may execute the file.

Bit 11	shall be set to ONE.
Bit 12	if set to ZERO, shall mean that any user may read the file.
	if set to ONE, shall mean that a user not a member of the group specified by the Group Identification field may not read the file.
Bit 13	shall be set to ONE.
Bit 14	if set to ZERO shall mean that any user may execute the file.
	if set to ONE, shall mean that a user not a member of the group specified by the Group Identification field may not execute the file.
Bit 15	shall be set to ONE.

9.5.4　File Creation Date and Time (BP 11-27)
This field shall specify the date and the time of the day at which the information in the file was created.
This field shall be recorded according to 8.4.26.1.

9.5.5　File Modification Date and Time (BP 28-44)
This field shall specify the date and the time of the day at which the information in the file was last modified.
This field shall be recorded according to 8.4.26.1.

9.5.6　File Expiration Date and Time (BP 45-61)
Ths field shall specify the date and the time of the day at which the information in the file may be regarded as obsolete. If the date and time are not specified then the information shall not be regarded as obsolete.
This field shall be recorded according to 8.4.26.1.

9.5.7　File Effective Date and Time (BP 62-78)
This field shall specify the date and the time of the day at which the information in the file may be used. If the date and time are not specified then the information may be used at once.
This field shall be recorded according to 8.4.26.1

9.5.8　Record Format (BP 79)
This field shall contain an 8-bit number specifying the format of the information in the file.

Number 0	shall mean that the structure of the information recorded in the file is not specified by this field.
Number 1	shall mean that the information in the file is a sequence of fixed-length records (see 6.10.3).
Number 2	shall mean that the information in the file is a sequence of variable-length records (see 6.10.4), in which the RCW is recorded according to 7.2.1.
Number 3	shall mean that the information in the file is a sequence of variable-length records (see 6.10.4), in which the RCW is recorded according to 7.2.2.
Numbers 4-127	are reserved for future standardization.
Numbers 128-255	are reserved for system use.

This field shall be recorded according to 7.1.1.

9.5.9   Record Attributes (BP 80)

This field shall contain an 8-bit number specifying certain processing of the records in a file when they are displayed on a character-imaging device.

Number 0	shall mean that each record shall be preceded by a LINE FEED character and followed by a CARRIAGE RETURN character.
Number 1	shall mean that the first byte of a record shall be interpreted as specified in ISO 1539 for vertical spacing.
Number 2	shall mean that the record contains the necessary control information.
Numbers 3-255	are reserved for future standardization.

If the Record Format field contains zero then the Record Attribute field shall be ignored in interchange.

This field shall be recorded according to 7.1.1.

9.5.10   Record Length (BP 81-84)

This field shall specify a 16-bit number as follows.

If the Record Format field contains the number 0, the Record Length field shall contain zero.

If the Record Format field contains the number 1, the Record Length field shall specify the length in bytes of each record in the file.

If the Record Format field contains the number 2 or 3, the Record Length field shall specify the maximum length in bytes of a record in the file.

This field shall be recorded according to 7.2.3.

9.5.11   System Identifier (BP 85-116)

This field shall specify an identification of a system which can recognize and act upon the content of the System Use fields in the Extended Attribute Record and associated Directory Record.

The characters in this field shall be a-characters or a1-characters.

9.5.12   System Use (BP 117-180)

This field shall be reserved for system use. Its content is not specified by this Standard.

9.5.13   Extended Attribute Record Version (BP 181)

This field shall specify as an 8-bit number the version of the specification for the Extended Attribute Record.

1 shall indicate the structure of the present Standard.

This field shall be recorded according to 7.1.1.

9.5.14   Length of Escape Sequences (BP 182)

This field shall specify as an 8-bit number the length in bytes of the Escape Sequences field in this Extended Attribute Record.

This field shall be recorded according to 7.1.1.

9.5.15   Reserved for future standardization (BP 183-246)

This field shall be set to (00).

9.5.16   Length of Application Use (BP 247-250)
This field shall specify as a 16-bit number the length in bytes of the Application Use field in the Extended Attribute Record.
This field shall be recorded according to 7.2.3.

9.5.17   Application Use (BP 251-BP(250+LEN__AU))
This field shall be reserved for application use. Its content is not specified by this Standard.

9.5.18   Escape Sequences   (BP(251+LEN__AU)-BP(250+LEN ESC+ LEN__AU))
This field shall be optional. If present, it shall contain escape sequences that designate the coded character set to be used to interpret the contents of the file. These escape sequences shall conform to ECMA-35, except that the ESCAPE character shall be omitted from each escape sequence. The first or only escape sequence shall begin at the first byte of the field. Each successive escape sequence shall begin at the byte in the field immediately following the last byte of the preceding escape sequence. Any unused positions following the last escape sequence shall be set to (00).

9.6   Consistency of File Attributes between Extended Attribute Records of a File
The following fields of the Extended Attribute Record associated with the File Sections of a file shall contain the same values:
- Record Format field
- Record Attributes field
- Record Length field, if the records are fixed-length records (see 6.10.3).

10.   LEVELS OF INTERCHANGE
This Standard specifies three nested levels of interchange.

10.1   Level 1
At Level 1 the following restrictions shall apply:
- each file shall consist of only one File Section;
- a File Name shall not contain more than 8 d-characters or 8 d1-characters;
- a File Name Extension shall not contain more than 3 d-characters or 3 d1-characters;
- a Directory Identifier shall not contain more than 8 d-characters or 8 d1-characters.

10.2   Level 2
At Level 2 the following restriction shall apply:
- each file shall consist of only one File Section.

10.3   Level 3
At Level 3 no restrictions apply.

SECTION III: SYSTEM REQUIREMENTS

11. REQUIREMENT FOR DESCRIPTION OF SYSTEMS

This Standard specifies that certain information shall be communicated between a user and an implementation (see clauses 12 and 13).

An information processing system that conforms to this Standard shall be the subject of a description which identifies the means by which the user may supply such information, or may obtain it when it is made available, as specified in this Standard.

12. REQUIREMENTS FOR AN ORIGINATING SYSTEM

12.1 General

The implementation shall be capable of recording a set of files, and all descriptors that are specified in this Standard, on a Volume Set in accordance with one of the interchange levels specified in this Standard.

12.2 Files

The implementation shall obtain from the data preparer the information that constitute the set of files to be recorded.

12.3 Descriptors

12.3.1 The implementation shall allow the data preparer to supply the information that is to be recorded in each of the descriptor fields below, and shall supply the information for a field if the data preparer does not supply it.

For the Primary Volume Descriptor:
- System Identifier
- Volume Identifier
- Logical Block Size
- Location of Occurrence of Type L Path Table
- Location of Optional Occurrence of Type L Path Table
- Location of Occurrence of Type M Path Table
- Location of Optional Occurrence of Type M Path Table
- Volume Set Identifier
- Publisher Identifier
- Data Preparer Identifier
- Application Identifier
- Copyright File Identifier
- Abstract File Identifier
- Bibliographic File Identifier
- Volume Creation Date and Time
- Volume Modification Date and Time
- Volume Expiration Date and Time
- Volume Effective Data and Time
- Application Use

For each Path Table Record:
- Extended Attribute Record Length
- Location of Extent
- Parent Directory Number
- Directory Identifier

For each Directory Record:
- Extended Attribute Record Length
- Location of Extent
- Data Length
- Recording Date and Time

- The Existence bit of the File Flags field
- The Directory bit of the File Flags field
- The Associated File bit of the File Flags field
- The Record bit of the File Flags field
- The Protection bit of the File Flags field
- File Unit Size
- Interleave Gap Size
- Volume Sequence Number
- File Name of a File Identifier
- File Name Extension of a File Identifier
- File Version Number of a File Identifier
- System Use

12.3.2 The implementation shall allow the data preparer to supply the information that is to be recorded in the descriptor fields listed below, and shall not record the Supplementary Volume Descriptor if the data preparer does not supply the information.

For each Supplementary Volume Descriptor:
- System Identifier
- Volume Identifier
- Logical Block Size
- Location of Occurrence of Type L Path Table
- Location of Optional Occurrence of Type L Path Table
- Location of Occurrence of Type M Path Table
- Location of Optional Occurrence of Type M Path Table
- Bit 0 of the Volume Flags field
- Escape Sequences
- Volume Set Identifier
- Publisher Identifier
- Data Preparer Identifier
- Application Identifier
- Copyright File Identifier
- Abstract File Identifier
- Bibliographic File Identifier
- Volume Creation Date and Time
- Volume Modification Date and Time
- Volume Expiration Date and Time
- Volume Effective Date and Time
- Application Use

12.3.3 The implementation shall allow the data preparer to supply the information that is to be recorded in the descriptor fields listed below, and shall not record the Volume Partition Descriptor if the data preparer does not supply the information.

For each Volume Partition Descriptor:
- System Identifier
- Volume Partition Identifier
- Volume Partition Location
- Volume Partition Size
- System Use

12.3.4 The implementation shall allow the data preparer to supply the information

196

that is to be recorded in the descriptor fields listed below, and shall not record the Boot Record if the data preparer does not supply the information.

For each Boot Record:
- Boot System Identifier
- Boot Identifier
- Boot System Use

12.3.5 The implementation shall allow the data preparer to supply the information that is to be recorded in the descriptor fields listed below, and need not record the Extended Attribute Record if the data preparer does not supply the information for any of the descriptor fields listed below. If the Extended Attribute Record is recorded, the implementation shall supply the information for a field if the data preparer does not supply it.

For each Extended Attribute Record:
- Owner Identification
- Group Identification
- Permissions
- File Creation Date and Time
- File Modification Date and Time
- File Expiration Date and Time
- File Effective Date and Time
- Record Format
- Record Attributes
- Record Length
- System Identifier
- System Use
- Length of Escape Sequences
- Length of Application Use
- Application Use
- Escape Sequences

12.3.6 The implementation shall allow the data preparer to supply the information that is to be recorded on the Logical Sectors with Logical Sector Numbers 0 to 15.

13. REQUIREMENTS FOR A RECEIVING SYSTEM

13.1 General

The implementation shall be capable of reading the files and the recorded descriptors from a Volume Set that has been recorded in accordance with one of the interchange levels specified in this Standard, except Associated Files.

13.2 Files

The implementation shall make available to the user the information that constitutes the recorded files, except any Associated File.

If the implementation allows the user to specify that the information constituting a file is to be interpreted according to 6.10, the implementation shall make available to the user the length of each record in the file.

13.3 Descriptors

13.3.1 The implementation shall allow the user to supply information sufficient to enable the implementation to locate the files required by the user, and to locate the volumes on which these files are recorded.

13.3.2	The implementation shall make available to the user the information that is recorded in each of the descriptor fields listed below.

For the Primary Volume Descriptor:
- Volume Identifier
- Volume Set Identifier
- Copyright File Identifier
- Abstract File Identifier
- Bibliographic File Identifier

For each Supplementary Volume Descriptor:
- Volume Identifier
- Bit 0 of the Volume Flags field
- Escape Sequences
- Volume Set Identifier
- Copyright File Identifier
- Abstract File Identifier
- Bibliographic File Identifier

For each Path Table Record:
- Parent Directory Number
- Directory Identifier

For each Directory Record:
- File Name of a File Identifier
- File Name Extension of a File Identifier
- The Directory bit of the File Flags field

13.4   Restrictions

The implementation may impose a limit on the length of a record to be made available to the user. The implementation is not required to make available to the user any byte beyond the first n bytes of a record, where n is the value of the imposed limit.

13.5   Levels of Implementation

This Standard specifies two nested levels of implementation.

13.5.1   Level 1

At Level 1 the implementation need not make available to the user:
- the information that constitutes the files identified in a Directory Hierarchy that is identified in a Supplementary Volume Descriptor,
- the information that is recorded in the descriptor fields of a Supplementary Volume Descriptor and of the associate Path Table records, of associated directory records, and of Extended Attribute Records identified by the associated directory record.

13.5.2   Level 2

At Level 2 no such restrictions apply.

b7 b6 b5 →	000 (0)	001 (1)	010 (2)	011 (3)	100 (4)	101 (5)	110 (6)	111 (7)
b4 b3 b2 b1 / row								
0000 — 0	NUL	DLE	SP	0	@	P	`	p
0001 — 1	SOH	DC1	!	1	A	Q	a	q
0010 — 2	STX	DC2	"	2	B	R	b	r
0011 — 3	ETX	DC3	#	3	C	S	c	s
0100 — 4	EOT	DC4	¤	4	D	T	d	t
0101 — 5	ENQ	NAK	%	5	E	U	e	u
0110 — 6	ACK	SYN	&	6	F	V	f	v
0111 — 7	BEL	ETB	'	7	G	W	g	w
1000 — 8	BS	CAN	(	8	H	X	h	x
1001 — 9	HT	EM	)	9	I	Y	i	y
1010 — 10	LF	SUB	*	:	J	Z	j	z
1011 — 11	VT	ESC	+	;	K	[	k	{
1100 — 12	FF	IS4	,	<	L	\	l	|
1101 — 13	CR	IS3	-	=	M	]	m	}
1110 — 14	SO	IS2	.	>	N	^	n	~
1111 — 15	SI	IS1	/	?	O	_	`	DEL

The d-characters are those which are not shaded in the above table.

b7			0	0	0	0	1	1	1	1
b6			0	0	1	1	0	0	1	1
b5			0	1	0	1	0	1	0	1
b4 b3 b2 b1			0	1	2	3	4	5	6	7
0 0 0 0	0		NUL	DLE	SP	0	@	P	`	p
0 0 0 1	1		SOH	DC1	!	1	A	Q	a	q
0 0 1 0	2		STX	DC2	"	2	B	R	b	r
0 0 1 1	3		ETX	DC3	#	3	C	S	c	s
0 1 0 0	4		EOT	DC4	¤	4	D	T	d	t
0 1 0 1	5		ENQ	NAK	%	5	E	U	e	u
0 1 1 0	6		ACK	SYN	&	6	F	V	f	v
0 1 1 1	7		BEL	ETB	'	7	G	W	g	w
1 0 0 0	8		BS	CAN	(	8	H	X	h	x
1 0 0 1	9		HT	EM	)	9	I	Y	i	y
1 0 1 0	10		LF	SUB	*	:	J	Z	j	z
1 0 1 1	11		VT	ESC	+	;	K	[	k	{
1 1 0 0	12		FF	IS4	,	<	L	\	l	|
1 1 0 1	13		CR	IS3	–	=	M	]	m	}
1 1 1 0	14		SO	IS2	.	>	N	^	n	‾
1 1 1 1	15		SI	IS1	/	?	O	_	o	DEL

The a-characters are those which are not shaded in the above table.

Appendix B
CD-ROM Suppliers

Access Innovation
P.O. Box 40130
Albuquerque, NM 87196
505-265-3591
A-V Online

ADP
920 East Algonquin
Schaumburg, IL 60173
312-397-1700
Onsite Plus

American Psychological Assn.
1400 North Uhle St.
Arlington, VA 22201
800-336-4980
PsychLIT

Bell & Howell
5700 Lombardo Court
Seven Hills, OH 44351
Chrysler Parts Catalog
GM Parts Catalog
Honda Parts Catalog

Bowker Electronic Publishing
245 West 17th St.
New York, NY 10011
800-323-3288
Books in Print Plus
Books Out of Print Plus
Books in Print Plus
w/Books Reviews
Plus
Ulrich's Plus

British Library
Boston Spa, Wetherby
West Yorkshire, England
LS23 7BQ
Blaise Files

Brodart Automation
500 Arch St.
Williamsport, PA 17705
717-233-8467
LePac: Govt Documents Option
LePac: Local Public Access Catalog

BRS Information Technologies
555 East Lancaster Ave.
Saint David, PA 19087
800-468-0908
BRS/Colleague

Cambridge Scientific Abstracts
5161 River Road
Bethesda, MD 20816
800-843-7751
MEDLINE
Aquatic Sciences and Fisheries Abstracts
Life Sciences Collection

Canadian Centre for Occupational
    Health and Safety
250 Main St. E.
Hamilton, Ontario L8N 1H6
416-572-2981
CCINFO Disc

CCOHS
250 Main St.
Hamilton, Ontario
Canada L8N 1H6
416-571-2981
Ccinfodisc

Cornell University
English Dept.
Rockefeller Hall
Ithaca, NY 14853
607-255-4390
Black fiction

DataTimes
1400 Quail Springs Parkway
Oklahoma City, OK 73134
405-751-6400
Daily Oklahoman

Datext
444 Washington St.
Woburn, MA 01801
617-938-6667
CD/Corporate
CD/CorpTech
CD/Banking
CD/Private+
CD/International

DeLorme Mapping Systems
P.O. Box 298
Freeport, ME 04032
207-865-4171
DeLorme's World Atlas

Dialog Information
3460 Hillview Ave.
Palo Alto, CA 94304
800-3-DIALOG
ERIC
Medline

Digital Diagnostics
601 University Ave.
Sacramento, CA 95825
916-921-6629
BiblioMed

Digital Decus Corp.
Boroughs Plaza
219 Boston Post Rd.
Marlboro, MA 01752
617-480-3418
Decus Fall 1986 #1
Decus Spring 1987 #2

Disclosure
5161 River Rd.
Bethesda, MD 20816
800-843-7747
Compact Disclosure

Donnelley Marketing Information
  Services
70 Seaview Ave.
Stamford, CT 06904
203-353-7474
    Conquest

Dun's Marketing Service
49 Old Bloomfield Ave.
Mountain Lakes, NJ 07046
201-299-0181
    Million Dollar Directory

EBSCO Electronic Information
P.O. Box 13787
Torrance, CA 90503
213-530-7533
    The Serials Directory
    Medline

Elsevier Science Publishers
52 Vanderbilt Ave.
New York, NY 10017
212-370-5520
    EMBASE
    Ca-CD

ERM Computer Services, Inc.
999 West Chester Pike
West Chester, PA 19382
800-544-3118
    ENFLEX INFO

Facts on File
460 Park Avenue S.
New York, NY 10016
212-683-2244
    Visual Dictionary

General Information Inc.
401 Park Place
Kirkland, WA 98033
206-828-4777
    Hot Line
    World Almanac

General Research Corp.
5383 Hollister Ave.
Santa Barbara, CA 93111
800-235-6788
    LaserQuest
    LaserGuide

Geovision, Inc.
270 Scientific Drive
Norcross, GA 30092
404-448-8224
    GEOdiscs

Grolier Electronic Publishing
95 Madison Avenue
New York, NY 10016
212-696-9750
    Electronic Encyclopedia

Highlighted Data
P.O. Box 17229
Washington, DC 20041
703-241-1180
    Merriam Webster Ninth
        New Collegiate Dictionary
    Map Cabinet

Info Globe
444 Front St. W.
Toronto, Ontario M5V 2S9
416-585-5250
    Globe & Mail

Information Access Company
11 Davis Dr.
Belmont, CA 94002
800-227-8431
    Magazine Index Plus

Information Handling Services Inc.
1300 Charleston Road
Mountain View, CA 94039
415-969-7990
    Zip + 4

Information Handling Services
15 Inverness Way East
Englewood, CO 80150
800-241-7824
Personnet
CrossLink

Ingram Book Company
347 Reedwood Dr.
Nashville, TN 37217
615-361-5000
LaserSearch

Innovative Technology Inc.
2927 Jones Branch Drive
McLean, VA 22102
703-734-3000
TLRN

I.S. Group
948 Springer Dr.
Lombard, IL 60148
312-627-0550
Oncodisc

JA Micropublishing Inc.
271 Main St.
Westchester, NY 10707
800-227-CIRR
CIRR

KnowledgeAccess Inc.
2685 Marine Way
Mountain View, CA 94043
415-969-0606
Your Marketing Consultant

Lasertrack
6235B Lookout Rd.
Boulder, CO 80301
303-530-2711
LV Services

Library Association Publishing
   Ltd.
7 Ridgmount St.
London WC1E 7AE
England
01-636-7543
LISA

Library Corp.
P.O. Box 40035
Washington, DC 20016
800-624-0559
Any-Book

Lotus Development Corp.
55 Cambridge Pkwy.
Cambridge, MA 02142
800-554-5501
One Source

McGraw Hill Book Co.
11 West 19th St.
New York, NY 10011
212-512-2000
Science & Technical Reference Set
Electronic Sweet's

Micromedex Inc.
6600 Bannock St.
Denver, CO 80204
303-623-8600
Drugdex
Emergindex
Identidex
Poisindex

Microsoft Corp.
16011 NE 36th Way
Redmond, WA 98073-9717
206-828-8080
Bookshelf

MicroTrends Inc.
650 Woodfield Dr.
Schaumburg, IL 60195
312-310-8928
Biolibe
FastPast
LinguaTech Bilingual Dictionaries
Menu
Nature Plus
Versa Text

National Information Center for
   Educational Media
P.O. Box 40130
Albuquerque, NM 87196
505-265-3591
A-V ONLINE

National Standards Assn.
5161 River Road
Bethesda, MD 20816
800-638-8094
Parts-Master

National Decision Systems
8618 Westwood Dr.
Vienna, VA 22180
703-883-8900
Infomark

NewsBank Inc.
58 Pine St.
New Canaan, CT 06840
800-223-4739
NewsBank Electronic Index

Newsreel Access Systems
885 3rd Ave.
New York, NY 10022
212-230-3250
News Scan

OCLC
6565 Frantz Rd.
Dublin, OH 43017
614-764-6000
Agricola
ERIC
NTIS

Online Computer Systems Inc.
20251 Century Blvd.
Germantown, MD 20874
301-428-3700
Tax Forms on Demand

Optical Media International
495 Alberto Way
Los Gatos, CA 95032
408-395-4332
Universe of Sounds

ORI, Inc. Information Systems
4833 Rugby Ave.
Bethesda, MD 20814
301-656-9723
ERIC

PCI Inc.
80 Bloor St. W.
Toronto, Ontario M5S 2V1
416-928-6733
Remote Sensing On-line
Retrieval System (RESORS)

PC-SIG Inc.
1030 E. Duane Ave.
Sunnyvale, CA 94086
408-730-9291
PS-SIG CD-ROM
Science Helper
Biotech

Pergamon Press
13 Vandy St.
London, England EC2A 2DE
Encyclopedia of Information

Prentice Hall Inc.
1 Gulf & Western Plaza
New York, NY 10023
212-373-8600
   PHINet Tax Resource

Psychological Abstracts Information Services
1400 North Uhle St.
Arlington, VA 22201
703-247-7829
   PsycLIT

Reference Technology Inc.
5700 Flatiron Pkwy.
Boulder, CO 80301
303-449-4157
   Software Library DataPlate

SilverPlatter Information, Inc.
37 Walnut St.
Wellesley Hills, MA 02181
617-239-0306
   AGRICOLA
   CHEM-BANK
   COMPU-INFO
   MEDLINE
   NTIS
   ERIC
   PsycLIT
   Ca-CD
   OSH-ROM
   A-V ONLINE
   CIRR

Sociological Abstracts
P.O. Box 22206
San Diego, CA 92122
619-565-6603
   Sociofile

Standard & Poor's Compustat Services, Inc.
1221 Avenue of the Americas
New York, NY 10020
212-512-4900
   Compustat PC Plus

Tax Analysts
400 N. Washington St.
Falls Church, VA 22046
703-532-1850
   Tax Library

Tescor Inc.
461 Carlisle Dr.
Herndon, VA 22070
703-435-9501
   First National Item Bank &
   Test Development System

Tetragon
5455 Pare St.
Montreal, Quebec
Canada H4P IR1
800-363-2372
   Businessbase
   Homebase

Tri-Star Publishing
475 Virginia Dr.
Fort Washington, PA 19034
215-641-6000
   Trademark Information Database
   Oxford English Dictionary

University Microfilms
300 N. Zeeb Rd.
Ann Arbor, MI 48106-1346
800-521-0600
   Dissertation Abstracts Ondisc

U.S. Bureau of Census
Data Users Service Div.
Washington, DC 20233
202-763-4100
   Census Test Disc

U.S. Geological Survey
804 National Center
Reston, VA 22092
703-648-4000
   Prototype Geological Information

Wiley Electronic Publishing
605 Third Ave.
New York, NY 10158
212-850-6331
Kirk-Othmer Encylopedia
of Chemical Technology
Int'l Dictionary of Medicine
& Biology
Encyclopedia of Polymer
Science and Engineering
1987 Registry of
Mass Spectral Data

Year Book Medical Publishers
35 East Wacker Dr.
Chicago, IL 60601
312-726-9746
Ca-CD

Appendix C
CD-ROM
Drive Manufacturers

AMDEK
1901 Zanker Road
San Jose, CA 95112
(408) 436-8570

Denon
27 Law Drive
Fairfield, NJ 07006
(201) 575-7810

Digital Equipment Corporation
2 Mount Royal Ave.
Marlboro, MA 01752
(617) 480-4820

Hitachi
401 West Artesia Blvd.
Compton, CA 90220
(213) 537-8383

JVC Corp.
41 Slater Drive
Elmwood Park, NJ 07407
(201) 794-3900

LMSI/Philips & Du Pont Optical
4425 Arrows West Dr.
Colorado Springs, CO 80907
(303) 593-4269

LoDown Corp.
10 Victor Square
Scotts Valley, CA 95066
(408) 438-7400

Panasonic Corp.
1 Panasonic Way
Secaucus, NJ 07094
(201) 392-4602

Reference Technology
5700 Flatiron Parkway
Boulder, CO 80301
(303) 449-4157

Sanyo Electronics
200 Riser Rd.
Little Ferry, NJ 07643
(201) 440-9300

Sony Corp. of America
655 River Oaks Parkway
San Jose, CA 95134
(408) 432-0190

Toshiba America
9740 Irvine Blvd.
Irvine, CA 92680
(714) 583-3117

Appendix D
Systems Integrators

AMTEC Information Services, Inc.
3700 Industry Avenue
Lakewood, CA 90714-6050
213-595-4756

Knowledge Access International
2685 Marine Way
Suite 1305
Mountain View, CA 94043
415-969-0606

KnowledgeSet Corporation
60 Garden Court
Building A
Monterey, CA 93940
408-375-2638

Online Computer Systems, Inc.
20251 Century Blvd.
Germantown, MD 20874
301-428-3700

Reference Technology Inc.
5700 Flatiron Parkway
Boulder, CO 80301
303-449-4157

Reteaco Inc.
716 Gordon Baker Road
Toronto, Ontario M2H 3B4
Canada
416-497-0579

SilverPlatter Information Inc.
37 Walnut Street
Wellesley, MA 02181
617-239-0306

TMS, Inc.
110 W. 3rd Street
P.O. Box 1358
Stillwater, OK 74076
405-377-0880

Index

Index

Million Dollar Directory, 92
minimizing, 12
moulding, 14
multilevel zoom and pan, 27
multimedia CD-ROM, 21
multimedia interactive CD-ROM, 93-106
  applications for, 94
  benefits of, 101
  IXP for audiovisual tapes and, 102
  man-machine interface for, 96
  production of, 96

N

National Decision Systems, 90
National Information Center for Educational Media, 84
NewsBank Electronic Index, 91
NewsBank Inc., 91
NTIS Bibliographic Database, 80

O

Online Computer Systems, 71
online database services, 2
OPTI/Search, 78
optical disc technology, 1, 93-142
optical requirements, 18
optionally limited color, 26
ORI Inc., 79
OSH-ROM, 83
outer diameter, specs for, 17
overlays, 29

P

Paisley, William, 106
pan, 27
Personnet, 86
photon shot noise, 12
physical structure of CD-ROM, 4
  technical highlights of, 7
pit, 4, 6
players, 48
pre-mastering, 3, 13, 72
professional markets, 139
program area, 16
program image, 100
prototype configuration, 30

prototype functionality, 28
Psychological Abstracts Information Services, 80
PsycLIT, 80
publishing, 2
  electronic, 122-127
  integrated text and image database CD-ROM in, 21
  revolutions in, 109
pulse code modulation (PCM), 31, 32

Q

quantization, 32

R

radial deviation of track, specs for, 20
radial tracking, recording format, 11
readout system, specs for, 17
recorded area, specs for, 19
recording format, 5
  data layout in, 10
  error correction in, 8
  error sources in, 12
  radial tracking in, 11
  scrambling/control, 10
  technical highlights of, 7
Reference Technology, 76
replication, 3
RESEARCH Retrieval, 74
Reteaco Inc., 65
retrieval engine, 72
retrieval software, 99
retrieval systems, 72
rotation, specs for, 19

S

sampling rate, 32
Sanyo, drives from, 58
scrambling/control, recording format, 10
search template, 28
signal-to-noise ratio (SNR), 12, 32
SilverPlatter Information Services, 68, 79-84
Sociofile, 85
Sociological Abstracts, 85

Sony Corporation, CD-ROM drives from, 52
spot diameter, 7
stamper making, 14
Stand Alone CD-ROM drive, 56
Standard & Poor's Compustat Service Inc., 89
Standard ECMA-119, 143-198
suppliers, 201-207
system description, 16
system design, 98
system integrators, 63-78
  suppliers of, 210

T

technical highlights of CD-ROM, 7
technology and hardware overview, 1-41
telephone technology, 110
text database sizing, 24
thickness, specs for, 17
Time Management Software, 74
titles, 79-92
Tivona, Elissa J., 132
TMSFAX, 75
track pitch, specs for, 19

U

Ulrich's Plus, 85
University Microfilms International, 91
user requirements, 97

V

vertical deviations of information layer specs for, 20
visual-oriented interface, 25
volume and file structure file for information interchange, 143-198

W

WORM technology, 44
  optical discs using, 45-47

Y

Year Book Medical Publishers, 82

Z

zoom, 27

Other Bestsellers From TAB